Page

Teresa Helena Higginson

Teresa Helena Higginson
Servant of God
"The Spouse of the Crucified"
1844–1905

Cecil Kerr

De torrente in via bibet; propterea exaltabit Caput
Psalm CIX.

With an Introduction by
Paul Haffner

GRACEWING

This edition first published in 2008
by

Gracewing
2, Southern Avenue
Leominster
Herefordshire
HR6 0QF
www.gracewing.co.uk

The right of Paul Haffner to be identified as the author of the
Introduction has been asserted in accordance with the Copyright,
Designs and Patents Act 1988.

ISBN 978–0–85244–181–7

Concordat cum originali: Christopherus Findlay–Wilson
Die 21 maii 2008

For the original version:
Nihil Obstat: Georgius H. Joyce, S.J., Censor deputatus.
Imprimatur: Edm: Can: Surmont, Vic. gen.
Westmonasterii, die 2 Septembris 1926

Cover design: From a photograph taken after the visit of Teresa
Higginson to Rome, 1900.

Contents

Introduction

MORE than one hundred years have elapsed since the holy passing from this world of the Servant of God, Teresa Helena Higginson (1844–1905). Teresa was a saintly Catholic schoolteacher. She was born in Holywell, North Wales and grew up in Gainsborough and Neston. As an adult she lived in Bootle, Clitheroe, Edinburgh and Chudleigh in Devon where she died. It seems she received many supernatural gifts from God, such as healing, prophecy, bilocation and the stigmata and attained the mystical marriage. It is claimed that she was chosen by Christ to make known his great desire for his Sacred Head to be worshipped as the Seat of Divine Wisdom. The principal biography written by Lady Cecil Kerr has been out of print for some time, and we have thought it opportune to republish it with minor corrections.

It is just over a century since Teresa's death and she seems to have faded from view to some degree. There was a time when she was very well known. Mary Cahill wrote in the *Tablet* of 8 January 1938: "By means of articles, lectures and meetings, teachers all over the country have been invited to take up the cause of Teresa Higginson." Another letter from Monsignor O'Brien (the vice–postulator for her cause) tells us that he had received letters bearing witness to her sanctity and petitioning for her beatification from all parts of Great Britain and Ireland, France, Germany, Italy, Holland, Belgium, Malta, USA, Canada,

West Indies, Brazil, India, China, Burma, Borneo, South Africa, Uganda and New Zealand. Today her memory is perhaps kept alive in fewer places. Yet perhaps as with the case of St Maria Faustina Kowalska of the Divine Mercy, her cause has been delayed for the appropriate time when her name would be universally known and honoured. Indeed St Faustina's devotion to the Divine Mercy was blocked by the Holy Office in 1959, and images of the said devotion were prohibited.[1] This ban was later lifted on 15 April 1978, considering further documentation and the changed circumstances.[2]

The Cause for the canonisation of Teresa Higginson went to Rome in 1937, and it reached the stage of her being declared Servant of God. In the 1930's there was much interest in this Cause of Teresa Higginson, and a series of letters in *The Tablet* from November 1937 to March 1938 evince an incredible display of devotion to her. Even famous figures like Evelyn Waugh entered into the discussion.[3] On 21 February 1938 Monsignor O'Brien, the vice–postulator, was sent a letter from the Secretary of the Congregation informing that the Holy Office had pronounced the *Non Expedire* on the introduction of her Cause. The Secretary privately made it known that it was not the Congregation of Rites that had pronounced the *Non Expedire*. If there had been anything by reason of heresy or moral disorder, a *Reponatur* would have completely ended her Cause. So the *Non Expedire* was a kind of "shelving".[4] The Secretary also implied that it was

---

[1] See the *Notificatio* in *AAS* 51 (1959), p.271.

[2] See the *Notificatio* in *AAS* 70 (1978), p.350.

[3] See E. Waugh, "Teresa Higginson" in *The Tablet*, 180 (11 December 1937), p.803.

[4] In a protocol (Prot. N° Dev. V. 20/1942), the Holy Office made it clear that there are no errors against the faith. However, there is always danger that from such a devotion error might arise. There does not seem to be any superstition involved, but there is some element which is not consonant with the traditional piety of the Church. Unfortunately there seems to have been some negative aspects on the part of a person or persons who may have illicitly

Teresa's emphasis on the public honour due to Our Lord's Sacred Head that had had its part to play in shelving her Cause and that a major miracle would go some way to overturning the decision. There had been several appeals for devotions to different parts of Our Lord's body at the time, so that Rome probably reacted against it. Dr Cartmell explains some of the reasoning behind Rome's decision in the *Clergy Review* of 1937. A further letter from the Vatican in February 1949 confirmed that there was no insurmountable obstacle to the Cause.

However, within the tradition of the Church there is a strong basis for devotion to the Sacred Head of Our Lord. A church dedicated to the eternal Wisdom of Christ, the Light of the world (John 8:12), who is the Way the truth and the life (John 14:6), was built at Byzantium by the Emperor Constantine. After this church was destroyed, a second one was built and inaugurated on 10 October 405. The second church was also destroyed and Emperor Justinian I took the decision to build a third and entirely different basilica, larger and more majestic than its predecessors. This church retained its dedication to Holy Wisdom (Ἁγία Σοφία in Greek).[5]

Theologically the head carries great significance. In the Sacred Scriptures, heads are crowned with glory, raised in exultation, lifted in expectation, bowed in worship, covered in submission, turned in repentance, hanged in shame, hidden in disgrace, dusted with ash in mourning, and crushed in defeat. It happened that the ultimate act of humiliation you could visit on your defeated enemy was to put your foot on the back of his head, thus making your enemy's head your footstool (Psalm 110:1). The word *head* has more than one meaning. In the case of Christ,

---

used this devotion for financial gain. A final point made was that there are already enough pious devotions approved by the Church, like the Sacred Heart, the Holy Face and the five Holy Wounds.

[5] The Greek name in full is Ναός τῆς Ἁγίας τοῦ Θεοῦ Σοφίας, Church of the Holy Wisdom of God.

it refers to the physical Head of the crucified Lord Jesus, and also to Christ in his role as Head of the Church whose body we are.

Christ is the divine Physician who heals all the ills of the mind and the heart. He it is who refocuses the unity between the mind and heart which was lost through the Fall, and which is damaged through personal sins. At a particular stage in the Church's history, there developed the devotion to the Sacred Heart of Jesus. Worship is rightly paid to His Heart of flesh, inasmuch as it symbolises and recalls the love of Jesus. Thus, although rightly directed to the material Heart, adoration does not stop there: it also includes love, that love which is its principal object, but which it reaches only in and through the Heart of flesh, the sign and symbol of this love. Devotion to the Sacred Heart already existed in the eleventh and twelfth centuries, where the wound in the Heart of Christ symbolised the wound of love. St. Bonaventure was one of the medieval writers who dealt with the theology of the Sacred Heart.[6] However, it was during the period when Jansenism had turned cold the sense of God's love, that the devotion really developed as an antidote to this heresy and its effects, proposing the Heart of Jesus as the universal symbol of love. Devotion to the Heart of Jesus is a recognition of that love which is central to the Christian faith: "The Sacred Heart is...quite rightly considered the chief sign and symbol of that love with which the divine Redeemer continually loves the eternal Father and all human beings without exception."[7]

Now it could well be asked whether the human mind needs a similar healing from the coldness of rationalism by means of the parallel devotion to the Sacred Head of Jesus, which could be seen as a complement to devotion to the Sacred Heart. Devotion to Our Lord's Sacred Head already existed in the medieval hymn, attributed to St. Bernard:

---

[6] See St. Bonaventure, *Lignum vitae*, 29–30, 47 in St. Bonaventure, *Opera Omnia* vol. 8 (Quaracchi: Collegio San Bonaventura, 1898), pp.79–80, 85.

[7] CCC 478.

O sacred Head ill–uséd,
by reed and bramble scarred,
that idle blows have bruiséd,
and mocking lips have marred,
how dimmed that eye so tender,
how wan those cheeks appear,
how overcast the splendour,
that angel hosts revere.[8]

In possibly the earliest text which forges this link, St Bridget of Sweden (1303–1373), closely associated a devotion to the Sacred Heart of Jesus with a veneration of His Sacred Head. She prayed to Christ as Head of all men and angels, and universal King, whose Head was crowned with thorns, and whose Heart is praised by all creatures in heaven and on earth.[9]

---

[8] The translation is by Ronald Knox. The original Latin runs:
Salve, caput cruentatum,
Totum spinis coronatum,
Conquassatum, vulneratum,
Arundine verberatum,
Facie sputis illita.
Salve , cuius dulcis vultus,
Immutatus et incultus,
Immutavit suum florem,
Totus versus in pallorem
Quem coeli tremit curia.

[9] See the following texts in a prayer attributed to St. Bridget, in Bridget of Sweden, *Revelaciones* ed. B. Bergh and S. Eklund (Uppsala: Almqvist and Wiksells, 1977–1992) Book 12, "Four Prayers", Prayer 3, line 66: "Domine mi Ihesu Christe, tu vere es caput omnium hominum et angelorum et dignus rex regum et dominus dominancium, qui omnia opera facis ex vera et ineffabili caritate. Et quia caput tuum benedictum corona spinea coronari humiliter permisisti, idcirco caput et capilli tui benedicti sint et honorentur gloriose dyademate imperiali celumque et terra et mare et omnia, que creata sunt, in eternum tue subiaceant et obediant potestati. Amen." Also *ibid.*, line 77: "Domine mi Ihesu Christe, quia benedictum cor tuum regale et magnificum numquam tormentis

The devotion existed in Klagenfurt in Austria in the nine-teenth and twentieth centuries.[10] It was also spread in England around the same time by Teresa Higginson. She received a private revelation from Christ to make known that His Sacred Head be worshipped as the Seat of Divine Wisdom, to atone for a time of extraordinary intellectual pride and apostasy, and at the same time to be the healing antidote for that intellectual pride. It is true that the devotion to the Sacred Head of Our Lord does not yet enjoy the full approval of Church authorities. Nevertheless, at least one Archbishop of Liverpool had placed the imprimatur on the litany of the Sacred Head. Towards the end of last century there were rumours that Teresa's body had been exhumed and had been found to be incorrupt. However, official confirmation is lacking on this point.[11]

The essential content of this devotion can be summed up in Teresa's own words:

---

nec terroribus seu blandiciis flecti potuit a defensione regni tui veritatis et iusticie nec tuo sanguini dignissimo in aliquo pepercisti sed magnifico corde pro iusticia et lege fideliter decertasti legisque precepta et perfeccionis consilia amicis et inimicis tuis intrepide predicasti et pro defensione ipsorum cum tuis sanctis sequacibus moriendo in prelio victoriam obtinuisti, idcirco dignum est, vt inuictum cor tuum in celo et in terra semper magnificetur et a cunctis creaturis et militibus triumphali honore incessanter laudetur. Amen."

[10] In Klagenfurt, Austria, an image of the sacred Head of Christ was venerated after a miracle. See J. Maier, *Des heiliges Hauptes Mahnung und Trost* (Klagenfurt: Konrad Walcher, 1917) and G. Baumann, "Iconographische Betrachtung zum «Heiligen Haupt zu Klagenfurt». Ein volksbarockes Andachtsbild als Erbe alter europäischer Bildtraditionen." In *Unvergängliches Kärnten. Beitrage zur Heitmatkundige Kärntens. Die Kärntner Landsmannschaft* (10/1976), pp.57–71.

[11] See N. Parsons, "Teresa Higginson – A mystery unsolved" in *Catholic Life* (February 1996), pp.3–4.

I was considering the excessive love of the Sacred Heart and offering to my Divine Spouse this same love to make amends for our coldness, and His constancy and infinite riches to make up for our poverty and misery, when our divine Lord suddenly represented to me the Divinity as a very large bright crystal stone in which all things are reflected or are, past present and to come, in such a manner that all things are present to Him. This immense precious stone sent forth streams of richly coloured lights brighter beyond comparison than ten thousand suns, which I understood represented the infinite attributes of God. This great jewel also seemed to be covered with innumerable eyes which I understood represented the Wisdom and Knowledge of God....Our Blessed Lord showed me this Divine Wisdom as the guiding power which regulated the motions and affections of the Sacred Heart, showing me that it had the same effect and power over its least action, and raising it, as the sun draws up the vapour from the ocean. He gave me to understand that an especial devotion and veneration should be paid to the Sacred Head of Our Lord as the Seat of divine Wisdom and guiding power of the Sacred Heart, and so complete this heavenly devotion.[12]

Teresa clarified how this devotion would be the completion of devotion to the Sacred Heart. Devotion to the Sacred Head of Christ is an expression of adoration towards the Wisdom of the Father and of the Love of God revealed in the Light which shines in the darkness and enlightens every person coming into this world. Specifically the adoration of the Sacred Head of Our Lord is directed to the Seat of Divine Wisdom, for the Head of Christ is the sanctuary of the powers of His Soul and the faculties of His Mind and in these the Wisdom which guided every affection of the Sacred Heart and the motions of the whole Being of Jesus our Lord and God. This devotion does not separate the attributes of His Soul or Mind, or of the divine Wisdom which guided, gov-

---

[12] C. Kerr, *Teresa Helena Higginson* (London: Sands and Company, 1927), p.104.

erned and directed all in Christ, true God and true Man, but gathers them all together to be specially honoured, with His sacred Head adored as their Temple. Just as the head is the centre of all the senses of the body, so this devotion is the completion, not only of the devotion of the Sacred Heart, but the crowning and perfection of all devotions. The devotion to the Sacred Head would seem to be truly the crowning of devotion to the Sacred Heart and to have come at a most apposite time: it shows how Love is ordered through Wisdom.

Furthermore devotion to the Sacred Head of Jesus would constitute the atonement for man's intellectual pride in this modern era, and would be the antidote to this sin. Man offends the divine Wisdom by the abuse of the powers of his mind and by his sins, thus tending to erase the image of the triune God in himself. Also by wild folly, man tries also to rob creation of its God. If the sun be taken away we cannot have light or heat. If faith, the light of the soul, is taken away, then humanity suffers decay and desolation. Purely worldly wisdom which is in fact folly has, since the Enlightenment, drawn people into an abyss of darkness which is Hell.

In the past, when the heart of man set his affections against God, the Sacred Heart of Jesus really human yet divine, united to the Divine Person of God the Son, was the source of healing grace. Jesus revealed the burning love of His Sacred Heart and complained of man's coldness and demanded a reparation, and people were warmed in that furnace of divine love and souls glowed again with charity towards the God of Love. In our own time, infidelity, pride of intellect and open rebellion against God and His revealed law damage the minds of people, and draw them away from the sweet yoke of Jesus, binding them with the cold heavy chains of self–seeking, private judgement. People thus reject all right to be guided and wish to govern themselves in disobedience to God and to His holy Church. In the face of this great need for spiritual healing, Jesus the incarnate Word, the Wisdom of the Father who became obedient even unto the death of the Cross, again offers an antidote, devotion to His Sacred Head, which is an expression of the infinite mercy and justice of God.

Christ is the Head of Creation, as St Paul made clear in his letters to the Ephesians and to the Colossians (Ephesians 1:10; Colossians 1:15–20). This tradition was continued in St Irenaeus, who described how Christ, "as the eternal King, recapitulates all things in Himself."[13] St Maximus the Confessor also developed this idea:

> This is the mystery circumscribing all ages, the awesome plan of God, super–infinite and infinitely pre–existing the ages. The Messenger, who is in essence Himself the Word of God, became man on account of this fulfilment. And it may be said that it was He Himself Who restored the manifest innermost depths of the goodness handed down by the Father; and He revealed the fulfilment in Himself, by which creation has won the beginning of true existence. For on account of Christ, that is to say the mystery concerning Christ, all time and that which is in time have found the beginning and the end of their existence in Christ.[14]

For Blessed John Duns Scotus, the Incarnation of the Son of God is not seen as a contingency plan when the original creative process of God is affected by sin: it is the very reason for creation. In the Divine plan of creation, it was the Incarnation that came first, and it was only for the sake of this that there was creation at all.[15] According to Pope John Paul II, Jesus comes as the cosmic "Principle and Archetype of everything created by God in time", as "Lord of Time and of History", and as the "New Man" who

---

[13] St Irenaeus, *Adversus Haereses*, III, 21, 9. See also J.-F. Bonnefoy, *Christ and the Cosmos* (Patterson, NJ: St Anthony Guild Press, 1965).

[14] St Maximus the Confessor, *Questio 60 ad Thalassium*.

[15] See Bl John Duns Scotus, *Opus Oxoniense*, 3, dist. 19.

calls humanity to the goal of divinization.[16] Christ reveals to us also the true face of man, "fully revealing man to man himself".[17]

Christ is now crowned in glory and His sacred Head also represents the Kingship which He exercises over the Church as well as over all of creation:

> The Head that once was crowned with thorns
> Is crowned with glory now;
> A royal diadem adorns
> The mighty Victor's brow.[18]

St. Thomas Aquinas distinguishes a twofold function of this grace of Headship, analogous to the double role exercised by the head with regard to the members of the body. "The head," he says, "has a twofold influence upon the members: an *interior* influence, because the head transmits to the other members the power of moving and feeling; and an *exterior* influence of government, because by the sense of sight and the other senses which reside in it, the head directs a man in his exterior actions."[19] St. Thomas then goes on to remark that Christ also, by His grace of Headship, has a twofold influence upon souls: an *interior* influence of supernatural life, because His Humanity, united to His Divinity has the power of justification; an *exterior* influence by His government of His subjects. The role of justification and sanctification is that of Christ as Priest, while the second prerogative of government and direction constitutes the spiritual Kingship of Christ. We have said the "spiritual" Kingship of Christ, for we must distinguish between the spiritual and the temporal Kingship of Christ or between His Primacy in the supernatural order and His Primacy in the natural order. We

---

[16] Pope John Paul II, *Tertio Millennio Adveniente*, 3; Idem, *Centenary of the Consecration of the human race to the Heart of Christ*, 1; Idem, *Novo Millennio Ineunte*, 23.

[17] Pope John Paul II, *Novo Millennio Ineunte*, 23. See also Vatican II, *Gaudium et Spes*, 22.

[18] Hymn by Thomas Kelly (1769–1854).

[19] St Thomas Aquinas, *Summa Theologiae*, III, q.8, a.6.

deem it important that the theological foundations of devotion to the Sacred Head of Christ be further deepened, as this would increase and foster devotion to Christ at this present time.

This new publication is presented in the hope that the figure of the Servant of God, Teresa Higginson may come to be better known and loved, and that her cause may be re–examined. The Second Vatican Council reflected on a renewed awakening of the laity to a sense of holiness and of community within the Church:

> The laity, by their very vocation, seek the kingdom of God by engaging in temporal affairs and by ordering them according to the plan of God. They live in the world, that is, in each and in all of the secular professions and occupations. They live in the ordinary circumstances of family and social life, from which the very web of their existence is woven. They are called there by God that by exercising their proper function and led by the spirit of the Gospel they may work for the sanctification of the world from within as a leaven. In this way they may make Christ known to others, especially by the testimony of a life resplendent in faith, hope and charity.[20]

These words of the Council are particularly meaningful in the life of Teresa Higginson, who exercised the lay apostolate in a special and profound way. Moreover, the Council also pointed out that the Holy Spirit endows the faithful with particular gifts. Allotting His gifts "to everyone according as He will" (1 Corinthians 12:11), the Holy Spirit distributes special graces among the faithful of every rank. These charismatic gifts, whether they be the most outstanding or the more simple and widely diffused, are to be received with thanksgiving and consolation, for they are exceedingly suitable and useful for the needs of the Church.[21] Christ continually distributes gifts in His Church, in which, by His own power, we serve each other in the way of salvation so that, carrying out the truth in love, we might through all things

---

[20] Vatican II, *Lumen Gentium*, 31.

[21] See *ibid.*, 12.

grow unto Him who is our Head.[22] Clearly, the discernment of these charisms is the task of the Church, and in this regard it is to her that we entrust the final word on the private revelation received by Teresa Higginson. We do not intend to anticipate or prejudice the decision of the Church in this regard.

Private revelations have been made in every age. These revelations do not form a part of the deposit of truth contained in Scripture and Tradition, and which has been confided to the Church for interpretation. Even when the Church approves them she does not make them the object of Catholic faith, but she simply permits them to be published for the instruction and edification of the faithful.[23] Nevertheless, as in the case of devotion to the Sacred Heart and to the Sacred Head of Christ, such devotions are closely intertwined with beliefs in Scripture and in the Tradition of the Church. Indeed the devotions to the Sacred Heart and the sacred Head of Christ taken together emphasize the Love and Wisdom of the Saviour and Redeemer of mankind. The wisdom and love of God are indeed correlative as is seen in the full divine economy, spanning from Creation to the final consummation: "In wisdom He made the heavens, for His faithful love endures for ever" (Psalm 136:5).

Clearly, God can make revelations to whoever He pleases, even to sinners; but invariably, He makes them only to persons who are not only fervent, but already raised to the mystic state. Moreover, even for the interpretation of true revelations, it is necessary to know the qualities and defects of those who think themselves favoured with revelations. Hence a careful analysis must be made of their natural and supernatural qualities. As to natural qualities one must ascertain whether the persons concerned are sincere, well–balanced or affected by psycho–neurosis or hysteria; for it is evident that in the latter case there is ground for suspecting the alleged revelations, such tempera-

---

[22] See *ibid.*, 7.

[23] See A. Tanquerey, *The Spiritual Life: A Treatise on Ascetical and Mystical Theology* (Tournai: Desclee, 1930²), 1490.

ments being subject to hallucinations.[24] As to supernatural qualities, the Church must examine whether the persons concerned: are endowed with solid and tried virtue, or merely with more or less sensible fervour; whether they are sincerely and deeply humble, or whether on the contrary they delight in being noticed and in telling everybody about their spiritual favours; true humility is the touchstone of sanctity and the lack of it argues against a revelation; whether they make the revelations known to their spiritual director instead of communicating them to other persons, and whether they readily follow his advice; whether they have already passed through the passive trials and the first stages of contemplation; especially, whether they have practised the virtues in a heroic degree; for God generally reserves these visions for perfect souls.[25] The presence of the aforementioned qualities does not prove the existence of a revelation, but simply renders more worthy of credence the word of those who claim to have received it; their absence does not disprove the fact of revelation, but makes it quite unlikely. In the case of Teresa Higginson, as the following pages will show, we think that the conditions are met for the validity and veracity of the private revelation in question.

As regards the object of private revelations, all visions and suchlike contrary to faith or morals must be rejected, according to the unanimous teaching of the Doctors of the Church based on the words of St Paul: "But even if we ourselves or an angel from heaven preaches to you a gospel other than the one we preached to you, let God's curse be on him" (Galatians 1:8). God does contradict Himself, nor does He reveal things opposed to what He teaches through His Church.[26] In the case of Teresa Higginson, her many letters deal with the Incarnation, the Most Holy Trinity and the spiritual life; she writes about these mysteries with great fidelity and accuracy.[27]

---

[24] See *ibid.*, 1498.

[25] See *ibid.*, 1499.

[26] See *ibid.*, 1501.

Concerning the effects of private revelations, Our Lord Himself has supplied us the fundamental rule of thumb: "By their fruits you will know them" (Matthew 7:16–20). According to St Ignatius of Loyola and St Teresa of Avila, a divine vision causes at first a sense of wonderment and fear, soon to be followed by a sense of deep and lasting peace, of joy and security. The contrary is true with regard to diabolical visions; if at the outset they produce joy, they soon cause uneasiness, sadness, and discouragement. It is thus that the devil brings about the downfall of souls. True revelations strengthen the soul in humility, obedience, patience, and conformity to the divine will; false ones beget pride, presumption, and disobedience.[28] Above all, the effect of a genuine revelation should draw the recipient and others closer to Christ. We believe this to be the case with the devotion which Teresa Higginson received and which we are now promoting.

For this new edition of Cecil Kerr's major work, we have kept to the original format as much as possible. A few minor corrections have been made. Also, the citations of letters have been taken from the text and placed in footnotes, as this allows a smoother read. We have added a third appendix containing some prayers and devotions composed by Teresa Higginson; these give some idea of the flavour of the spirituality of devotion to the Sacred Head of Our Lord. As regards the renewed publication of this work, many thanks are due to Fr Christopher Findlay–Wilson for his generous help in the preparation of this volume, and to Mr Tom Longford, the publisher, for his encouragement.

Paul Haffner
Rome
6 June 2008

---

[27] See F. W. Kershaw, *Teresa Helena Higginson. A Short Account of her Life and Letters* (Neston: Carston Print Services, 1999), p.10.

[28] See Tanquerey, *The Spiritual Life*, 1503–1504.

Foreword

THE following pages relate the history of a simple English-woman – a humble teacher in our elementary schools who, not long ago, passed unnoticed and unknown among the crowds of our busy streets and along our lonely country lanes. It is but twenty years since she was laid to rest in the little village church-yard at Neston. Her sisters and one friend only were present at the funeral: she shared her mother's grave: her name was not even added to the tombstone. And yet today this name is on many lips, and a memorial bearing numerous and influential signatures has been addressed to the Archbishop of Liverpool, praying him to institute a preliminary canonical enquiry into her virtues, with a view to her ultimate exaltation to the altars of the Church. The evidence must be duly weighed and sifted, and until the Church has spoken none may venture to pass judg-ment; but some record, however inadequate, of her life will doubtless be acceptable to those who are interested in her cause. The account here given has been taken entirely from her own writings, from the statements of her confessors, and the lips of those who knew her, many of whom are still alive. It is given without commentary or attempted explanation. Much of it is very wonderful: some of it is startling – to many minds it may be even distasteful – much will no doubt be criticised and contro-verted. But, in the words of her own Bishop: "If this is the work of God, it will prosper in spite of opposition." And while the

Process is being carried on, her friends are asked to pray that, if it be indeed the work of God, He will speedily exalt His humble servant, so that, ere long, through the voice of Holy Church, all nations may call her blessed. Should such prove to be His Will, we, in these Isles, shall surely be glad and rejoice that after the lapse of so many centuries yet another English name is invoked among the saints of God. For with what confidence might we not turn to one who so lately trod our great cities, spoke our own tongue and shared our life and customs, begging her by her prayers to hasten the day when her dear native land may once more find shelter in the one true Fold.

Feast of the Exaltation of the Cross, 1926.

Sources of Information

1. – Teresa's own letters to her directors, Fr. Powell and Canon Snow.[29] These were all carefully collected by Canon Snow and left by him to Fr. O'Sullivan, OSB, who entrusted them to the author with a view to the compilation of the Life. The following are Canon Snow's instructions to his executors with regard to these papers:

To my Executors,

The whole contents of this drawer are the letters and writings of the Servant of God, Teresa Higginson, copies of them, and various writings concerning her and the Devotion to the Sacred Head of Our Lord, Jesus Christ. None of these papers must be destroyed but carefully preserved together, and God in His own time and His own way will bring them to light and cause them to be used to His own honour and glory and the good of souls.

It is right for me to leave it on record that I was her director from September 1883, till her death on the fifteenth of February, 1905. During that period she lived in various places (eleven years at St. Catherine's Convent, Edinburgh) and went to confession to the local priest, but she was in constant communication with me and always regarded me as her director to whom she was under her vow of obedience.

---

29 Father Edward Powell, the rector of St. Alexander's, Bootle, was Teresa's director from 1879–83. He afterwards went to Lydiate but remained in close touch with her until his death in 1901. Father Alfred Snow, of St. Mary's Aughton, succeeded Father Powell as her director and remained so till the end of her life. He was made a Canon in 1901, and later Chancellor of the archdiocese. He died in 1922.

Since Benedict XIV in his essay on canonization says that great weight ought to be given to the opinion of the director of the Servant of God, I feel I should do wrong if I died without leaving behind me a declaration, which I now make, that it is my strong conviction that Teresa Higginson was from her very childhood called to a very high degree of sanctity, that she was led by extraordinary ways; that she went through, one after another, the various degrees of prayer and union up to and including the Mystical Marriage. (This last she beautifully described in a letter to Fr. Powell and in one to me.) This conviction was formed by my intimate knowledge of her, her interior, her way of life, her heroic virtues, her sufferings and trials, her writings, the analogy between her life and the lives of the saints, all combined with my knowledge of mystical theology of which I made constant and close study.

2. – "Observations on the life of the Servant of God, Teresa Higginson, Spouse of the Crucified", by Canon Snow.

3. – Notes on her life till she went to Bootle in 1879, by Canon Snow.

4. – A diary kept by Canon Snow from 1883 to 1885.

5. – Letters from Canon Snow to Fr. O'Sullivan, OSB.

6. – Letters from her earlier directors, Fr. Wells and Fr. Powell.

7. – The statements of her fellow lodgers with regard to the attacks of the Devil.

8. – Notes taken by Miss Ryland and Miss Woodward of Teresa's condition and conduct when participating in the Passion during her ecstasies at Wigan.

9. – Letters of Bishop Knight, Fr. Wilberforce, OP, Mons. Weld, Fr. Hall, OSB, and others who were asked to investigate her case.

10. – Written and verbal statements of her sister, her friends and those who lived with her, many of whom are still alive, not a few having since entered religion.

1

A Child of Promise

"I FEEL it right to say that I have the firm conviction that Teresa was not only a saint but also one of the greatest saints Almighty God has ever raised up in His Church." These striking words, written of Teresa Helena Higginson, express no mere passing opinion, but are the weighty judgment of the wise old priest who, for the last twenty–two years of her life, was the director of her soul.

In the year 1844, when so many hearts in England were turning with hungry longing to the ancient Church, a little girl was born at the famous shrine of Holywell. The child of a Catholic father and a convert mother, she inherited from the one the heroic traditions of the dark ages when the light of faith had so nearly been extinguished, and from the other the bright hopes of a future when it was once again to illuminate the land. And she herself, though destined to play no public part in the world's history, may yet prove to have been one of those special instruments whom Almighty God from time to time selects for the fulfilment of His secret purposes.

Her father, Robert Francis Higginson, was born in Preston in 1816, and educated at Stonyhurst. He then went to Ireland as agent to Lord Dillon at Loughlyn House, Roscommon, and while on a visit to Dublin, was taken to a ball at Viceregal Lodge. Here he was introduced to Miss Bowness, a young English lady a few years older than himself, the romantic story of whose conversion

at once excited his attention. Her family came from the town of
Bowness in Westmorland, and she had been brought up in
staunch old–fashioned Protestantism. Her father had a hearty
hatred of the Catholic Church and more especially of the Jesuits,
but in spite of this he allowed his daughter to travel with some
cousins to Rome, where they were much attracted by the great
churches and basilicas. Having wandered one day into the Gesù,
they met a kindly English priest who offered to show them
round. They were deeply interested and liked their guide so
much, that they begged him to come and see them at their hotel.
During his visit, Mary Bowness alluded to her intense dislike of
the Jesuits. To her no small embarrassment, her new friend
quietly observed that he himself was one. Closer acquaintance
apparently removed her prejudices, for before leaving Rome, she
asked to be instructed, and was finally received into the church.
When she told her father what she had done, he was terribly
angry and turned her out of house and home, declaring that he
would rather see her dead at his feet than a Catholic. She took
refuge with some friends in Dublin and so met a fellow English
Catholic, Robert Higginson. They quickly fell in love and were
married at Loughlyn in October, 1841. Their first child, a daughter, was born in the following year, and soon afterwards, they
returned to England and settled down at Gainsborough in Lin-
colnshire, where Mr. Higginson took up business as a wharfinger. The quiet little town of Gainsborough was a place of
considerable note at a time when so much of the country's traffic
was conveyed by water. The Chesterfield, Keadby, and other
canals brought goods from all parts of the country to its wharfs,
whence they were shipped down the river to the open sea. The
duty of the wharfinger was to control and regulate this traffic, a
busy and important post, and Mr. Higginson was able for some
time to maintain his fast growing family in very comfortable
circumstances. But with the advent of railways, things began to
change. Commerce on the canals gradually died down and, in

the end, ceased altogether, and in 1857 he found himself obliged to remove to Whalley Bridge in Cheshire.

But it was at Trent Port Wharf in Gainsborough that the little Higginsons spent the first happy years of their lives. Teresa was the third child. Before her birth, Mrs. Higginson being in a poor state of health went on a pilgrimage to Holywell, and so it came about that this child of special destiny was born at the ancient shrine so famous in the days of faith, on May 27th, 1844. Priests were few and scattered, and it was not till June 22nd, that the baby was baptised. The ceremony was performed by Father O'Carrol, and it was surely not mere chance which prompted the selection of her names. Saint Teresa, the great mystic of Avila, and Saint Helena, the British princess who searched so diligently for the Cross, were the patrons chosen for this child who was herself to walk the heights of mysticism and to prove so true a lover of the Holy Cross.

Catholic life was at a low ebb in the east of England in those days, and the Higginsons who were so devout must have felt themselves sadly isolated. There were a few scattered Catholics round Gainsborough when they first went there, and a priest visited the place at intervals. The second entry in the baptismal register is that of Robert Francis Higginson, son of Robert Higginson and Mary Higginson, formerly Bowness. He was born in April, 1848, and nearly two months elapsed before a priest came to baptise him. It would appear that the Rev. J. B. Naughton was appointed to the district shortly afterwards, for the last three children of the family were baptised by him within a few days of their respective births. In the year 1850, a room was taken in Whitehorse Yard which was used as a chapel until the building of the present church, but before this took place it is probable that the Higginsons' house was the chief Catholic centre of the neighbourhood. They had an oratory where Mass was said as often as possible and where the vestments and other altar requisites were kept. Dr. Roskell, the Vicar Apostolic of the northern district, was a frequent visitor, and they numbered many well known priests among their friends. These were stirring times for the little band of Catholics, and we can easily imagine the eager conversations that were carried on, and how their hopes for the return of England to the Faith rose high, as day by day the roll of Oxford converts mounted up with steady tide. Not least welcome of their guests was the Venerable Dominic Barberi, the famous Passionist, who in all likelihood will soon be raised to the altars of the Church, and by whom Newman himself and so many of his followers were received. One of the children, Louisa, was privileged to receive baptism at his hands, and he often carried little Teresa in his arms. Did he, to whom the future was so often shown, perhaps foresee the heights of sanctity to which this child would reach — how steadfastly she would scale the path to Calvary, there to be ennobled by our Lord Himself with the sublime title of "Spouse of the Crucified"? Surely we cannot doubt that his fervent prayers won for her a share in his own heroic zeal for souls, and that his burning words sank deep into the opening mind of this little one whose infant heart was aflame already with the love of God.

There are no outside records of Teresa's early days. Our only sources of information are two accounts written by herself, in obedience to her directors, Father Powell and Father Snow, and from her simple pages we gather many glimpses of a very perfect Catholic home. The children led a sheltered life; they had no playmates, but the five sisters and three brothers formed a happy, merry little band among themselves, and Teresa seems to have been the ringleader in all their games and romps. Their education was entrusted to nursery governesses, but their good parents themselves watched closely over them and trained them carefully in the fear and love of God. Although with few spiritual advantages — until she went to school Teresa had never been either to Benediction or the Stations of the Cross — they learnt to follow closely in the spirit of the Church and to enter fully into all her feasts and seasons. They were trained too, to have true charity for the poor. Each day at dinner the first helping from the dish was set aside for the next beggar who might ask for alms, and, if by evening none had come, the good parents would say: "We have had no visit from Our Lord today." Teresa used in after years to tell how to her confusion, when carrying the dish to the kitchen to be kept warm, she once fell and smashed the plate and scattered all the food.

One of the lessons their mother impressed most deeply upon their young minds was the practice of the presence of God. She would bid them picture Our Lord as standing always at their side, and Teresa told a priest in her last illness what consolation this had brought her throughout life. "I had but to put out my hand to find it ever in His", she said.

The good seed took deep root in the fertile soil of little Teresa's soul. Lively and intelligent, thoughtful beyond her years, with a very tender heart and great force of character, her whole being from the very cradle was centred in the thought of God. Her parents early realised that it was no ordinary soul whom He had entrusted to their care. Indeed all who knew her looked upon her as a child of special promise, one whom God had marked in a peculiar manner for His own. Bishop Roskell watched with loving solicitude over this lamb of his flock; Father Dominic, as we have seen, loved to take her in his arms; and Father Ignatius Spencer, another well–known Passionist, used to call her his little apostle, from the zealous way in which she tried to spread his league for the conversion of England.

One of her earliest recollections was of hearing a priest (possibly Father Faber) say of her, that she would be either a great saint or a great sinner, and would lead many souls to God or away from Him. "This I think had a great impression on me though he did not think I heard it, yet it sank deep down in my soul, for that night when we received our parents' blessing, when Papa put his hand on my head, he sighed and it went through me. Then that same night when Mama came to look at us last thing, she knelt down by my crib and cried, and when she kissed me the warm tears fell upon my face, and I was too much ashamed to open my eyes and felt unworthy of so good a mother. I mention this fact for it has never been forgotten, and I think our dear Lord had a great deal to do with it, though I did not then understand the meaning of it all, but I did beg of the dear little infant Jesus to help me to be more like Him and never to let me do anything that would make my dear parents cry, for I loved them so tenderly. I don't know how old I would be then, but I must have been very young."[1]

It is clear that even at this early age, Teresa possessed a dominant personality and remarkable strength of will. "The Kingdom of Heaven suffereth violence and the violent bear it away", said Our Lord. It is not the feeble of will and the faint of heart whom He chooses to accompany Him on the way to Calvary. And certainly Teresa was no weakling. From the first she seems to have held complete sway, not only over her brothers and sisters, but also over all those with whom she came in contact. She describes herself as very headstrong and self–willed, though the objects she pursued so resolutely were no mere childish whims, but matters she had pondered deeply in her little mind, and which conscience told her to be right.

"I was a great source of anxiety to my parents for though I did not disobey them, yet I was very headstrong and almost always contrived to get my own way. I had such control over all in the house, and even strangers that dear Papa and Mama say I led them whichever way I pleased, in spite of themselves, and this self–will grew as I grew. I used to weigh a thing well in my own mind and if I thought it should be, I would not rest until I had achieved my point. I used to propose it and if I thought there was opposition, for a little I might argue it over, but dear Papa often said as long as I argued there was some chance, but when I became silent I had made up my mind, cost me what it would, I would do it (through God) and invariably I got what I wanted. I

---

[1] Letter 269. The figures give the reference to Teresa's letters to her directors which are numbered in chronological order. In every case the number is given of each letter quoted in the text.

was glad of obstacles and thought I had then something to give Him who had given me so much. Oh my Beloved, when I look back and see all the dangers you have led me through and removed from my path I rejoice and bless Thy Holy Name for Thou hast ever been mindful of me."[2]

In all the records of the saints there is hardly one more beautiful than Teresa's own description of her first realisation of the Blessed Trinity. This sublime revelation was granted to her at a very tender age.

"I think I would not be four years old when He brought me to the full use of reason and I fancy it was on the feast of the Purification (Presentation?) of our Blessed Lady. I must have been told a great deal about it and I wished very much to please and honour our dear Mother Mary, for I thought if I did she would let me nurse her dear little infant Jesus, and how ardently I longed for Him He only knows. But something must have been said to me also about our Blessed Lady being the Temple or Tabernacle of the most Holy Trinity and her giving herself to God when she was only as old as I was, for I remember going before the image of Mater Dei and telling our Blessed Lord I wished to say to Him all that our dear Blessed Lady said to him, and I promised to do all that she then promised and gave myself to her that she might offer me up with her own offering. And I think Almighty God accepted my poor offering and gave me grace to make a profound act of faith which I shall never forget, though I don't know in which way it was that thou Oh Beloved of my soul, then revealed to me for the first time the great mystery of the Blessed Trinity (not anything distinctly about it) but prostrating myself to the ground I felt surrounded by an overwhelming power and majesty and when I was able to speak, I said over and over again: 'Blessed be the most holy and undivided Trinity, now and forever more. Amen.' And although I did not understand the vows I then made, still I renewed them every

2   Letter 56.

day and night, and as I grew older and prepared for the sacraments I felt more and more my obligations of love and fidelity."[3]

There is a further account of this wonderful event in the memoir she began to write for Father Snow.

"It was the feast of the Presentation of our Blessed Lady in the Temple, and we had been told all about it and the four Hail Maries been said as Daughter of God the Father, Mother of God the Son, and Spouse of God the Holy Ghost, and Tabernacle of the adorable Trinity, and we were told that Mary was *all these* because she gave herself so entirely to God on that day, and a strange feeling began to work within me. I thought all over again and again and thought that I too must give myself to God as Mary did, and yet a strange feeling of dread was over me and I dare not. A real struggle was going on in my soul and at last Thou, oh my King, conquered: I stole into the oratory and bowing myself down to the ground I offered myself to God to be all His for ever. I told our Blessed Lady to say to God for me all that she said that day in the Temple. Then I realised God for the first time. I seemed to see and know the great Mystery of the Blessed Trinity and how Mary was the Tabernacle of the thrice Holy Trinity. I then really bowed in adoration and saw how the soul is made after their Image and Likeness. It seemed to me that God was in my soul in a mysterious manner, yet I knew Him and loved Him and gave myself to Him. I would be then about four years old and though I did not understand all the offering I made yet I daily renewed it."[4]

Where could be found a more touching scene than that of this tiny child prostrate before the altar, lost in adoration of the infinite majesty of God? "Venerable old age is not that of long time nor counted by the number of years; but the understanding of a man is grey hairs", says the Book of Wisdom. Young as she was, Teresa understood the Voice that spoke to her; she made her choice and henceforth she belonged to God for ever.

---

[3] Letter 38.
[4] Letter 269.

But to this wonderful grace there was soon added the realisation of evil, for she goes on to tell of her first sin — a mere childish act of disobedience it may seem to us, but to her whose soul was so illumined by the light of Grace, it was revealed in all its horror as a deliberate offence against Almighty God. Father Snow, for so long her director, used afterwards to say that in his opinion this was the only true matter she could ever have had for confession, and it would almost seem as though Almighty God had allowed this fall, in order that she should realise to the full the horror and malice of sin and the anguish of repentance.

"Oh my Spouse and my only Delight, how closely Thou hast guarded Thy poor weak child", she writes. "How often would I have strayed from Thee if Thou hadst not made Thyself so attractive to me and imprinted Thy beautiful Face on all things, so that looking at earthly things I might see in them Thy beauty, Thy wisdom, Thy power and Thy love. And yet in spite of all these yet in Thy very presence would I dare to offend Thee my Lord and my God. Ah who but Thou wouldst have borne with me in my wickedness for at the very time Thou wert lavishing favours upon me I dared to disobey my parents and thus break Thy Holy command. One day we had all been out for a walk as usual, and when we returned I stayed behind a little till the rest had all gone upstairs and, instead of hanging up my hat, I was dragging it after me or something of the kind, and dear Mama saw me and called to me and I pretended not to hear her, but went on humming something to myself and trusting that she would call me again, but she did not and I did not go to see what she wanted or tell her how naughty I was and that I was sorry, for I really was grieved the moment after it happened. The next minute I was called into the nursery but I could not do anything I was so ashamed of myself and so sorry I could not learn my lesson, play, or take my tea, and they all thought I was sick and everyone's kindness made me worse and worse. I felt they really would cry if they knew how wicked I was and I longed to tell them and beg pardon and yet I felt they would be so hurt with me, and when they nursed and kissed me I felt as though my heart would break, not so much because I had offended my dear Jesus, as it was for the wrong I had done to so good a mother and I felt I was so ungrateful to her. Oh how I longed to put my arms around her neck and tell her all, but I was put to bed, and of course I could not rest, so after a while I crept out of bed and came partly down the stairs and there I sat crying to myself, till someone saw me and told Mama and I was carried into the room where Rev. Father Smith etc. were playing whist. I said I wanted to tell Father Smith something and he took me on his knee and when supper was ready he said he would stop a few minutes and see what I had to say, and there and then I made my first confession though I did not get absolution from Father Smith, yet I felt so happy again, and he took me down with him and I told my dear parents, and Father Smith, Papa, and Mama all cried, and I cried too, but now they were tears of joy for me and I promised that I would not be such a naughty girl again."[5]

In a letter to Father Powell she writes in allusion to her sin: "Oh what a day of misery that was for me. I was afraid of our dear little Infant Jesus and His holy Mother, and I was ashamed before my dear good angel and my friends, and I thought the clock was telling everyone what I had done. And now I bless You for this fall, for it showed me how much and how truly you loved me (by allowing me to make my first confession so soon) and Father Smith and my parents cried to think I should so soon offend our Blessed Lord, and it made such an impression on me then, a new world seemed open to me and I felt that I had been the cause of all that our Blessed Lord suffered and I tried each day to hurt myself in some way. I have cut my fingers and scalded and burnt myself as if by accident trusting that, in union with His bitter torments, these little things would be acceptable in His sight. I often used to put my finger ends in between the door when it was about to be shut and try to get my feet trodden on. I would entangle my hair purposely, so that when it was

---

[5] Letter 269.

combed it would hurt my head. I am sure you will laugh at these little things, but little minds and hearts can only contrive little ways, and little as they were I always felt I was pleasing Him whom I love above all things. And I wonder He never told me I should ask about things, for our Blessed Lady several times brought Him to me that I might look into His little Face and see how beautiful and good He is. He showed me Himself to me in such a manner even then, that I could not help but love him. I mean there was no virtue on my part."[6]

The horror of sin and the awful price it had cost Our Blessed Lord were indelibly impressed upon her mind, and her one desire henceforth was to share His pain and to help Him to win back the souls He held so dear. So at four years old, the little girl took up her cross and set out resolutely to accompany Our Lord on the long road to Calvary, and as she grew, her love of suffering for His sake also grew until it filled her with such insatiable desire that, as she said, she craved for it more than for meat and drink. The penances invented by her childish mind sound almost incredible, but none knew of them. She never spoke of them regarding them as precious secrets with her Jesus, sure that He too loved to share them, for she noticed that He often helped to hide them when others might have found them out. One of her favourite ways of mortifying her natural inclinations was to take upon herself the misdeeds of her companions, a practice for which she used afterwards to blame herself severely, but one which at the time must have cost her many a bitter fight.

"My dear Lord how often I have offended Thee I know not, for many and many times I have said that I committed faults that I never did, for if little things sometimes were denied by the others, I would not tell of them but would say that I did it, to save them the punishment, and this I did many times even after I made my first holy Communion and thought I was doing something for God, when all the time I was offending Him in Him Infinite Truth. Oh that I could cry aloud to the whole world and

6   Letter 56.

say how base and ungrateful I have been and how sorry I am. Oh my dear Lord how ungrateful I have ever been to thee, and though I have always had a great desire to please Thee yet how little have I done. My dear sisters and brothers were always a great deal better than I was though I do not think Thou gavest them, Oh my Spouse, and only Treasure, such a knowledge of Thy beauty and love as Thou gavest to me. For my infant heart was all on fire for Thee and Thy Blessed Mother and I longed at times to shed my blood for Thee. And our play as little ones was very often little instances from Your holy Childhood and lives of the Saints and martyrdoms, and we used to save our pocket money to buy Chinese children, for we were all in the Holy Childhood and used to have the little stories read from the Annals of that Society, which gave us a great zeal for the souls of pagan children etc. And many times in the day ever since I have prayed, and always teach the children under me to say, 'Oh divine Child Jesus save us and all other poor children, especially those of pagan parents. Oh Virgin Mary, St. Joseph pray for us and them, Hail Mary etc.'

"When I was about five, my little brother died and this made a great impression on me, for the whole house was in great mourning; and I think someone must have said something about what a soul must feel when it has to be separated from Almighty God, when we feel so keenly the death of a person we love — but I don't remember who said it, only that ever after I used to beg of Our dear Lord never to let me be sent away from Him for one minute, though I don't know that I did anything extra to try and please Him more. Though a little later on just before we went to the convent, when my eldest sister who was about seven made her first confession, I renewed all my good resolutions and gave myself to my dear Divine Lord, promising Him to be for ever more and more His own, and that I would never again say what I liked, but for the sake of Him who denied Himself all things I too would henceforth mortify myself in every way possible, keeping a strict guard over my senses and watching for chances to prove how earnest I was in doing little things for him whom I felt burning my poor little heart away. And though I often did little things, yet Oh my God how frequently and basely I offended, slighted, and neglected Thee and how ungrateful I have ever been towards Thee, my loving Lord. I was never very strong and our dear Lord gave me a great many chances of suffering patiently and silently for love of Him, and I know I used to feel so grateful to Him if He could give me some painful suffering that no one knew about only Himself.

"Then in 1854 Dr. Roskell gave confirmation in Gainsborough and I think he remained over night at our house; however he heard us our prayers and catechism (as Miss Featherstone was obliged to go to her aunt who was sick) and he advised dear Papa and Mama to let us go to the convent at Nottingham where I remained for eleven years."[7]

---

[7] Letter 269.

2

The Convent School at Nottingham

IT must have been with heavy hearts that these good parents made up their minds to the parting with their children, more especially with their little Teresa over whom they had watched so anxiously. However, acting on Dr. Roskell's advice, they decided to send the three eldest girls to school at Nottingham, where the Sisters of Mercy had a fine convent. It was built by Pugin and had a sheltered garden overlooked by a wide cloister, round which the children used to walk, singing their hymns, during the month of May. There was a beautiful chapel where Teresa spent many hours before the Blessed Sacrament, and where too she made her first confession and communion and was confirmed. She was ten years old when she arrived with her two elder sisters, on the 3rd of March 1854, and she ever remembered the impressions of that day. It was Friday in Lent and "The Stations of the Cross was the first devotional exercise I performed in the convent, and I had never heard them said before. Oh my Crucified Jesus when I think of the innumerable ways you sought after me and drew me in Thy wondrous love to compassionate Thee in Thy sorrow, and Oh my God no one will ever know until the last great day all you gave your poor weak child on the first day I followed Thee on Thy way of the Cross."[1]

Sensitive and tender–hearted, the little girl felt keenly this first parting from her mother and, try as she would, she could

---

[1] Letter 269.

not help being terribly homesick; "Though I tried to bind myself very closely to Him and tried to love and serve Him better, yet at this time I seemed to forget everything and fret very much to go home again. Then the beautiful month of May came which was kept with very great devotion and then I began to settle and really love the convent, for I remember one of the dear nuns telling me that when our Blessed Lady was taken to the Temple at three years old, she never cried for Saints Anne or Joachim nor wished to go home again, and then I began to feel how ungrateful I was and self seeking and made acts of contrition and told our dear Lord since He had loved and thought so much for me, I could never love or think of anything out of Him and begged of Him to give me some little suffering as proof of His love."[2]

Teresa remained at Nottingham on and off for about eleven years though her education was much interrupted by illness, for her health, always delicate, was permanently injured by the severe mortifications she secretly practised. All who knew her during her school life are now dead and very little is remembered of her in the convent, but her own story, written for Father Snow, throws much light on those early days. She speaks of course chiefly of her spiritual life, but we can none the less fill in a good deal between the lines. In the picture thus presented to us she stands out as a highly sensitive, intelligent child, brimming with life, quick to see and enjoy the surprise of the good nuns at her wild spirits and love of play, differing so widely from the proper conduct for which they looked. Her personality quickly made itself felt and she soon became the leading spirit among her schoolfellows, as she had always been with her brothers and sisters at home. But following her usual practice she made use of this as a further means of self–denial. "As I grew older I thought I would never say what game I wished to play at, for everyone of the children used to consult my wishes in nearly everything and I was a great romp at play time and I know the nuns were

---

[2] Letter 269.

often astonished at me for they expected me to be quiet at all times and I was a real tomboy."[3]

But her most striking qualities were her force of character and her amazing strength of will. Young as she was, she had deliberately chosen her part in life and given herself without reserve to God, and she now set out to conquer self and subject nature by practising the most severe austerities and mortifying herself in every way. Some people would appear to think that saints are ready born, that they are made of different clay from common men and rise almost without effort to the heights of sanctity. But rather is it true that those who walk upon a loftier plane and are endowed with greater light must gird themselves for a sterner fight, for their warfare will be waged upon a wider scale. What heroic courage is required utterly to conquer self, only the Saints can tell. "God gave him a strong conflict that he might overcome" is written of the just man, and it is "he who could have transgressed and hath not transgressed, and could do evil things and hath not done them" who shall have glory everlasting.

And so with Teresa the battle was fierce and unremitting, and the child at first was often disheartened and tempted to give up. But her courage never failed, for day by day her love grew stronger and she rejoiced in everything that brought her nearer to the holy Cross. This strange passion for suffering, which she shared with her great patron and so many of the saints, arose from no mere morbid craving for the pain itself, but from the feeling that by this alone could she assuage the agonising fires of love which were burning up her very soul. She was often left in darkness; we find her kneeling for hours before the Blessed Sacrament, her soul steeped in desolation, and when her prayer was hard and dry she did but kneel the longer. And far from making a display of sanctity, her one endeavour was to hide the little secrets she loved to share only with Our Lord. Among the features that stand out most clearly in her narrative are the sober sense and balanced judgment which marked her even as a little

---

[3]   Letter 56.

child. Though she realised that Our Lord was favouring her beyond her fellows and that others held her in such high esteem, she calmly went her way. She saw all things through the sure perspective of humility, knowing that her very weakness was her strength, for it made her cling to Him and feel that "I was truly His and that nothing in myself was my own, only my sins and wickedness."

The simple story of her convent days — so like in many ways to that of the little Saint of Lisieux — must be given in her own words that the reader may form for himself his own picture of her character.

"On the feast of Corpus Christi all the cloisters and every place through which the Blessed Sacrament was carried was beautifully decorated, and archways were left till morning when fresh lilac, laburnum etc. were gathered and I climbed up the tree to bend the branches for Sister to break off small branches and I fell and hurt myself. Though Sister was much alarmed, I persisted in saying it was not much, for I thought our dear Lord had allowed it to happen that so I might have some little thing to offer Him. It went on increasing in pain till at last I could not get out of bed, and the doctor was sent for and he was very angry and said he should have been sent for before, that inflammation of a very serious kind had been doing its work for some days and he was afraid he had no chance to do anything effectively, it was too late and they must telegraph home at once. So you see how early I began to get others into trouble, and though I was sorry for the dear nuns and poor Papa and Mama, yet I felt so happy and thought I would soon really possess my dear Jesus and see His Blessed Mother and mine and I felt quite disappointed when I got better. I was ill for six or seven weeks at the Convent in bed and when I got up the doctors said I was in a decline and I was taken home for some time. I had had a fall previous to that at home in a sawpit that was made when they were enlarging the house and building new warehouses."[4]

---

[4] Letter 269.

She tells the story of this fall more fully in another letter: "A few weeks before I went to the convent I threw myself down into a sawpit which hurt me severely and through this fall, when I got to the convent, I had inflammation in my left side and as soon as I was able I was taken home again. (They were enlarging the house and a number of men were busy there and they had to saw up a quantity of wood so they made this pit.) I did not say anything about it and my sisters dare not, until the doctor said I had been severely bruised. I was questioned and I said I did fall down in the pit but I had done it purposely. I thought about the dreadful agony Our Blessed Lord must have felt when His Cross was fixed on Mount Calvary and I longed for a chance to feel that dread shake and I thought I could then easily stumble as if by accident and so I did."[5]

"I don't know exactly how long I remained at home, but I think I did not go back for a year, but my sisters remained. I have never been strong since, however I got stronger and begged so hard to go back that at last I was taken, but I did not have regular lessons, I had to be out in the open air as much as possible, and dear Reverend Mother (Sister M. Aloysius Perry) had had her leg cut off and had to be out in the garden also, so I was very much with her, and as she was so holy everyone looked upon her as a saint. She used to tell me beautiful things about the love of God and teach and question me about Him and what I did for Him, and, seeing her suffer so patiently, I began to have a very great thirst for suffering and felt it so sweet, and I begged of Our Dear Lord never to leave me without and ever to give me more and more. I think the reason dear Rev. Mother liked me to be with her was because I hurt her most, for I used to jump into her chair and sit down at the side without the leg to thread daisies and jump in and out. I never was still and then I used to say I was our Blessed Lord crowning her for being so good and suffering so much, and she would caress me, I think now, because I caused her greater pain when I stood up, perhaps kicking or knocking

---

[5]   Letter 56.

against the stump, for she used to smile so sweetly and often kiss her crucifix and let me do the same."[6]

It was a close friendship which sprang up between the patient, saintly nun and the restless little girl who played beside her chair; and who can tell what influence the prayers and example of her old friend may have had upon the child whose mind was even then so fixed upon the things of God? She continues: "While I was out with her these times she prepared me for the Sacrament of Penance and Oh with what tender love she spoke of the Passion of our dear B. Lord, and the great love of His sacred Heart in forgiving His little children etc. and I was very much moved to sorrow and made many resolutions to try and serve Him better, and prove my love for Him. And I began to set myself certain time for meditation of which I often grew very weary and I was not much improved. And all this time I was a very self–willed child, though our dear Lord hid my many faults, and others had a high esteem of me, yet I knew my own misery and often wondered how God and others could put up with me and how it was that they could be so really good and kind to me. But I think now it was because I was very delicate and they knew I suffered a good deal, so in charity they looked over all my faults, and though by His grace He kept me from mortal sin, yet all I did was most imperfect and I used to beg of my dear good angel to help me to do at least one action really well, and yet I do not remember *once* succeeding and so I had nothing ever to offer Our dear Lord and His Blessed Mother but imperfections. At last I made my confession and the Precious Blood of my dear Jesus was poured out upon my poor soul and new light and strength were given to me. Oh wondrous love of the Sacred Heart, Thou who in death didst pray for thy executioners, are ever renewing it in this great Sacrament and raising the dead to life and making the blind to see and the lame to walk, and oh my God how can I ever thank Thee for Thy mercy and love to me the least and most ungrateful of Thy children?

---

[6] Letter 269.

"When I saw myself so self–seeking and having such little thought for others and on the other hand Jesus so forgetful of Himself and so loving and generous to all (for He made me see and feel very plainly His great love and gentleness and kindness to others) and how I was always studying myself, and others giving up their will and pleasure to me, and I taking it all as a matter of course, for I have often since considered over their generosity and kindness, for they always were, or very often would be, guided by me as to what game we should play at, and gave up their wills in many things so cheerfully.

"I think it was at or about this time, that I made the resolution of rising in the night for the sorrowful mysteries of the Rosary and half an hour's meditation and then go back to bed. This was very hard for me, and I was often tempted to give it up, especially when our dear Lord tried me with dryness which He frequently did and sometimes for months, but when I felt this very much I would prolong instead of shortening the time and looked carefully after opportunities of denying and mortifying myself, for I wanted to try and prepare well for my first Holy Communion. On one occasion we had Exposition of the Blessed Sacrament and I went with the rest to make a visit, and I had been very full of desolation and could not form a single prayer, which was a great trial to me; but I tried to adore and love Him and kept my eyes upon Him in the sacred Host, but I had no satisfaction in my prayer. And after we went out of chapel dear Rev. Mother asked me what I saw and if our dear Lord had told me anything, so then I told her how I had not been able to say my prayers etc. for a long time; that I had not seen anything, not even the angels which I frequently did, but that I had promised our dear Blessed Lord that I would not move or take my eye off Him. I was only therefore keeping my promise for so well I remember how I felt — that I could not make one act of love nor feel sorry about it. I was so indifferent that of course I took it as a sign that He had left me on account of my wickedness and sin, and as I could not adore Him in very truth I would so far as outward acts went.

And Rev. Mother told me that I had pleased Our Lord more, and perhaps adored and loved as well as any of the nuns, and she said I was a good little girl and did love God very much and that I was very dear to the Sacred Heart of Jesus. This was I think the only time I ever told anyone about my soul, for I thought Our dear Lord liked to have secrets and I therefore tried to hide things, instead of asking advice and getting permission to do things... Oh my God how can I write of the great things Thou hast done for me — when the prophet's mouth was burnt to cleanse it, I the poorest and most wretched worm of the earth. Oh if it were not in holy obedience how I would shrink away from it, knowing how unworthy I am and how I marvel at the wondrous love of the Sacred Heart in Its patience and condescension to this vile and ungrateful wretch, for it seems to me that I have always been the same sneaking coward, taking everything and giving nothing but empty words and desires even to the present, only that now I have all His own riches and infinite perfections to offer Him as my own. Oh what depths of love and generosity on the part of the most High."[7]

"I did not undertake any regular corporal punishment until I was preparing for my first holy Communion. Then I began to rise and lay under the bed (after Sister had put out the gas and gone down) till the bell rang at five in the morning for the nuns to rise — then I used to get into bed. Then I managed to get a piece of sacking and I pushed in bits of old knitting needles, little tacks, etc. I used to put it under me on the floor, but I did not do this long for fear of being found out. I was so often sick and the nuns took such great care of me that they seemed to notice every little scratch or mark, but I had an opportunity one day of getting some red hot cinders from the fire and I only just had time to pick them from the grate when Sister entered. I put them down my breast and they set my things on fire, but when I made the holy sign of the cross on the flames they went quite out, but Sister scolded me very much and told me never to do such a thing

---

[7]   Letter 269.

again. I begged her not to say anything so as she gave me her word I feel sure she never did."[8]

Teresa tells how Father Faber once visited the school while she was there:

"When I was at the convent I don't know what year, but Fr. Faber came round and asked the children their birthdays and as mine was on St. Philip's feast he said, 'You should be called Philippa. What is your name?' And when I told him Teresa he said: 'See that you are a Teresa.' And I wondered much what he meant and I was greatly afraid and thought it a great pity that I had a name of such an extraordinary saint, and I asked our b. Lord to make me love Him, not only with the love of St. Teresa but with that of the Holy Ghost and our b. Lady. And I began to think I had been guilty of great presumption in calling myself Teresa of Jesus when I had done nothing to prove my love, and from that time I have said instead, 'Lord I am Thine; do with me what Thou wilt.'"[9]

"Then I was preparing to make my first Holy Communion and several times I was put back on account of my age, and I shall never forget how I longed to receive Him and begged of Holy Simeon to intercede for me, for I thought he would understand my feelings knowing how he yearned with desire to see Him, and Mary too; oh how I begged of her to give Him to me. And it was this that made Dr. Roskell (R.I.P.) say that I should make my first Communion, for my prayer was heard and I was promised to make it on Easter Sunday April 12, 1857. Oh my God how I lived those days I hardly know, that week seemed as though it would never come to an end. Though I was so unworthy (though I know He preserved me from mortal sin) I seemed to forget all but Him, and in spite of my many miseries I received Him over and over again in spirit and adored and entertained Him with all the court of Heaven. I felt nothing but His love and saw nothing but His beauty and goodness. He let me suffer too,

---

[8]   Letter 56.
[9]   Letter 54.

for I remember being very ill and the doctor said I had low fever, but as I wished so much to be up he said it would do me more harm to stop in bed. He was a good Catholic and perhaps he had felt the same desire himself. Well the dear nuns allowed me to be the nearest our dear Lord on Maundy Thursday though Rev. Mother would not let me kneel or stay very long, though I told her it did not tire me. I am sure you will think I prayed well and made many good resolutions, but oh my Father, how all my misery stands out at this time. Neither then or after my first Communion did I, although Rev. Mother and all the Sisters asked me to pray for them, I don't think I asked anything, my heart seemed too full, all I could say as far as I remember was: 'Jesus my love, my Jesus I am all Thine, even as Thou art all mine, do with me now and always as Thou willest.' I had so much to say, so much to ask and I said not one word more, but I felt He knew all — all I wanted for others and all the graces I needed for myself. And yet how much He did for me and how He gave to others the things they wished me to ask for. I know now how He read all my desires and knew what I would say; how from the centre of my soul I wished to give and consecrate my whole being to Him, to be His and His only in thought, word and deed, for time and eternity: and though I was not able to renew my vows in words, yet from that day I felt that I was really His and that nothing in myself was my own, only my sins and wicked-ness. All the good resolutions I had wished to make I felt that they were sealed as it were with His most Precious Blood, and I tried to check my will and tried to empty myself of myself to live a life of self–denial, and as I was so self–seeking and so full of self–love oh my dear Father, you cannot understand what a battle I had to fight, how often I felt disheartened and tempted to give up; for things that others would have esteemed and been glad of the opportunity of doing, I shrank from in my cowardice and would often have really given in but for my promise to Him. And then I would thank Him even for my weakness for I felt it made me cling to Him whereas if I had been like others, generous and strong, noble and self–sacrificing, I might have done more in act for Him, yet as it was I had to get Him always to do it for me and so He made me feel that He was ever near and taught me how I could not do one thing good. And my weakness has been my greatest gift, for it has taught me to know Him and myself, to see that I was emptiness, and it was on that account that He has done what He has, for He said: 'Because thou art empty — — .'"[10]

"I knew not what saint to take as my patron when I was to be confirmed, so the right Rev. Dr. Roskell gave me the name of Agnes and I remember telling our dear Lord how much I loved His Holy cousin Saint John the Baptist and the great Saint Joseph and I did not know which I should choose. And I excused myself as it were for taking (Mary) Agnes, saying the Bishop gave me that name. And He then made me understand that Agnes meant lamb, and how the little lamb gave its wool to clothe its master, gave its life and shed its blood to give its flesh as food to its master, how it loved and followed its master and how its shepherd loved it, and I thanked Him and felt to love Him more for allowing me to be called His lamb. And on another occasion our dear Lord showed me that He wished to offer me in sacrifice as it were as His little lamb, and now I think it was after these things that I began to suffer for Him. I think it would be about 1859 or 60."[11]

"Ah dear Jesus even after Thou hadst given Thyself to me in Holy Communion and made me the living Temple of the Holy Ghost by confirmation, yet I remained the same vile, empty good–for–nothing as ever. Though you kindled within me the fire and opened wide my eyes to the light, and I professed and made great promises and told You again and again how much I loved Thee and would rather die than offend Thee. Yet when I remembered the words: 'By their fruits ye shall know them,' I found that I was just as empty–handed as ever, that I was as a

---

[10] Letter 269.
[11] Letter 110.

hollow vessel making much sound and really doing nothing; and though if I had looked far into myself I should have been too disheartened, I used to try and hide myself with all my faults in His Sacred Wounds, and even thank Him for my weakness and offer Him the hatred He has, and the pain occasioned, and the Precious Blood shed from those Sacred Wounds, and beg of Him to pardon and pity His poor blind child. Oh how often I thought it is no use crying over spilt milk — try and live this hour as if it were the only one I had. My weakness, etc. was so deeply impressed upon my soul that I tried to shut my eyes to myself and open them wide in God and would say: 'Oh my dear God, You know how much I wish to love You and all I wish to do for You. I am weak but You are the Holy and strong God, help me to live this hour for Thee alone. I am all Thine, do with me what Thou wilt Oh my Lord and my God, my Father, my Jesus, my Emmanuel. Dear Jesus grant that I may never betray Thee. Out of the depths of my nothingness I have cried to Thee oh my Lord, and Thy Name is magnified in Thy works. I am needy and poor. Oh God help.

"On the 17th of May of the same year, 1857, that I made my first Communion, our dear Rev. Mother (Sister M. Aloysius Perry) died and this was a great trial to me, for she had been such a great help and so excessively kind to me, and the dear Mother who succeeded her thought I had been too much made of and tried me in very many ways for my good; and when I felt things very hard (for you know being cowardly many things proved hard to me that would not have been noticed by a generous soul), I used to say to Our Lord: 'I know Thee and I love Thee Lord and yearn to shed my blood for Thee.' telling myself it was only Our Lord in disguise, for I always tried to look on everyone as Jesus Christ Himself. I was obliged to do these things to keep myself at all within bounds, so from these little instances you may form some idea how weak and wretched I was. Oh my Love, when I look back I marvel more and more how Thou hast borne with me. Have mercy on me dear Jesus and forgive me through Thy precious Blood.

"In the year of my first holy Communion, towards the close, a great feeling of indifferentism came upon me and lasted for many months and what I went through then, our dear Lord only knows. I felt as if I had no power to do anything for God, that I really did not love Him, and I seemed to care very little about whether I did love Him or not, I used to think, 'oh if I could only be sorry for not loving Him that would be a consolation in itself, but I was too cold and callous for anything good, my prayer was hard to make and dry, and so far as I could see without fruit. I was sick too in myself and I know I felt weary and worn, tired of everything and seemed to have no power to exert my will to act or heart to love; I was too afraid to look either before or behind. Instead of being open with my Confessor I hid everything concerning my soul from him and told him only my sins of thoughts, words, deeds and omissions, but not one word of struggle or temptation or of things which it is wise to get permission for. And whatever I felt was hard to my self–love or that I shrank from doing, anything that disgusted me I used to take upon myself to promise our dear Lord I would seek every opportunity of overcoming myself, and this was really necessary for me because I was always so self–seeking, so mean, that I was obliged to pledge myself to do this and not to do that and then I felt I should be less likely to offend Him mortally. For I would not break my word no matter what it cost me if I could help it, and if it were not that He had given me this little good I fear that today I should have been in Hell. He made me realise when I was very young that He was Truth as He confirmed in me some years after. I felt that everything that was not Truth was the Devil and I hated anything that bore the appearance of a lie, and when I would take blame for others if not actually telling a lie, I used to act one and I was so blinded with self–love etc. that I did not consider it a lie. Oh my dear Jesus forgive me and save me and all poor sinners. For instance I remember once Sister having to speak about something that was very disagreeable, and I felt what a pain it must be for her to have to do so, and so sorry for the poor child who had done it. I felt all her confusion and prayed that she might own it at once, and when she did not Sister said she was very sorry to have to put the whole school in penance but she felt obliged to do so. For an instant I struggled with myself and then I stood up as if I had done it, but I was so filled with shame that I reeled over, and when I came to myself I found that the poor child had owned, and Sister said, 'How could you stand up and own to doing what someone else had done?' But mind, it was not sin that had been committed. I would not say I did not do it for I was trusting she would think I did. — From all these evils in me Our dear Lord drew and impressed a lesson on my soul. I thought thus: If we are so confused when thought guilty of a fault before man, how terrible will be the anguish of a soul who appears before the God of Infinite Purity with mortal sin upon it. How I dreaded to be a castaway; how I prayed for poor sinners in words at least, for I was too dry to pray with heart and mind, so I thought. And these things and the like gave me a great insight of myself and urged me to undertake little acts of mortification and charity, for Our dear Lord impressed the words: 'In this shall all men know that you are my disciples, that ye have a love for one another.' And when I hardly knew which would be more perfect of two actions, I used to try and chose that that appeared to me to be the act of charity to my neighbour, and in this you see selfishness again, for naturally I took pleasure in these things, so I always was very suspicious of these seeming kindnesses to others, for I doubt not that in many cases it was a greater kindness to myself.

"As for my prayer, it was made without order or method. I used many vocal prayers which were said without any senti-ment (except of disgust) and with few affections. My meditation was hard and irksome. I tried to follow the prescribed rules in order and method and tried to force myself to do so, and for many years I used to accuse myself of not making my meditation every time I went to confession. And yet I never seemed to mend though I was really in earnest, at least so I thought. Yet all this time how close our dear Lord must have been to me or I should certainly have perished. I feel certain too that different things that then happened in the convent were done by the Devil, for sometimes the whole building seemed to have fallen in by the noise that was made, and the place shaken to its foundations, and on more than one occasion all the nuns as well as all the children were so afraid that they got up and dressed. The nun who is Rev. Mother there now, was a boarder at the time. She, I am sure will remember it well (she is my Godmother in confirmation). Her name was Eliza Cowlam, in religion Sister M. Xavier. For it was always worse when I made an especial offering of myself in reparation or for the conversion of sinners, and I noticed how enraged the Devil was in after years when I really saw and felt him, and so I connect the two facts, though I really don't know.

"When I look back it seems to me that in spite of the ungenerous manner in which I did everything, yet our dear Lord seemed waiting to lavish His favours upon me. To show how pleasing little acts of kindness are though done most ungraciously, I will relate a little instance.

"There was a child who sat near me in class, I think she was No. 4, who hated sewing and did it very badly. She had very hot hands poor child, and on this occasion, a very bad hand — we were making things to give to Rev. Mother on her feast and this child had done the whole of the top of a nightdress and she was delighted when it was finished. But when Sister saw it she said she was so disappointed, it was so badly done, it must all be unpicked and stitched over again. Poor child she cried so bitterly and commenced to unpick, but she could not see very well and she was making a terrible mess of it. I thought I would take it and do it for her and give her mine, but we were going to Robin Hood's Cave that afternoon, and I thought, 'No, I won't, it serves her right for not taking more pains', and though I felt very sorry for her you see I thought more of myself though I now had a great chance to overcome myself. Without saying a word to anyone this struggle went on within me for a while, then I took my name off my work and stitched it on hers, took her work and said I wanted to stop in so she might let me have her work as an excuse, for Sister wanted it all finished that evening. She poor girl was overjoyed and said: 'How can you do it for me when I am always so unkind to you?' (She really was not unkind though I often did things that provoked her.) Then M. M. Walburga came in to see if we were all ready and right for going out, and when she saw me sitting sewing she came up to me and looked at the sewing and said she was ashamed of me, it was disgraceful for a child who had been so long at school to produce such work, and she said I must have tried how badly I could do it, and she scolded me very much and said I was not to go out the whole week for a walk (as a penance) nor go to the playground but stay in and learn to sew. They all went off and I was left by myself and when they had all gone I began to cry, for I was much disappointed at being deprived of the walk and play, for I was a great romp and loved play. But I looked up at the statue of our dear Blessed Lady and the Holy Child, and I said: 'I unite every stitch with those you took when making the seamless garment, and the little disappointment as an act of atonement for sins against charity committed by children in this school, especially my own self–love.' I looked at our dear Lord and a thrill of pleasure passed through me that I had never experienced since the day of my first Communion, and I felt (although I did not see or feel anything outwardly), I felt that Jesus was really and truly by my side both God and Man, I mean in His sacred Humanity, that He watched every stitch I took and searched into the very depth of my heart. This was the first time I experienced this kind of vision for I often had afterwards though I never felt able to express it to myself in words, for I saw without seeing and heard without hearing, but I was most certain that He was there and my whole soul lay prostrate in adoration at His Sacred Feet. And

He made me feel that as I chose to remain in and do this little act of kindness for Him He would stay and keep me company. For I really did for Him and He amply repayed me for my little nothing. It seems that Sister knew all about it, that the other nun had told her, but she wanted to see if I was really doing it for Our Lord, and if so she would give something else to offer, for she told the Bishop about it though they never spoke to me, but good Dr. Roskell, when I was at Sabden mentioned it to me and said I never should know how much the good God had given me through this little act, for he said Sister told him of it at the time and that Our Dear Lord was sure to bless me for it.

"It may seem strange to you, dear Rev. Father, for me to say or think that our dear Lord was actually by my side in the manner I have described, particularly as the Church teaches our dear Lord is only in Heaven and in the most Blessed Sacrament of the Altar in this manner. Yet I have felt His real bodily presence, present with me, going with me where I went, and watching with His sacred human Eye everything I did — not by His presence in my soul, but standing by my side and listening to every word and counting every notion of my whole being. I don't know that I have mentioned this before, but it has very frequently happened to me, though I could not see or hear yet being more certain than if I really saw or heard.

"Things went on much the same always, I doing little or nothing and our dear Lord loading me with favours on every side till the end of the years 1859 or 60, when I was taken very ill and given up by the doctors. I was in bed, I think, for nearly nine months, I was anointed and received all the rites of our Holy Church, and the nuns were waiting for me to die. I was consecrated a child of Mary and then became unconscious and remained so for some days. On the 13th of December the Bishop and Rev. Edward Smith who was in Rome with Father Powell both said a votive Mass of the Blessed Virgin for me. They all thought I must die and told me their little secrets that they wished me to ask our dear Lady to grant them when I died, but on the octave of the Immaculate Conception I came to myself again and began to get better. I consecrated myself again most solemnly to our dear Lord and His blessed Mother, promising to live and die for them, and begging them to let me work and suffer for the salvation of souls.

"I am sure dear Rev. Father, you will smile and think I have always been beginning and am doing so still. It seems to me that I am ever empty handed, always going to do, but never doing anything. It is a very true saying that empty vessels make much sound, for I am always saying and never doing.

"Oh pray hard for me dear Rev. Father, that in the end I may not be a castaway."[12]

Whether there was anything miraculous in Teresa's recovery from her severe illness, as in the case of her little namesake, we cannot tell. She remained on at the convent for several years, but we have no further details of her life there, for her own story here comes to an end.

It was written by wish of Father Snow in 1888, when she was at Saint Catherine's Convent in Edinburgh, but finding how much it cost her, he thought that perhaps Our Lord did not wish her to continue it and told her she need carry it no further.

---

[12] Letter 269.

3

The Call to Teach

IN 1865, when twenty–one years of age, Teresa finally left the convent and returned home. Her family were now living at St. Helen's, in Lancashire, where Mr. Higginson was engaged as a commissioner or forwarding agent. He went out to his office every morning, and, evening by evening, his wife stood waiting at the garden gate to welcome him on his return. One day he came home looking deadly pale and evidently in great distress. He walked straight into the house and began pacing up and down the dining room. Mrs. Higginson, seeing he could not speak, waited outside the door for a few minutes to give him time to recover. Teresa happened to be in the room and watched her father anxiously. At last, thinking that sin alone could cause such anguish, she threw her arms round his neck and kissed him saying: "Oh, Papa, even if you have committed mortal sin, God will forgive you. Only do not lose your trust in Him!" He put her aside and, turning to his wife who at that moment came into the room, said: "I am ruined! I have ruined you all!"[1]

Teresa afterwards told Father Snow that these words pierced her heart like a sword. She had always had a great dread of riches and had prayed much that her family might be poor, and now, when she saw her father's agony and realised all the anxiety and distress her dear ones would have to undergo, she felt that

---

[1] Notes on Teresa's Life by Father Snow.

her prayer had indeed been answered. Mr. Higginson had been involved in some dealings in cotton which had turned out disastrously owing to the American War and he had lost everything. He went bankrupt and for a time it was impossible for him to find employment, so they removed to Liverpool where they suffered many hardships from their poverty. Teresa, who was a beautiful needle–woman, used to go from shop to shop asking for work. She was often laughed at or refused, but she obtained a few orders, and the nuns at the convent in Beacon Lane were very good to her. After a time, the family settled at Egremont in Cheshire, and gradually their circumstances began to improve. Mr. Higginson was able to resume business at St. Helen's; one of his daughters, Louisa, trained as a school teacher with the Sisters of Notre Dame at Mount Pleasant, and another, Frances, gave lessons in music. Teresa remained at home with her parents who seem always to have been very loath to part with her, both, no doubt, on account of her delicacy and because they realised the very special treasure Almighty God had committed to their care.

In the year 1871, a terrible epidemic of smallpox and cholera broke out in the western counties and spread with great rapidity in Liverpool and the neighbouring towns. One of the most severely affected was Bootle, where the schools had to be closed for want of teachers. The rector of St. Alexander's church at Bootle, the Rev. Edward Powell, was a zealous and holy man who came from a family of corn merchants at West Derby, Liverpool. He had the interests of his parish very much at heart, and the story is told of how he once went to seek advice from the saintly Curé d'Ars. He explained how he had prayed and even fasted for the good of his people, but apparently with small result. The saint looked at him and said simply: "Have you tried blood?" When Father Powell came to die many years later he was found to be wearing a hair shirt.

This zealous priest was much distressed at the state of his children who, owing to the closing of the schools, were running wild and becoming utterly undisciplined. He applied for help to

Sister Mary Philip, then in charge of the training college at Mount Pleasant. She had no qualified, or even experienced, teacher, available, but recommended Miss Teresa Higginson, the sister of one of her students who had a wonderful influence with children. Teresa, as may be imagined, far from being scared by the fear of infection, was delighted at this opportunity of sacrificing her life in the cause of charity and eagerly offered her services. Father Powell gratefully accepted the offer, and two souls destined to play a great part in each other's lives, were thus brought together. The appointment proved a great success. Teresa quickly won her way with the children and remained at Bootle for about a year. Father Powell became more and more impressed with her as he recognised the great heights of virtue to which she had already attained, and the special graces with which Almighty God had endowed her. He allowed her to communicate daily, a thing most unusual in those days and one for which she was ever grateful to him. He soon discovered her wonderful gift for teaching. When she was giving her catechism classes on a Sunday he used to watch the benches fill with grown–up people as well as children, all listening to her with rapt attention. After a time he told her he thought Almighty God was calling her to serve Him in this way and sent her to consult the Sisters of Notre Dame. Sister M. Philip told her that she would require a year's study before going in for the necessary examination, but Father Powell, finding that one was to be held in the following week, bade her go in for it at once. She obeyed and passed successfully. Throughout her life it was remarked that her learning never came from books. She was hardly ever seen to read, a point on which she was often affectionately teased by her fellow–teachers in later years. They used to say that it was hardly fair that she should be able to give her lessons with so little trouble when they had to spend such long hours in preparation. A gentle smile was Teresa's only answer.

Mr. and Mrs. Higginson were opposed to the idea of Teresa's adopting the teaching profession, for they did not think her health would stand it. She herself was in much anxiety as to her vocation in life. As a tiny child she had dedicated herself entirely to God, and she only longed to know along which path she could follow most closely in the steps of her suffering Lord. In her trouble she went to consult Father Ignatius Spencer, the venerable Passionist who had been so fond of her in her childhood, and who was then at Sutton. When she went in he said aloud the Gloria Patri, adding: "Thank God, my child, you have come to me." He encouraged her to continue her teaching and told her she had no vocation to be a nun, though she would later on live in a convent. He assured her that God had special designs on her, and that she must be very faithful and very open with her confessor, adding that if she were lost her damnation would be awful. He also warned her against making friends, promising that when our Lord saw it was necessary for her to have a friend He would send her one.

Teresa's doubts were set at rest. She felt, as she expressed it, that "Almighty God was calling her to teach little children how to love Him", and she entered eagerly on her profession. In 1872, she went as mistress to the village school of Orrell, near Wigan, and having satisfied the government inspector, was granted her certificate, and sent early in the following year to the more important post of St. Mary's, Wigan. Here she remained for three years, leading to all outward appearance the ordinary uneventful life of a schoolmistress, but in the inner history of her soul these years were to prove of vast importance. It is at Wigan that we first come into touch with friends and fellow teachers, from whose living lips we are able to gather many details of Teresa's daily life. But it must be borne in mind that her constant aim was to avoid notice and to disguise as far as possible from others the favours which Almighty God was lavishing upon her soul. And thus it is that, with few exceptions, her companions, while they could not fail to note many strange occurrences, little guessed their true significance, and when, in after years they learnt the stupendous truth about the retiring little woman they thought they had known so well, they could but wonder at their blindness. Even the chosen few who were admitted to her confidence were far from knowing all — this was revealed to her director alone and then only in virtue of obedience. Still, her friends have much to tell that is of interest, both as depicting the external history of her life, and as lending confirmation to her own statements.

One of her fellow teachers has described her appearance when she was at Wigan:

"She appeared about thirty years of age (though I have since learnt that she was much younger than she looked. She was about five feet two inches in height, her body seemed much emaciated though her face was not too thin. She had what the people here call a wizen face, i.e. shrivelled and sallow. Her hair was dark, eyes also dark, small, very quick and bright, her general expression very pleasing; in conversation she was animated, witty and humorous. Her movements were quick and sprightly and she seemed always on the alert and entered heart and soul into everything she took in hand. Her dress was often odd. She never cared whether her clothes were in taste or well–fitting, in fact never seemed to have a new costume and as she had literally no regard for money I came to the conclusion that her clothes were simply her sisters' cast off clothing, and that she squandered her salary in buying books and objects of piety for others and in charity, so that she never had the wherewithal to buy a decent outfit. Such was Miss Higginson as I remember her... From the first day I met her until we parted I could never find fault with her in any way. She was never cross–looking or out of humour and her pupils idolised her. She seemed to live in the presence of God and always introduced some religious topic into the conversation without boring one with an overdose of piety, or seeming to preach."

The little staff of St. Mary's school were on very happy, intimate terms. One of the things which attracted their attention with regard to Teresa was the strange attacks of what they called debility to which she was subject, especially of a morning. She went to daily Mass but was often so weak that she had almost to be carried to the altar rails; then, after receiving holy Communion, her strength returned and she would walk back unaided to her place and be able to carry out her duties for the rest of the day as though in normal health. They noticed too, how rigorously she fasted. There were times when she seemed literally to live on the Blessed Sacrament alone, for three days at a time taking no other food.

Towards the end of 1873, a new teacher was appointed to the staff, Miss Susan Ryland. She spent a day at Wigan to visit the school, and Teresa told her later how, before her arrival, the Devil had tormented her, saying that she would no longer be able to keep her secrets as the new teacher would soon find them out. Miss Ryland took up her duties on January 5th, and Teresa soon recognised in her the friend Father Spencer had promised her our Lord would send her in her need. For the next eighteen months they were seldom parted, and during the holidays Miss Ryland accompanied Teresa to her home. Mrs. Higginson met her with open arms, saying: "I have longed to meet you. You are the only friend Teresa has ever had." And Mr. Higginson bade his family do all they could to welcome Teresa's friend.

Miss Ryland and Teresa at first shared a lodging and then removed to the little schoolhouse attached to St. Mary's school, where they occupied the same room and even slept in the same bed. Hard–worked and poorly paid, there was much of sacrifice and no little heroism in the life of the Catholic teacher of those days. The year 1874 was to be one of the most eventful in Teresa's life, and our Lord had provided her with a friend after her own heart, loyal, silent, and above all not inquisitive! Living in such close intimacy it would have been impossible to hide all trace of the mysterious events of those months, and Teresa gladly gave up all attempts at secrecy and, though she never spoke of her inner life, Miss Ryland was the silent witness of many marvels concerning which she drew her own conclusions. Yet even so, on looking back, she can but wonder at the simple way in which she took these things and at her utter want of curiosity and surprise concerning them.

"I became acquainted with Teresa", she writes, "at the end of December, 73. It was on January 5th, 1874 that I began my life with her. I remained with her at Wigan until July 1875. During that time she received to my knowledge many favours from God; visitations from the evil One in person, also from our Lord, our Lady and the saints. In Lent, 1874, she was granted the following of our Lord in the details of His sacred Passion, the Crown of Thorns, like St. Rose of Lima, the sacred Stigmata and many other favours."

From their first meeting Miss Ryland was strangely attracted to Teresa and soon began to suspect that there was something very remarkable about her. Her first experience of anything out of the common was after she had been at Wigan a fortnight. It was about ten–thirty and they were going to bed, when she looked round and found Teresa lying on the floor, unconscious. Being unable to move her she called for help and lifted her on to the bed. She saw that this was no ordinary illness, and when, by one p.m. there was no change, she went for Father Wells. He came at once though she was surprised to see the calm way in which he took the matter. Teresa was still unconscious, but when he gave her some Lourdes water she immediately came to herself. He then sent Miss Ryland for the doctor, who expressed astonishment at Teresa's excessive weakness and could make nothing of the case. Miss Ryland herself soon realised that these strange illnesses were supernatural — Teresa was in fact, in ecstasy, a condition which became very constant at this time. Her friend has described her outward appearance on these occasions:

"There were two ways in which Teresa was taken. In one the body was supple and she showed either excessive grief or excessive joy. In the other the body was quite rigid and it was almost impossible to move her. That state did not last long. Twice she was like that in the street. Fortunately it was in a lonely part or it might have proved awkward. I could do nothing but stand at her side till she became conscious. During the early part of 1874, there was something in the paper about Louise Lateaux[2] in France being in ecstasy every Friday and we passed the remark (I mean Miss Woodward and I), 'That is nothing to this house. It is a daily occurrence here', which it was at that time. Teresa must have had some kind of communication with her, for she said one day after coming to herself: 'Louise Lateaux told me to read something in the life of St. Teresa.' So I brought the book to her but I don't know what she read. She had the same favours as that saint, one being the seraph's dart of love, but she said it did not seem to come from an angel, it was our Lord Himself. Once she saw something (I don't think it was the Passion) that caused her great grief and a little while after something that brought on excessive joy and I heard her say (for she spoke rather loudly), 'I can bear the grief but I cannot bear this joy.' At another time she experienced some terrible fear, she was for a long time as pale as death and as if in an agony. She held her crucifix in her hand at a distance and passed it round in front as if to ward off someone. I got the holy water and used it freely. It brought about no change, so Miss Woodward went for Father Wells. He came down, watched her for a while, then called her by name when she immediately came to herself. I have only thought since what it might be. As the holy water did no good I am of opinion that she was resisting our Lord because I know that she had after-wards something of the same kind to do and it was distasteful to her, but of course she always obeyed.

"There was another state she was in but I think that was only recollection. When we said the rosary together she would suddenly stop and I had to wait a long time for her, so I made up my mind not to wait but to continue taking both sides. That night in the middle of the first mystery, she stopped and began again when I was finishing the fourth. She touched me gently when I began the fifth and said: 'It is only the second.' I replied: 'It is the

---

2   Louise Lateaux was a famous Belgian Stigmatic living at this time.

second for you, but for me it is the fifth, and I don't want to be here all night.' That sounds irreverent, but I was dealing with her then not as a saint but as a familiar friend.

"I have said little of our Lord's visits. They were frequent but, as a rule, Miss Higginson did not speak to Him in such a way that I could hear. She told me once, however, that she was longing for the Day of Judgment that He might show men how much she had loved Him. I recognised these words as having been said to St. Teresa.

"On four occasions, to my knowledge, our Lady appeared to her. I give an account of two. I saw she was talking to someone. Of course, at these times she was unconscious of anything else. When our Lady went away she said to me: 'Isn't she beautiful?' I asked: 'Who?' 'Our blessed Lady. Didn't you see her, dear?' When I said no, she was very quiet and only said: 'She has told me I love Him more than I can tell.'

"The second apparition was at a time when she was very ill and not able to help herself. I was kneeling by her side when she sat up and said: 'Our Lady says I am cured, and I shall go to holy Communion on Thursday morning.' That was Tuesday night, and I wondered why not the next morning since she was better, but in the morning I found she was weak as ever. I got her up before dinner and brought her downstairs. After dinner she became unconscious again. I had to leave her and go to school. Miss Woodward remained with her. A little before four o'clock, she (Teresa) came up to the school to me although she had to mount a flight of stone steps. I said: 'You have no right to come up here when you have been so ill.' She said: 'What God does He does well. I am all right', or words to that effect. She had also been to church, and to see Father Wells. Miss Woodward told me that at three o'clock she came to herself and said: 'Didn't our Lady say three o'clock?' She then put on her hat and came out, going first to church.

"St. Joseph was with her once and St. Peter once. There were other visions which she only told me of, but I mention only those which I was present for."

Teresa's great wish was ever to remain hidden and unknown, and never throughout her life did she do any startling public work, but while in Wigan she seems to have performed a number of what might be called minor miracles, of which Miss Ryland gives a few examples.

"At the bidding of Father Wells she cured a child of some chest disease. She used common lard (as an excuse I suppose). The child's mother asked her afterwards for some of the ointment. Teresa said to me: 'What shall I do? It is only common lard.' One night she came from church where she had been doing the altar, etc., bringing with her a duster or so to wash. There was no common soap in the house. I suppose we had forgotten it. She asked me had we nothing but the good soap and when I said no, she remarked it was against holy poverty to use that for dusters. I turned away but happened to turn back just in time to see a pound of common soap on the table and Teresa stretching out her hand to take it, as it was nearer to where I was standing than to her. I am not sure but I think she laid down the money necessary to pay for it. I am quite certain there was no soap on the table when I turned away. Another time I had forgotten, or did not notice, that there was no wood in the house. In the morning I wanted to light the fire. Teresa was in bed. I went in to her and said: 'We have no wood and I want to light the fire.' She said: 'There is plenty in the sacristy.' But I said: 'The church is not open yet.' 'Very well', she said, 'ask St. Joseph for some.' I said: 'You ask him, he won't do it for me.' Then she said: 'Have you been to such a cupboard?' I said: 'Yes, and there is none there.' 'Well, go and look again.' I went and found a quantity of nice pieces not like the wood we bought.

"The key of her school was once lost. We kept it in the school–house, and when she wanted to enter it was not to be found. I searched the house for it, so did she. She then went up to the parlour and I think knelt by the table. Presently she came out with the key in her hand and looking very pale. I said to her: 'What on earth is the matter with you? You look frightened to death.' (It was unusual to see her like that.) 'Yes', she said, 'I was frightened because I saw nothing, but a white hand put the key down.'

"Another day after coming from Holy Communion she lighted the fire on the spur of the moment by making the sign of the cross over cold cinders. She said: 'This would warm the children's cans.' Then made the sign of the cross and I saw the flames come into the cold cinders. She did the same thing at home. Her sister Fanny said to me in Teresa's presence (they, like myself, used to tease her sometimes): 'Our Tess is very clever, she can light a fire without coal or wood.' I asked Teresa what she meant and she told me her Mama was ill that morning and Fanny wanted the fire quickly. Hence the result. Her brother said to me one day: 'Tess can do wonderful things. She can send up a tray before her.' He was teasing her. I asked her what he meant. She told me she was going to bring up the tray but it was too heavy for her, so her guardian angel took it from her and put it into her brother's hands. Then he saw her at the bottom of the stairs.

"The Maundy Thursday I spoke of I was preparing the room for holy Communion and had nearly finished, when the bell rang for Mass and I had to leave to see to the children. There were clean sheets downstairs which I was airing at the fire the day before, and a white counterpane we used only when she received. That was in my box. As I went downstairs I said to our Lord: 'I cannot do any more. I must go now to my duty.' I locked the door of the house. When I came back the sheets and counterpane had been put on. It was done for her, but certainly not by her as she was unable to leave her bed. Besides the undersheet was only halfway as is sometimes done in case of sickness."

Miss Ryland noticed that Teresa seemed often able to read her thoughts and even knew what happened in her absence. As a little instance she tells how she was once making pastry and dropped the rolling pin on the floor. She washed it and having wiped it with a cloth went on with her work. When she went upstairs, Teresa, who had all the time been in her room, said with a smile:

"My dear, never roll out pastry with a damp roller."

Others of her friends had like experiences, and an amusing story is told of two old priests on their way to visit her who thought it wise to go to confession to each other before seeing her!

But ecstasies and visions notwithstanding, Teresa never for an instant thought that she could slacken in her battle against self. To the end she feared she might turn traitor, and often begged for prayers lest she should become "a castaway". One of her favourite sayings was: "Small straws show which way the wind blows", meaning that it is the little things which prove our attitude towards God. The following incidents related by Miss Ryland show the close watch she kept and how sternly she exercised her rare powers of self–control. One day in conversation something was said about Father Wells. Teresa jumped up and ran out of the room. Miss Ryland followed her and found her in the school–yard with her lips tightly closed and her hand pressed over them. She asked what was wrong. 'Oh', said Teresa, 'I was so afraid I should answer back!'

Another night she came in looking much disturbed. "I did not speak to her", says Miss Ryland, "as I thought it best to leave her until she recovered. In a few minutes she said to me: 'I was nearly overcome that time!' meaning that she almost gave way to nature. I said: 'I thought you were put out. What happened?' She then told me that she had gone as usual to ask Father Wells' blessing before retiring to rest and he had ordered her out of the room, and she said: 'I think he would have thrown me over if I had not got off my knees quickly.' Father Wells, of course, did these things to try her."

No detail was too trifling to be turned to use in the conquest of nature. When asked to admire a lovely sunset she took one glance and did not look again. She delighted to obey the wishes of her junior teachers, and would often stand waiting at the door that Miss Ryland might enter first. Tiny straws indeed! but it is by the lightest touch that the masterpiece is brought to its perfection, and what iron mastery of self does such unceasing watch entail!

Miss Ryland has often been asked whether she did not find life with Teresa sad and painful, but she will not have it so. Teresa herself was so ideal a companion, ever kind and thoughtful, bright and full of interest, by nature very quick and active, except when overtaken by her mysterious weakness. Even then she took no thought of self nor was she in any way hysterical. Calm and self–controlled, she was never known to cry or make a scene, and the doctor, puzzled though he often was at her condition, never made mention of hysteria as its cause. Her very illnesses gave way before the call of duty and, except towards the end of Lent, she was seldom absent from her place in school. Her influence with the children was very great and they quickly fell under the charm of her personality, so strongly felt by her companions in her own childhood. She seemed to see into their minds and to know if they were speaking the truth, and they soon found that the most elaborate excuses were of no avail, though in any pain or trouble they had a ready listener. One who was a pupil teacher at the time, describes Teresa's lively interest in her pupils and remembers specially some game of railways in the school–room wherein she played a leading part, puffing up and down the room in vigorous imitation of an engine!

4

St. Mary's, Wigan

THE little incidents related in the last chapter give the picture of Teresa as she appeared to the eyes of her friends and companions. We must now turn to the more important events of this time, and Canon Snow[1] supplies the clue which sets them in their true perspective. He says that Teresa was essentially a contemplative, and as such was being led along the path of Mystic union. He goes on to explain how, the closer the union to which a soul is called by God, so much the more intense is the purification to which it is subjected. Teresa, he says, during these months at Wigan, was being prepared for that degree of union known as the Mystical Espousals which was accomplished on the Feast of the Sacred Heart, 1874. "During this period", he says[2], "she underwent many trials and much suffering. Our blessed Lord allowed her more fully than before to participate in the sufferings of His Passion. She suffered much from the obsessions of the Devil. She was also subjected to many trials and tests on the part of her director.

---

[1] As the name of the Rev. Alfred Snow will figure largely in these pages, it may be well to explain at once that he later on became Teresa's director, when, finding himself called upon to guide so gifted a soul, he set himself to make a special study of mystical theology.

[2] Notes on the life of Teresa by Canon Snow.

"To begin with the last of these trials", he continues, "Father Thomas Wells, the rector of St. Mary's and her director, was a holy, zealous and devoted priest, faithful in the discharge of every duty and withal a humble man. Finding himself in charge of so gifted and holy a soul, a position so remote from any experience he had hitherto had, in his humility and diffidence he sought advice and considered it his duty to follow it in all respects. Hence he came to guide her soul by proxy. He consulted and was in frequent communication with the Rev. James Lennon, D.D., professor of moral theology at St. Cuthbert's College, Ushaw. This is a situation that has often arisen in the lives of the saints and other holy souls, arisen no doubt by the Providence of God for the greater purification of the soul, but one which in itself can hardly be considered consonant with the principles which should guide the confessor in his dealings with his penitent. It invariably happens in such cases that the priest consulted is never satisfied, especially where he has no personal knowledge of the penitent. He is ever in doubt and orders one test after another to be applied, one humiliation and trial after another, until the penitent and director are robbed of all peace. This is precisely what happened in the present case. Father Wells was one of those men, and there are many like him, who think that when they ask advice they ought conscientiously to take it. Hence he appears to have imposed upon Teresa all the trials and humiliations that Dr. Lennon suggested. At one time, he insulted her in public and drove her out of the church. This little affected her for she and all who witnessed the event, knowing as they did the habitual kindness and gentleness of Father Wells, would know that he was only acting. The humiliation was too apparent. What proved to be a real trial and suffering was a much more simple thing. He put her under obedience to take off her scapulars and medals and carry no pious object on her person. This caused her very great suffering as she considered she must in some way have made herself unworthy to wear them, and, moreover, thought that they were means of grace which she had thought necessary for her salvation."

Among the trials to which Father Snow alludes are the obsessions of the Devil. "Our wrestling is not against flesh and blood but against principalities and powers, against the rulers of the world of this darkness, against the spirits of wickedness in high places", says St. Paul, and the greater the saint the sterner will be the conflict. So we find Satan bringing all his forces to the attack against this unknown little teacher. He mocked and beat her, ill–used and tempted her, even as he had done to the great Fathers of the Desert, and to the saintly Curé d'Ars. She told it all in obedience to her directors, and her own account is fully borne out by the witness of her friends. There is no stronger proof of her rare powers of attraction than the fact that the young girls who were her companions should none the less have had the courage to remain with her, but their trust in Teresa was unshakable and as long as she was near they knew full well no harm could come to them.

The following letter describes some of her experiences in this respect.

"AMDG et in hon B V M et Bt. J.
"Bootle June 20 1880

"Dear rev. Father

"In honour of the Seat of divine Wisdom and in the holy name of Jesus and Mary I will relate the principal temptations at Wigan by which the Devil by the permission of God assailed me.

"I think the first visible temptation which I had at Wigan was as soon as I went. I think you know that without any permission I used to rise as soon after twelve as I conveniently could (I had not a bed to myself) to make my meditation etc. and each time I commenced the Devil used to beat and ill use the body, and spit horrible filth upon me in the face and eyes, in fact, completely cover me which made me very sick, and the stench was almost poisoning. And this I told to rev. T. Wells who told me he thought I had a very fertile imagination, and as far as I can judge he did not believe me, but he told me to tell him each time I fancied it, and when he saw that it still continued he asked me could he write to some priest of great experience about it. But in the meantime, he said, you must not rise to make your meditation. Night is the time to sleep and rest so that you may be able to do your work as duty requires. And so I did not rise intentionally, but several times I found myself rising, and when I at once returned the devils would shriek and yell and laugh in a most dreadful manner and mock me and say: 'Most obedient maid how firm are your words of promise to the King of heaven!' But I did not notice him. Of course each time I found myself getting out of bed I told my confessor as soon as I could see him and he said if the will was really desirous of being entirely obedient he did not see how I could be so continually rising; but I begged and prayed our Lord and His b. Mother to help me to accomplish perfectly and promptly whatever my director would wish, cost it me what it would. And so by degrees I did not rise, but I seldom slept, I could not help myself making my meditation though I think I strove hard to resist, and so I told Father Wells. Then he said I must sleep a certain time, I forget now but I think he said four hours, and under obedience I did so, and when I slept the Devil would rouse me. Sometimes he cried as though some poor child were out upon the doorstep; sometimes he used to throw me completely out of bed, throw things at me that were in the room, and make awful noises, and I used to be afraid at first that Miss Gallagher or the people of the house would hear. And several times when I awoke I perceived a smell of something burning, and the house being filled with smoke and brimstone, I thought surely the house was on fire. And other times I saw the whole bed and room full of flames and heard the crackling and I am afraid in this case I proved a coward, for I was frightened more than I can tell at first for there was no holy water: the Devil threw something against the bottle and broke it. But Mary and St. Michael were ever near and when I called upon her I knew he had no power to hurt. But I thought the house

might really be burnt and I think it was the Devil so I told Fr.
Wells that I felt afraid and he said I must tell the Devil he must
not do it again. And any temptation I always noticed stopped at
the command of my director. Fr. Wells told me to ask our b. Lord
to change the temptation.

"When Fr. Wells told me not to make my meditation I thought
that was just what the Devil wanted, but I did not say so for I
knew that obedience and giving up my own will was more
pleasing to our b. Lord and more to my own good than anything
else.

"Our Lord kept these temptations secret till we went to the
school–house and then they were soon known. The Devil knew
I did not like anyone to know these things and so he often told
me he would let the other mistresses see and know all; but I
knew he had no power of himself so I never heeded him, and I
used to say to our dear b. Lord when he said these things to me:
'Thou knowest best oh Lord what is good for me. I am Thine do
with me what Thou pleasest."

"At length Miss Ryland (who is now a nun) and Miss Woodward (at Burscough Hall) soon saw and heard everything almost; at least I don't know what they knew, but as they were
frightened Fr. Wells told them the Devil could not hurt them etc.
I think I had temptations against every virtue while there and I
seemed entirely abandoned by God and His holy Mother, and at
these times Fr. Wells on more than one occasion would not hear
what I had to say. He used to tell me to go to holy Communion
as usual which was then only four times per week."[3]

Teresa always felt herself called in a special manner to make
reparation for sinners, and she used often to beg to be allowed to
take on herself the punishment due to them in order to secure
their salvation. This seemed to infuriate the Devil, and at such
times he would attack her with redoubled fury.

"I think the reason why the Devil used to spit and throw that
abominable filth of such awful stench at me was because at that

3   Letter 55.

time I resolved to mortify the senses more rigorously and never to gratify them in the least, or rather to do all that I could that was disagreeable and hurtful to them. Certainly at times I was almost suffocated but the holy and strong God never forsook me and Mary was ever a tower of strength against all the wiles of the wicked one. And when ever our dear good God accepted my poor prayers and little nothings in behalf of poor sinners he, the Devil, used to be infuriated, and beat, drag and almost choke me. He used to tell me it was no use me trying to save souls when my own was lost, that God had already given him power over me, that it was far better for me to live a very ordinary life, that such things that I took upon myself were more than the greatest saints attempted, that it was mad presumption on my part to expect that God would work continual miracles in my behalf...

"When our dear Lord tried me with great desolation, he appeared with numberless demons and tempted me as I think they would tempt the poor souls whose guilt I took upon myself, with, I think, every description of sin — against charity, with envy — hatred I may say, and against holy Purity, against Faith and to a dreadful despair. For when I was really worn out with continual struggling and I knew not whether I had sinned or no and I cried out to God for pity and pardon, and to Mary, Joseph, and St. Michael for protecting help, the fiends laughed and cried as with one voice: 'Where is now Thy God who has hitherto helped you? In what a true friend you confide, see now what effect your prayers have. Most compassionate friend, generous and charitable soul, perhaps now you will learn that charity begins at home. Learn wisdom if it is not too late; see what a reception you will have, angelical Teresa, humble and beloved Spouse of the Almighty One. Who will now help you? Where are the souls you have saved? Where is your loving Mother now? Where the God you thought to serve? Where is your God?'

"And bowing to the august and thrice blessed Trinity I answered the wicked One by saying: 'Ah my Jesus, my God, my only Hope! Surely Thou art here in Thy Justice. Spare me not oh

Lord, but save them whom You desire I should help. Remember Thy most Precious Blood is the price of each soul! Look on Thy gaping Wounds! See Thy Mother's heart is breaking. Look on the work of Thy Hands, and when Thou lookest have mercy and spare!'

"Whatever temptation I had our b. Lord once told me to offer to the Eternal Father at once the sufferings and the Precious Blood that was endured for that particular sin, and make an act of the opposite virtue, uniting it to the perfection of that virtue in Jesus Christ and His b. Mother. Four or five times when I was fasting for sins of drunkenness and self–indulgence, and perhaps I fainted or so, the Devil would come as a friend to give me food and drink and tell me in a most compassionate manner I was too weak for such excessive mortifications. And I used at times to suffer greatly from a burning thirst and my tongue used to swell very much, and he often would bring me water and other things and wish me to slake my thirst and say: 'You are really destroying your health, you are now in a burning fever' etc. And he would make others notice it, and someone told Fr. Wells that I was so thirsty that I could not speak and I would not drink, and he asked me to take a drink any time Miss Ryland wished me so then I did. I know it is more pleasing to our dear b. Lord that we give up our will in little things than fast or mortify ourselves for years. The Devil used to make me strike myself as I have seen children playing with each other. He used to appear in hideous forms sometimes and also as man very often (I think he used the bodies of damned souls), and I remember particularly on two occasions him opening the bedroom window and talking as if he had a companion. Miss Ryland heard him too but she did not see him and she became much alarmed. It was in the night and she said she could not help listening, and I asked her to say the Little Office of our Lady with me and she did so and I asked her to offer it up for all who might be specially tempted at that time, in union with all the glory that ascended to Almighty God in the immaculate purity of the B.V. Mary and the awful purity of God in Unity. And the Devil was so exasperated that he commenced to throw the things about the room at me and make a terrible noise. Then it seemed as though a great explosion was taking place and he seemed to set the room on fire — she could smell the burning and she said: 'Oh dear he is burning the bed, what shall we do?' I told her to take no notice, to sprinkle a little holy water and let us get on with our prayers, or else try to go to sleep, he could not hurt her and the bed was not mine, he had no power over Fr. Well's things. So he threw something against the holy water font and broke it. Sometimes he would follow me about as a fox, and sometimes as part a fish, part a fox, and part a pig, I mean a thing with a serpent's head, a pig's head and a fox's head and tail and a bird's wings and head with hooked bill, in church and out, but I never took much notice, I mean I appeared not to notice. I used to be much afraid at first, but Fr. Wells told me it was not sinful, it was the natural consequence of the supernatural coming in contact with the natural...

"I think I have now related the principal temptations, but they were many and seemed to my weakness to last a long time."[4]

The following is a letter written some years later by Miss Ryland to Father Powell in answer to his enquiries as to her experiences at Wigan.

"St. Paul's Convent,
"Selley Park,
"June 27, 1880.

"REV. AND DEAR SIR,

"In reply to your letter received on Friday last, I must say that whilst living with Miss Higginson at Wigan I heard at times extraordinary noises and saw her ill–used; I never saw by whom.

"In the first place you ask me to state what I saw, giving examples. I found the holy water stoop and bottle broken in a strange manner, I did not see it done. I have never seen Miss Higginson thrown out of bed, I have found her almost out and unable to replace herself. I have seen smoke, not flames. The bed

---

4   Letter 55a.

was not set on fire as far as I know for certain. I believe there were marks as if an attempt had been made to do so. I saw a strange light on the wall sometimes on the bed, and covering Miss Higginson's face. I saw, though indistinctly, because of the dark, things hurled at her which I picked up; I have seen her own hands thrown violently against her face, I saw no one there to do it. I found water which I left by her for the purpose of washing her thrown over her. I did not see it done.

"You next ask what I heard.

"I heard noises as if everything in the room above was being dashed against the ground and on going up the noise then seemed to be in the room below where Miss Higginson was. I heard at times a rushing noise as if animals were in the room — sometimes footsteps, knocking, voices of people (once only) speaking in an undertone. I heard a noise made by Miss Higginson as though someone had hold of her throat. I have been wakened by hearing shrieks, but when fully awake did not hear them. Once or twice during the day I heard a noise as if she was struck by a hand.

"As to the effects on myself. It did cause me fear which increased until I spoke of it in the confessional and received advice about it. Afterwards it was much lessened. You ask me what I did myself and by whose advice, whether by Miss Higginson's. I never asked Miss Higginson's advice. I told her in the beginning I was afraid of that strange light, that I did not know what it was but I don't remember ever asking her what I should do. I never asked anyone, I used holy water. I went at first once or perhaps twice, I forget now, to my confessor and hers in his room. I only told him what I had seen and heard the first and second nights and what I thought. I did not ask him what I should do.

"We had at that time a third person in the house who taught the night school. I told her also then, and I think asked her should I speak to my confessor, but I don't recollect so as to be sure.

"Trusting my answers to the questions you put will satisfy.

"I remain, dear Sir,

"Yours very respectfully

SUSAN RYLAND."

Besides this statement, Miss Ryland relates other instances of the ceaseless and petty attacks of the Devil during this time. Often there would come a knock at the door, and when Teresa went to open it she would receive a violent blow on the face from an unseen hand. When Miss Ryland went herself no one would be there. On one of these occasions Miss Ryland heard the blow, and Teresa came back into the room with a great swelling down one side of her face which gradually turned black and blue. One evening as they sat together in their house opposite the school they heard a child sobbing bitterly. Teresa, thinking it had been locked into the school by mistake, ran in great distress for the key and searched the whole building from top to bottom. No one was to be seen and suddenly the sobbing broke into mocking laughter. On another night when they were in bed, Teresa asked Miss Ryland if she heard anything in the room. She replied that there seemed to her to be two men whispering together at the foot of the bed as though they were hatching some plot. "Yes", said Teresa, "it is the Devil and he is planning to send a man in at the window to attack us." She then got up and fastened the window securely with a rope. A little later on there came a tremendous rattling and knocking on the pane. Teresa was always most careful on such occasions to use all human means at her disposal, and that done, she said the rest could be safely left in the Hands of God. She used to say too that it was best to pay as little attention as possible to the Devil when he tried to torment her — he just wanted to be noticed!

While Satan thus persisted in his futile persecutions, Teresa was undergoing other trials also in preparation for her closer union with her beloved Spouse. We have seen that from her infancy suffering had been her very life. This craving to participate in the pains of Christ was leading onwards to a special end.

It is in itself the true seal of those on whom He chooses to confer the singular favour of the Stigmata, and the time was now approaching when He would stamp Teresa with His Sacred Wounds and, so arrayed, claim her as His promised Bride. Dr. Imbert who has made a special study of the Stigmata and of the lives of those who bore it, writes: "The life of those who bear the Stigmata is but a long series of pains which lead up to the divine malady of the Stigmata and then form an escort as it were, continuing with it up to the hour of death."[5]

This was indeed proved true of Teresa.

The following letter to her director describes the penances she took upon herself in her attempt to control the flames of divine love which burnt so fiercely yet so sweetly in her heart — penances so terrible that they seem to us well nigh incredible, though to her they were but "little nothings", filling her with great delight.

"DEAR REV. FATHER,

"In obedience to your wish I will try and tell you all the little nothings I took upon myself without permission. Oh my dear good Jesus if these things were not according to your holy pleasure pardon me by Your obedience unto death...

"I could not adopt any method of mortification until after I had left the convent when I at first wore a cloth (in which I put twisted wire and tacks) but it was continually breaking, and I began to use a pair of goffering irons made red hot to burn myself and which I found very effectual, for when they would not really burn they would sear, and this I used in every part of the body that was not actually exposed to view. When I had a very sore burn I used to put on some cobbler's wax on a piece of leather which I had for the purpose, and once I had two large holes into which I used to pour turpentine. Two or three times when I had crushed toes and felt them sore, I pulled off the nails by wedging in small splinters and so dragged them out. Then another time I saw some of that steel wire cloth that I told you of

---

[5]   *Le Stigmatisme.* Vol. II, p.126.

and I got a small piece and wore it round my arms, then I procured enough for the waist, but I think the heat and discharge from the sores rotted it, for it broke into small pieces and it was sometime before I was able to get enough to make another. One reason why I thought these things were pleasing to our b. Lord was this, that on several occasions (when I have been taken suddenly ill and others have undressed me) He concealed them so perfectly that neither chain nor sores have been noticed. You know I always spent as much of the night as I could in prayer and I used to fast frequently without leave, and I made a rule never to take anything on the happy day that I communicated without I was put under obedience to do so. At first I used to feel fasting extremely, I was naturally very fainty, and I used to think the more I felt it the more it was pleasing to Him who was the suffering crucified Spouse of my soul. I made a vow too never to go to any public amusement unless forced through obedience or charity (when I left the convent). And although I always tried to mortify the senses, yet when I went to Wigan I made a vow never to indulge any of my senses, in anything that was pleasing only in obedience etc.; never to ask questions about ordinary things, I mean news; never to show if I was hurt; try always to be the same under every circumstance. I made most, and often renewed all my promises before this altar, I made the vows I put into practice at Wigan here before I left, for you were the first to allow me to communicate daily and I loved this church on that account. But although I felt fasting very much at first, sleep was the hardest enemy I had to fight against and when I used to prolong my hours of prayer I used frequently to go to sleep, but this did not dishearten me. He helped me to overcome it by little and little, and now I seldom sleep at all. I told you about the wire stays I wore without leave and which ate into the flesh so deeply that, when I was told to give up all corporal punishment till I got strong, I could not get it all out for months, it broke in little pieces. And I must be candid with you and tell you you have mortified me far more than I could think it possible to feel, for, although I know your word as my director is His word, yet writing what you have desired has almost annihilated me; if it is pride or human respect that is the cause I know He will punish it here, and although I try to obey cheerfully, yet I feel that my will is mortified and therefore I think not in perfect unison with His.

"Now oh my Father I think I have told you all the principal little nothings I have taken on myself to punish the body, but with great delight. I have often been tempted to give up little things through weariness or weakness, but I don't think He has ever allowed me, I have extended the time always instead of shortening it. These things are all His and I can truly say with the Psalmist: 'Not unto us oh Lord, not unto us, but to Thy name give the glory.'

"Oh my Jesus I considered all these things buried in Thy Sacred Heart, but since I am all Thine Thou canst do with me what Thou pleasest. May I accomplish Thy holy Will perfectly at all times and in the way Thou wishest. My will is Thine as my poor heart and soul are Thine. If I have not mentioned all it is in forgetfulness. I wish to lay all open to you even as I trust He will show you the very depth of my heart and centre of my soul. Never ask dear Father if you may do anything with me or about me. I have given myself entirely into His Hands and He expressly told me to do exactly what you desired me. I do not wish to be treated any other way than as a mother treats a very young child, she never asks its will. I do not wish to have any will but His, and now begging your prayers and blessing, I remain dear rev. Father

"Your obedient and devoted child in the sacred Head and loving Heart

"TERESA HIGGINSON,

"Enfant de Marie.

"I have written this first because I felt it most. Thank Him with me for this little humiliation."[6]

---

6   Letter 56.

5

The Spouse of the Crucified

CANON SNOW speaks of Teresa's frequent participation in the Passion. During this time at Wigan she seemed constantly, while in ecstasy, to be accompanying our Lord on His road to Calvary. These ecstasies of the Passion are a well-known feature in the lives of the stigmatics (St. Catherine of Ricci had them regularly for many years). In the case of Teresa, Miss Ryland gives a most exact description of what took place in Holy Week of 1874, though she says the same happened on other occasions also. Teresa was quite unconscious, but was evidently following our Lord step by step in all His sufferings, as was clear to those who watched from her actions and expressions, and from the exclamations which fell from her lips. Once Miss Ryland sent round for Father Wells. When Teresa seemed to have reached the third fall on the way to Calvary, she bent down as though to help our Lord to rise. Miss Ryland thought she was about to fall and put out a hand to help her, but Father Wells bade her sit still. Miss Woodward, one of the other teachers, spoke to her confessor, Father Gradwell, SJ, of the matter and he advised her to take notes of what occurred. Accordingly she and Miss Ryland took turns to watch and wrote down exactly what they witnessed. The notes on Tuesday and Wednesday in Holy Week were made by Miss Woodward, those on Holy Thursday by Miss Ryland who says: "I watched her actions and wrote them down. What I heard her say I put in brackets." The following are some extracts from these notes:

"Holy Thursday.

"Commenced at half–past four by asking our Lord to come to her. 'When wilt Thou come oh Lord? I am a sinful creature. Wash me in Thy Precious Blood oh Jesus. Ah Lord never permit me to betray Thee. I will never leave Thee.' Leans her head as St. John. 'Here let me rest oh Lord.' Raises her head a little. 'Ah Lord never permit me to betray Thee. Let me go with Thee. Oh my Jesus I will not leave Thee, oh let me. Oh Lord I cannot stay, let me go.' Head drops forward, slightly convulsed, shuts her eyes very closely as if to shut out some sight. 'Oh Eternal Father, if it be possible let this bitter chalice — Oh my God, my God, desert Him not. Ah pity Him. Thy Will be done oh Eternal Father, oh Angels come and help Him. Oh that I could help Him.' Groans for a few minutes. Head falls to right. 'Let me watch with Thee oh my Jesus.' Head falls on breast. Convulsions, head falls to right. 'Stay oh my Jesus.' Offers to hold Him. 'Hide. Hide, let me go.' Groans and works dreadfully, stretches out her hands. 'Oh Jesus stay. Stay for Mary's sake.' A look of great disappointment and groans. 'Do not permit them to rise again.' Turns her head from side to side with looks of horror. 'Ah my Jesus canst Thou bear this ingratitude?' Sees Him bound in the garden, stretches out her hands and begs to be bound instead. Blow on right cheek by the mouth. Blow on left eye. Heavy groans. A blow on mouth. Pulling of beard. Holds her chin. Low cries of pain. Sickness. A blow on left side of head. Beard is pulled. Appears to hear blasphemy, puts hands to ears to shut it out. Rests with head to right, hands to ears again. A blow on the right eye. Sickness, rests, head being inclined to right. Fingers to ears. 'Oh wicked Herod. Oh God of Wisdom. Clothed with scorn. Oh my Jesus.' Sickness, rests two seconds. 'Rest oh my Lord. Oh God Thou seest and knowest all things.' A blow on the right cheek. Rests, closes her ears, turns head away as if to shut out some sight. 'God of infinite Mercy show that there is no cause in Thee.' Turns head away. Rests for about three minutes. Turns aside in horror, gasps. Buffeted about the head. 'Canst thou stand with Him. Oh let me go with Thee, Lord Thou art too weak.' Turns in horror. 'Strip my heart of every affection. Oh let me, Lord Thou canst not bear it.' A tear drops from left eye. A blow on the face. Stretches out her hands in agony and begs for pity for Him. Writhes in fearful agony, apparently being scourged. Rests. A cry of pain, writhing again, rests, fearful writhing, rests. 'Oh see how torn He is, Ah find me something soft for mercy's sake.' Dreadful agony. 'Oh King of Heaven and earth, oh let me hold it for Thee. Ah King, God of Heaven and earth.' Puts hand to head with a look of great pain. 'Oh put it on me, You have done enough.' Crowning with thorns. Groans and writhes and clenches her hands. Raises her hand to her head and then to left cheek in great pain. 'Oh angels of Heaven adore Him.' Calls out: 'Show them all Thy wounds oh Lord and soften their hearts, oh lift Thine eyes blind with Thy Precious Blood, oh deafening yells.' Tries to shut them out. 'Oh Lord they know not what they do.' Is quite still for three minutes. Sees the drink offered. 'Oh take it Lord.' Calls out in agony. 'Oh stay him Lord.' Stretches out her hand for the Cross. 'Oh Lord let me bear it a little while. Thou art too weak. Oh lean on me. Thou art too weak oh Jesus lean.' First fall to the right. 'Oh Jesus let me raise Thee.' A blow on left cheek. 'Stand back.' A blow on right cheek. 'Oh Mary. Oh Jesus! Support her. Oh Jesus oh Mary?' Stretches her hands in agony. 'Oh Lord let me bear it, I can.' Lifts her right hand. 'Let me wipe it.' Sinks back. 'Lord I was not worthy.' Second fall. Five fearful blows about head and face, one on the mouth. 'Oh stand back! Oh trampled under. Oh my heart will break. Oh Eternal Father raise Thy Son.' A blow on the mouth. 'Oh how canst Thou forget. Oh compassionate heart, oh well may they weep. Oh lean. My Jesus lean. Let me guide Thy tottering steps, do not break the heart of Thy blessed Mother.' Fearful fall. Calls out in pain. Seven blows about head and face. One on the stomach. 'Stand back! Remember He is thy God.' Two blows. 'Raise Him gently.' Stoops to the ground. 'Ah

Jesus, lean on me Lord.' A blow on the right cheek. 'Ah lean on me Lord. Take it off.' Head falls to right. Rests about four minutes. Seems to see drink offered. 'Take it Lord. Oh Mary bid Him take it.' Stripping off garments. Begs to be allowed to take them off. 'Oh take them gently. Oh pure God.' Appears to feel garments torn. Holds them at the waist. 'Oh holy and pure God. Most keenly felt by Thee oh my Jesus.' Turns her head aside in anguish. Moans. 'I will not let Thee go.' Cries of agony. 'Oh Jesus say not Thou must go. I cannot leave Thee Lord. Oh Mary bid Him stay. He never disobeyed thee. Oh Jesus for Thy Mother's sake.' Goes prostrate and is still as death."

Teresa herself often speaks in her letters of how she had accompanied our Lord in the various stages of His Passion, and describes the anguish which inundated her soul: "She seems to forget that she is the sinner for which He is suffering and full of loving compassion she wishes to help Him. Oh that I could help Thee Dearest in Thy agony! I do not mean that we speak for I think it is impossible, but this is what is felt... Speaking about this kind of revelation of our B. Lord's Passion, it always creates a fresh and deeper horror of sin which I see is the cause of all, a great feeling of dread to offend the infinite Justice of God, and profound admiration of the awful purity of God. It fills me also with a thirst for suffering which nothing but the real pain which my crucified Saviour permits can appease and a burning desire and will to sacrifice myself with Him for the souls of all."[1]

It was in Passion Week, 1874, that our Lord conferred upon His chosen servant the special marks of His Sacred Wounds. In a letter written some years later in obedience to Father Powell, she thus simply tells him of the fact:

"And when I was at Wigan in 1874, on the Friday morning in Passion Week, my Lord and my God gave me the marks of His five Sacred Wounds which I earnestly begged of Him to remove, but to give me an increase if possible of the pain. During all the following week they bled, and Fr. Wells saw one of them on the

---

[1] Letter 26.

Good Friday[2], after which that disappeared, the others having done so earlier in the morning, and on several occasions they have reopened. This I think I have mentioned to you before but as I am not quite certain about it I thought it better to do so here."[3]

Again in another letter she says:

"I have suffered much in the head, chest and side since 1860 but the pains have been much greater since 1874 when our dear B. Lord conferred the great favour I told you of and in the centre of the hands, feet, head and heart they are at times very excessive, but I am relieved always when they bleed which does not happen very very often. I also have a severe pain in the shoulders. I feel ashamed of calling them pains for I know they are excessive favours which I could never merit or have anything to do with. They are all Thine oh my God as are all the favours Thou hast bestowed on me. I did not at first think what was the cause of these favours but some ten or twelve years back I noticed they were always worse on Fridays, feasts of our Lord and during Lent. I have always reaped great spiritual strength and benefit from them and often when I felt I could not overcome poor human nature in some way I have pressed these parts which were as fountains of life to me and I was always able to overcome. I mean my Lord gave me great help when I did so. But during this eclipse which last took place in the soul, our dear B. Lord has not pleased to give this help, they have appeared to me, vile coward, as mines of untold and almost unbearable suffering and torture. Yet oh Lord I know they are the pledge of Thy love to me, and I value them perhaps more than any other gift Thou hast bestown. May Thy Holy Name be forever blessed."

Miss Ryland gives a most interesting account of what she herself witnessed at this time.

"To begin with the receiving of the Crown of thorns. It took place on Passion Sunday, 1874. I was the only person present.

---

[2]   I certainly saw the signs of the Stigmata upon one of her hands upon the Good Friday afternoon of 1874. Father Wells to Father Powell.

[3]   Letter 11.

She asked me to come upstairs in the afternoon. She was apparently suffering and she went to lie down. She asked me to pray that she might be able to go to Sunday school and at night she would bear all our Lord wished. She added: 'He gave me this pain Himself.' She was able to get up, and went to Sunday school and also to Benediction. Towards night she got very weak and after we were in bed became very ill. I wanted to go for Miss Woodward who slept in the next room, but she would not let me so I returned to bed. All at once she sprang up and I am sure she left the bed, for I sprang up too to pull her down. For a while she spoke to her heavenly visitor. Then she put out her right hand towards our Lord (for it was He) and said aloud: 'No, not that, the thorny crown, give me the thorny crown.' Then in a few moments she fell back just as she had got up. I said to her: 'Teresa are you going to die? If you are I must go for Father Wells.' She did not seem to wish to get him up so I left it alone. Then she said to me: 'Our Lord has given me His Crown of Thorns, and also the Wound in the shoulder.' I saw no signs of it next day, except I thought there were pimples on the forehead, but I could not say whether they had anything to do with it or not.

"On the eve of Palm Sunday after going to bed (I think I had to take her as I often did on account of her weakness), I was kneeling by her side and she was unconscious (at least so far as I was concerned). She was speaking (to herself) to someone present. She raised her right hand and held it up quite firmly for a minute or two.[4] Then she let it drop. I did not examine it. I was strangely wanting (as I think now) in curiosity about these things, but the next morning she kept it closed, placing her thumb in the middle. I think she washed herself that morning

---

[4]   Miss Ryland at first thought that Teresa was then receiving the Stigmata but Teresa herself says that this took place on Friday morning and Miss Ryland adds: Perhaps when I saw her raise her right hand and hold it up so firmly on the eve of Palm Sunday she may not have been receiving the wound but offering it in some prayer for sinners.

with the left hand but I forget. However, when she handed me back the towel it was stained with blood. The morning after both hands were closed. I washed her and she said to me: 'I can wash my own hands, dear.' So I gave her the same towel and she returned it to me again spotted with blood. This happened every day...

"On Good Friday we went to the morning service leaving Miss Higginson in bed and the house door locked. When we returned we both ran up to her at once and found her stretched on the bed, her arms extended in the form of a cross, and wounds in her hands. As usual I did not go very near. I just saw Miss Woodward throwing up the clothes at the foot of the bed to see if the feet were the same, and I ran off to bring Father Wells. He came. She was still the same, and he said to me: 'Run for the doctor.' I went and when I got back accompanied by Dr. Hart she was natural again and talking to Father Wells. Dr. Hart found her extremely weak, but, as Father Wells said, he did not at all know what was the matter with her."

Teresa's longing for holy Communion when she could not get out was intense. "The sufferings she went through on that account I could only liken to a person dying of hunger with food before them which she could not touch. When I came from holy Communion you would think she would devour me and to listen to her craving was most painful. I went to Father Wells about it and all he said was: 'She has no business to go on that way. Tell her from me she is not to do it.' I had to tell her, of course, and after that she became perfectly silent."[5]

Sometimes Miss Ryland would beg of Father Wells to bring her Communion, but he would not always do so — no doubt to try her. On Holy Thursday, 1875, she waited all day long. She was in bed and whenever Miss Ryland asked her to take anything she would only reply: "He will come." At last, at nine o'clock at night, the curate who had been all day in Liverpool brought her the Blessed Sacrament. Then she got up but soon the

---

[5]   Letter 61.

weakness came over her again and she had to go back to bed. She remained there all next day and Miss Ryland never left her. She says that on that day a quantity of blood came from the mouth which she soaked up with a towel. She did not look at the hands and feet but nothing seemed afterwards to have come from them.

As was the case with most of those who bore the Stigmata, these sacred marks were a source of deep trouble to Teresa whose humility shrank from every outward sign. But, try as she would, she could not always disguise the fact, and several of her friends testify to having seen the wounds on her hands and feet and the thorn marks on her brow. Again and again she begged our Lord to remove the outward signs but to increase, if possible, the pain. In this she resembled St. Catherine of Siena who, when her request was granted, declared that the suffering from the invisible wounds was so terrible that only a miracle prevented her from dying. Teresa's prayer was also heard, for, towards the end of her life the marks completely disappeared, and the nurse who tended her during her last illness saw no trace of them either before or after death.

Teresa was now fittingly arrayed for the great event for which our Lord had been so long preparing her. This was the wonderful ceremony of her Mystical Espousals which St. Teresa calls the Spiritual Betrothal, saying that it is but the promise of what is to come, for it leads on to the Mystical Marriage wherein is accomplished the perfect union of the soul with her divine Lord. At the time none knew of this sublime event. Teresa never spoke of it even to Miss Ryland, and it was only after several years that she described it in two separate letters in obedience to her director, Father Powell.

"On the feast of the Sacred Heart of the same year, when I was making a visit to the most Blessed Sacrament, Our Lord placed a small crown of thorns, joined by a cross of unspeakable beauty, as a ring on the finger next to the little finger on my left hand, giving me to understand that thorns and crosses are the portion of those He chooses for His own, that He had accepted the offering I had so often made of myself and that I must consider myself for the future to be entirely His even as He had given Himself entirely to me, and as proof that this was no delusion, He told me that I should feel the thorns and cross which this little ring symbolised. And so I have, for since then He has sent me desolation and dryness and crosses of every description which before I knew not, and He has given me extraordinary help to bear them patiently and to love and cherish them next to Himself."[6]

"In the holy Name of Jesus our divine Spouse, in obedience to your wish and the honour and glory of the most Blessed Trinity, I will strive and relate that which Jesus my only Beloved has done for me, and in which I have no part or portion of merit and which it seems to me is a thing unheard of. It happened in the year 1874, I think on the feast of the S. Heart, after showing me very great favours which I am not able to relate (I mean what I saw or heard), that our dear B. Lord placed on the finger next to the little finger on the left hand a small circle of thorns with a small cross of magnificent stones in the centre, and He gave me to understand that I should suffer much for Him from that time to the end and that I must now regard myself as the 'Spouse of the Crucified.' Oh my God, how wonderful Thou art and how clearly dost Thou prove Thyself to be the Allwise and Almighty God, for I wondered much at the great things Thou didst to me and was not able to explain or express myself to anyone, and although I could not doubt about them coming from Thee, yet I thought that the Way of the Cross was a well beaten path and I was much afraid in times of dryness of the extraordinary favours Thou wert lavishing on me. And since Thou gavest me to sip of Thy bitter chalice in the garden my poor soul was thirsting and my heart burning with the desire of more and more suffering. And this thorny circle reassured me and bound me closer and closer to Thee the God of my heart, and from that time forth I have seen these words verified (I say words but I do not mean

---

6   Letter 11.

that He spoke but gave me to understand most clearly what I have said). I say *after showing me great favours*, for I do not think that at the time that the soul is lost in God that we can either see, hear, or understand anything either with the eyes of the soul or the body."[7]

---

[7] Letter 39

6

Direction

IN July, 1875, Miss Ryland left Wigan. Teresa walked with her to the station to see her off. Miss Ryland was in tears and on the way they met one of the curates who asked what was the matter. Teresa told him, adding with a smile: "I think it is rather I who should cry for I am losing my friend and being left all alone." But it was not her way to cry for any trouble of her own! The friends corresponded and met occasionally in the holidays, until a few years later Miss Ryland entered the order of the Sisters of Charity of St. Paul, helped no little in her vocation by Teresa. They never met again, but "Sister Barbara" has not forgotten her friend, and as the years draw on and failing sight entails many hours of enforced inactivity, she dwells more and more on the memory of those wonderful days when she was privileged to live in such close intimacy with one who was so near to God.

In the autumn of this same year Teresa wanted to return home, either on account of her health or by the wish of her parents, but Father Wells would not hear of her going. Miss Ryland says: "There was another younger girl[1] in the school with Teresa the last year and after I left I believed she stayed in the house with Teresa for company, but I don't think she slept in the

---

[1] This girl was a pupil teacher in the school. She did for a time share Teresa's room and it is no small tribute to the latter's success in evading notice that the child suspected nothing. She merely thought that at times Teresa suffered from a strange form of weakness.

same room. Father Wells would not let Teresa go, and the Sisters of Notre Dame took my place. She must have suffered a great deal that last six months all alone in that house.

She said she used a rope which she tied to the bedpost to raise herself in the mornings. She also told me that when she wanted to leave he would not give in, so at Christmas she took home the keys of the school and returned them to him saying she was not returning."

Father Wells finally accepted her resignation and sent her a testimonial: "Miss Teresa Higginson has, during three years, sustained a most exemplary character as a teacher in St. Mary's R.C. schools, Wigan. Signed. Thomas Wells, Manager. February 22nd, 1876."

A letter which he wrote some years later in answer to an enquiry from Father Powell shows his unshaken trust in her, in spite – perhaps on account – of the many and severe tests to which he had subjected her.

"Great Eccleston, Garstang.

"June 28, 1880.

"MY DEAR FATHER POWELL,

"Your letter to hand this, Monday, morning. As to the questions you ask regarding Miss Higginson, as far as I am able I am glad to answer.

"I certainly saw the signs of the Stigmata upon one of her hands upon the Good Friday afternoon of 1874, and I was quite aware of the many and extraordinary temptations to which she was subjected, and saw the effects, afterwards, as broken articles in the room she occupied, and notably the holy Water stoop. Upon one occasion she had been absent from school through sickness for nearly a week, and the doctor had been in attendance upon her at my request and seemed unable to afford her any relief, and was of opinion that her case was very obstinate and very dangerous. She was all but unconscious when I visited her at twelve o'clock, noon, and bedfast. I said, as I thought the school was taking harm through her absence, that she, must get up and take her place in school by three o'clock that afternoon. Though then unable to stand, I saw her at a quarter to three walking up alone to the school to make a visit, and by three she was teaching in the school apparently as well as ever. These things recurred repeatedly and I was in constant communication with Mgr. Lennon of Ushaw, who helped me by his advice very much. I wrote at once to the Bishop about her. I got Miss Ryland to write down the occurrences during Holy Week which she and I witnessed. The memorandum book which I forward you by this post is the matter she wrote down at my request. The slip of paper written upon in pencil is in Miss H's handwriting. I am anxious to have both back, and I hope that you will see I have them both returned. Mgr. Lennon's letters I still have by me.

"With my kind regards to Miss Higginson if she is still with you,

"Believe me my dear Father Powell,

"Yours very sincerely,

"THOS. WELLS."

Teresa could not remain idle, and, for a short time while living at home, she taught in Father Lynch's school at Seacombe. She then went to St. Alban's, Liscard, "but", says Miss Ryland, "she seems to have got on badly with the priest, for she told me he gave her a week's notice. I do not know whether it was from want of success in her work, or whether it was the commotion in the school — there, pictures were taken from the walls and thrown at her, and a slate was also taken from a boy's hand and thrown at her."

In 1877, the Jesuit Fathers opened a new mission at Sabden, a small village near Clitheroe. They had great difficulty in staffing the school, on account of the primitive conditions of the little place which had the reputation of being rough and godless. There was no proper teacher's house, the only available lodgings (kept by a non-Catholic) were very poor and the salary was small. Teresa was eager to undertake the work, though her parents, considering her delicate health, strongly opposed the idea. But she felt that charity and her vocation were calling her, and as in childish days when she thought a thing was right, nothing could turn her from her purpose, so now she won her way. Her father let her go, though he could not be persuaded to give his blessing on her undertaking. She said goodbye and went to Sabden. It was her last farewell to him for she never saw him alive again. On October 13th, 1877, he was taken with a seizure in the street and died almost immediately, having just been able to receive the Last Sacraments.

Teresa wrote to Miss Ryland telling her she had had a great cross and later sent her a mortuary card saying: "This is part of the cross I spoke of", adding that she had had a vision of her Father lying in the street in St. Helen's, dying, and that when the priest brought in the telegram, she said to him: "You need not tell me what it is, Father. I know Papa is dead." The memory of this dear Father never faded from her mind, and to the end of her life she used, year by year, to write to her priest friends begging prayers and Masses for his anniversary.

Mrs. Higginson's health was much affected by the shock of her husband's death and she longed to have Teresa with her. We may well believe that had Teresa followed the promptings of her own heart she would have hastened to her Mother's side, but in personal affairs she would decide nothing for herself. One of her sisters who was at home at the time wrote to Father Lea, the priest in charge of the mission at Sabden, telling him of her Mother's condition, and begging him to allow Teresa to return home. Father Lea's reply shows how highly he had learnt to value his teacher. He wrote on March 5th, 1878:

"I hardly know what to say about Teresa. If your Mother is ill and really requires her at home, there is nothing for her to do but to go home and help her Mother. It would be a very terrible loss to Sabden in every way, but duty to her Mother must hold the first place. If she does go home now, I am sure she will apply for another school as soon as her Mother can spare her. Now, under these circumstances, could you not as a great favour to me make arrangements for her to remain where she is if her Mother can spare her. As to her lodgings, I will do what I can to better them the very next time I go over to Sabden. With your well–known kindness, I am sure you will do all you can to oblige me."

This appeal had the desired effect and Teresa stayed on for the time at Sabden. The remark as to the lodging probably had reference to an incident which occurred while she was there. The woman with whom she lived lost one hundred pounds. Her suspicions fell on Teresa whom she accused of stealing the money and she called in a policeman, insisting that she should be searched. Teresa quietly submitted. The policeman refused actually to search her himself, but he stood by while the woman did so, and then together they ransacked the room. When the proceeding was over, Teresa asked him to produce his warrant. He had to confess that he had not got one, whereupon she severely reprimanded him and told him never to do such a thing again. It afterwards appeared that the woman had herself hidden the money in some safe place and forgotten where she had put it.

Teresa felt the insult very keenly. It must have been a bitter trial to one by nature so strong–willed and high–spirited, and there are several allusions in her letters to her confessor which give a hint as to her feelings. But she spoke of it to no one else, and not only did she forgive her accusers from her heart but, with sublime charity, she undertook to atone herself for any sin which might have been thereby committed, and begged special prayers for those whom she regarded as her truest benefactors.

She wrote to Father Powell:

"I think I told you before that I had been accused of stealing a bag of money containing over £100, I don't know the exact amount. I did not mention it to my friends, but someone has written and told my sister all about it which has put them dreadfully out of the way, and caused many unkind things to be said. Pray that charity may not be further broken or sinned against as they say here that Mrs. B. should be punished for saying and doing what she has. Pray fervently for her and all or any who may have said or done anything against me in this or any other case, that God will bless them a hundred fold. For I know they are only instruments in the hands of God, for I ask to atone for this sin and any sin that might be committed through it for it was a public scandal at the time, and He graciously heard my prayer. Blessed be His holy Name forever. Oh how weak is poor human nature and how keenly she feels all these little things, yet He knows how grateful I am to Him for allowing me to bear this for Him, all unworthy as I am and I esteem it as a great act of His love and I trust He will never more leave me without some such opportunity of proving my love for Him my crucified Spouse. I know you will join with me in praising and thanking Him for this and all other favours."[2]

The following recollections of one who remembers her at Sabden throw an interesting sidelight on her life at this time:

"When the Sabden Mission opened I was living at Clitheroe, and, as there was Mass but once a month, she came to Clitheroe each week–end. She had a standing invitation to come to our home, and a room was kept for her whenever she chose to come to us.

"My recollections of her are most vivid. She was sweet and gentle and quite homely, so much so that the younger members of the family usually found their way to her and they would crowd round her while she told them stories or sang hymns, sometimes amusing the babies by making her Child of Mary medal whistle.

"Her attitude at prayer specially struck me: she knelt motion-less, her eyes fixed on the tabernacle. If ever I chanced to go to Mass alone I invariably knelt where I could see her instead of going to our own bench in church. On one occasion she got permission to take myself and my eldest cousin to the Mass at Sabden. She entertained us the whole day showing us her school, etc. I well remember the caretaker of the school chapel, a woman,

---

2   Letter 14.

saying she spent the whole of every Thursday night before the blessed Sacrament, which at this time was reserved, and that she had seen drops of blood upon her forehead on the Friday. The children too, she said, saw it, and had become quite used to the sight.

"I remember hearing much of the instructions or expositions of the Catholic doctrine to non–Catholics which she used to give on some evenings in the week. Numbers came to listen to her but of the results I remember nothing."

She then recalls the mysterious conversations which went on with regard to the missing £100 of which the children were supposed to know nothing, but she well remembers her uncle exclaiming: "Nothing will convince me that Miss Higginson is in the wrong. She will come through this and prove she is the saint we believe her to be."

Teresa made many staunch and lifelong friends at Clitheroe, among the mill girls, especially one named Elizabeth Dawson, whose humble house was later on to be the scene of wonderful events. Teresa persuaded several of these simple pious girls to practise daily Communion, no light undertaking, for it implied starting work at the factory at six, and devoting the half–hour allowed for breakfast at eight to hearing Mass, leaving hardly a moment for food before resuming work. It was her own greatest trial that at Sabden she was deprived of daily Mass. She usually spent the Sundays at Clitheroe, but during the week she was unable to receive Holy Communion, the Food on which her whole life seemed to depend. At last her loving Spouse had compassion on her, and in answer to her ardent pleadings, came Himself to feed her with the Bread of Life. She told this later to Father Powell, adding that sometimes our Lord would grant her this wonderful favour three or four times in the same day. As will be seen, these miraculous Communions took place frequently in after years when they were attested by many witnesses.

In 1879, her health broke down and she had to return home. Father Lea was much distressed at losing her and wrote: "I am very sorry indeed that you have not the strength to go on with the school. It will be a very long day before we shall have another in Sabden like yourself. May God bless you." He also gave her a recommendation: "I have much pleasure in saying that Miss Higginson, during the eighteen months she had charge of our school at Sabden, gave every satisfaction, both to the children and to their parents. She was most devoted to her work and has a special talent for attracting children to her school. She left Sabden on account of illness.

"W. Lea, SJ, July 15th, 1879."

Mrs. Higginson was now living at Neston in Cheshire with her daughters who had charge of the village school, and they welcomed Teresa to the little school house which was henceforth to be their home. Gladly would they have kept her, but Teresa felt she could not settle there for good. She could not bear to be a burden on her family, and she knew too that, dearly as they loved her, they were often distressed and puzzled by her utter disregard of appearances and the strange stories that were beginning to be told about her. She had long ago taken a vow of poverty and given herself without reserve into the Hands of God, and she could not help but feel that at home she was under constant observation — though she used to wonder sometimes at the things that passed unnoticed and often thought our Lord Himself was helping her to guard her precious secrets. But the two things that specially weighed with her in her desire to return to work were, as she told Father Powell: "I cannot get regularly to Communion here and I feel too that I should be doing something more than I can do at home."[3]

However, for the moment no situation offered, so she spent the summer months at home, and about this time she came in touch once more with Father Powell who was still at Bootle. He again became her director, sent by divine Providence to lead her soul through deep and troubled waters, but her trust in his wise guidance was unfailing and became the source of the greatest

---

[3] Letter 3.

consolation. In fact her gratitude for the peace it brought her proves how terrible had been her former trials in this respect. She wrote on May 6th, '79:

"You cannot think what comfort your few words have given me. I know you will join with me in thanking our good God for that and the great consolation I have felt in finding myself so well understood. Blessed be His holy Name for ever."[4]

And again she wrote:

"You know before I came to confession to you again last year I was unable in any way to express myself to my director. I did not know what I wanted to say myself and was much troubled at not being able to tell what I felt was my duty (at times) and I wondered how it was that no body ever questioned me on these things. Then I would think perhaps I should not tell or speak of these things to anyone and I considered how secret our dear b. Lady kept those things which God did in her. Then I would be uneasy when I had tried to tell my director, I thought perhaps I had done wrong. And on one occasion when I was asking my divine Spouse what I should do (for I felt sometimes I should tell my director) our dear b. Lord impressed these words, I mean, breathed them into the very centre of my soul: "My loved One, all these troubles will soon be over." I thought I was soon to be united with Him forever. I mean I thought my death was not far off and I rejoiced exceedingly. He meant He would give me one who would understand me. Blessed be His holy Name for ever!"[5]

Whatever other trials awaited her, our Lord's promise in this matter was amply fulfilled, for henceforth, as regards the direction of her soul, she enjoyed unfailing peace. She placed herself in the hands, first of Father Powell, and later of Father Snow, with the utter simplicity of a child "even as He gives Himself into the hands of His priests at the altar" and to the end these two saintly men remained, not only her advisors, but her staunch and devoted friends. She took a vow of obedience to Father Powell:

---

[4] Letter 3.

[5] Letter 68.

"In the presence of the whole court of heaven, under the protection of the sacred Heart, our Lady and St. Joseph, and in union with the obedience unto death of our b. Lord and Saviour Jesus Christ, I renew my vow of entire obedience, and give myself entirely into your hands as my director, knowing that in following your advice, I am accomplishing the expressed Will of Almighty God. Trusting in our b. Lord's Passion and death and through His most Precious Blood to have grace and strength to persevere in this my vow until death."[6]

How faithfully she kept this vow is seen in her letters. All the secrets of her soul are laid bare to her directors and never would she undertake the smallest work without first obtaining their consent. During the months of inactivity at Neston the question of a religious vocation again came very much before her mind and she made enquiries as to the rule of various orders.

"Of my own choice I should certainly enter a convent in which prayer, austerities and mortification formed a great part of the rule, but I leave the matter entirely in your hands as my director, and feel sure that I am doing what is most perfect in following your advice."[7]

And again a few days later she wrote:

"How good God is and how miserable is this the least of all His poor creatures. Since you told me I should naturally have greater crosses in the world than in a convent, I began to consider that, as I knew what great good my poor soul had experienced under the cross it was greater perfection for me to remain in the world, particularly as I had made the religious vows many years back, and that perhaps if I entered a convent, even where they practised the greatest austerities, I should be missing greater crosses and so give less glory to God and rob those souls for which our bl. Lord shed the last drop of His most Precious Blood of help which I would be able to render them. Besides it seemed to me to be presumption of me to desire to live among those

---

[6] Letter 10.
[7] Letter 7.

whom our b. Lord had particularly chosen for Himself by the purity of their lives, — and so I went on harrassing myself ... and for this our dear blessed Lord has greatly rebuked me, showing me at the same time that I should give myself into the hands of my superiors without expressing a wish or a doubt, even as He gives Himself into the hands of His priests on the altar."[8]

Father Powell finally set all her doubts at rest by deciding that she was not called upon to enter the religious life.

One of the things which cost Teresa the most acute suffering was the effort to put into words the inexpressible things God taught her and the marvels He wrought in her soul. Not only did she shrink in her humility from speaking of them, but, as she said, they were beyond the scope of human language, and yet she felt bound to lay them before her director. At length, seeing her utter inability to do so by word of mouth, Father Powell put her under obedience to write them out and then, terrible as was still the effort, she found herself able in this, as in all else, to obey his command. The result is that from the year 1879 to 1883, her letters form the most wonderful and intimate autobiography of her soul. In the latter year, owing to the troubles which had arisen, the Bishop made her change her confessor and bade her write no more. Accordingly, Father Snow thenceforth became her director and these special letters cease. In 1886, she left Liverpool, and from this time to the end of her life she kept up a close correspondence with both Father Powell and Father Snow, but her letters with few exceptions, treat merely of the common events of everyday life. She did occasionally report on the condition of her soul, and Father Snow at one time made her write her own history (as already quoted, letter 269) up to the year of her leaving the convent school, but then, seeing the intense suffering it was causing her, he took pity on her and said she need write no further.

When Father Powell became her director in 1879 she wrote to him:

---

[8] Letter 10.

"There are several things of which I have never spoken to anyone, thinking that our b. Lord liked us to have little secrets that none but He knew of, but if you think it is more perfect to tell you everything I will try and do so as simply as I can. It is not that I have any lack of confidence in you still it seems that I cannot overcome the repugnance I feel in speaking of these great favours of our b. Lord. Perhaps it is that our bl. Lord wishes me to learn from it that they are the thorns that surround the sweet flowers of His grace."[9] Father Powell asked for further particulars and she replied:

"With regard to the 'little secrets' they are many but I will endeavour to tell you faithfully (with the help of Him who is all powerful) in obedience and to the honour and glory of His holy Name and the confusion of the least of His little ones.

"Our b. Lord frequently lays open to me His most sacred Heart, and shows and makes me feel all the indignities He has to endure in the most holy Sacrament, how He is insulted and neglected and He loudly complains many times of His priests and those specially consecrated to His service, and urges me to make Him some reparation, and He has told me at these times to offer Him all the love of His own most sacred Heart and the love which the blessed Trinity and His holy Mother have for Him in atonement for all this coldness.

"At other times He has shown me how He is abused and with what irreverence He is handled by His ministers, and how unworthily He is received by many who consider themselves His friends, for which He has told me to offer to Him all the glory with which His heavenly Father has clothed Him and all His elect, and also the glory which He continually offers to His Eternal Father to make a return for this disrespect. etc.

"At other times He fills my whole being with such a longing desire for Him and His glory that my poor heart seems breaking, and when I see how little He is loved and how useless I am in making Him known and loved I feel I could endure any torment

---

9   Letter 10.

if it were only to get His holy Name once said in respect and love. And it was this that seemed to force me to give the night to Him in prayer and little acts of mortification (instead of sleep) for I could not but incessantly implore Him to hasten the day of delivery of the poor souls that they at least might love and thank Him and beg of Him the conversion of all poor sinners. And our b. Lady once told me that the prayer most efficacious with the Eternal Father for poor sinners was: 'Father forgive them for they know not what they do.' And it was thus she pleaded for us. And when our b. Lord sees me almost expiring with a love and desire to render some service to Him by helping those souls for which He died and suffered so much, He seems to take compassion on me and allows me to be instrumental in bringing some poor soul back to Him; and frequently when I have besought Him to remember the price He has paid for the souls of heretics and pagans, He has allowed me to see an angel strewing beautiful flowers here and there and gives me to understand they are the flowers of faith and baptism which He has granted to my poor prayers. And for the last five or six years He has often shown me His most awful bitter Passion represented in a manner I cannot explain (for when I try to narrate it I find I can do nothing) and permitted me to feel some little of those most cruel torments which He then endured, particularly during the latter part of Lent."

Then follows the passage relating to her reception of the Stigmata and the account of her Mystical Espousals already quoted on pages 65 and 68–69, and she concludes:

"And last year He permitted me to be accused of theft and searched and this I felt very keenly, though with His help I blessed His holy Name feeling myself unworthy to bear this resemblance to Him, and I beg of Him earnestly to bless all those concerned in it and you to pray fervently for them. I have not time to write more at present and I humbly beg your prayers and blessing for your obedient and devoted child

"TERESA HIGGINSON,

Enfant de Marie."[10]

There still remained one precious secret which she treasured as her own – her miraculous Communions, and it was only some time later that she wrote of them to Father Powell in answer to his wish.

"In obedience I know He will explain what you desire and which I have never been able to put into words, and the one favour you now require I always felt He wished to keep as a secret for I could say so little about it really, and when I have been going to tell you it has always slipped my memory entirely, and if you had not now asked me so distinctly about holy Communion I don't think I should have told you ,— for you know I have frequently told you I don't know what I have told you, and as you seemed to say you knew the principal things you wanted to know, I was quite content and left all in the hands of my Lord and Master. Well, on Sunday the 18th Aug. Canon Daly gave out that there would not be holy Mass on Tuesday or Thursday next, and on Monday evening thinking I should not be able to communicate in the morning (for we were to leave by the first train for Burnley), such a burning flame of loving desire seemed to consume me that I knew not what I was doing or in what manner I besought Him, but I experienced that excessive pain which I think I have spoken of which pierces the very centre of the soul, and if it were not immortal would most surely destroy it. That night seemed to me like an eternity. Of course I was not able to raise myself from the ground I was so overcome with weakness, and if He had not come to me, I feel sure I should soon have died, or I mean I should have possessed Him forever. Early in the morning I know not the hour, but I think between two and three, my Lord and my God Jesus Christ appeared to me verily and indeed and His sacred Person shone with that brightness which is indescribable, and I think He wore a stole (but of this I could not be positively certain). He said to me, 'What wilt thou my loved One?' And I sinking in the depths of my utter misery could

---

[10] Letter 11.

have faded into nothingness before Him. Oh my God, who can describe this annihilation of the spirit? Then He said holding the sacred Host in Hand (I know it was a real Host), 'Ecce Agnus Dei' etc. and gave me the blessed Sacrament of His love. I did not see the sacred Host any more than I do when I receive holy Communion daily, I mean with the eyes of the body, but to me our dear b. Lord always appears in the b. Sacrament in a glorified Body as He was after the Resurrection (to the eyes of the soul). I felt at this holy Communion too that our dear b. Lady and holy Father St. Joseph were supporting me and St. Michael was near. When I had received Him, He drew me so entirely into Himself that I was lost in His immensity and infinite love. Then, when they came to call me in the morning at half past seven, I was quite astonished to find myself quite strong and able to go about more easily than ever, though I had no control over myself for days, or until at least the Devil came and tried to deceive me.

"I could not say how many times our dear b. Lord gave me holy Communion at Sabden, but He did it frequently, and some days three and four times the same day. I think the reason I did not mention it was that I saw so clearly before me the manner in which our dear b. Mother Mary hid as far as she could the secret of the Incarnation. I do not wish to excuse myself but pray God to show you the inmost workings of my poor heart and soul even as He sees and knows me Himself, and beg of you to chastise me as I deserve. I think I have told you that I seldom see the person of the priest at holy Mass (I mean in times of consolation) and whenever He has given me holy Communion He always appears as He does at holy Mass. And once just as Canon Pemberton left Neston and I was left in charge of the church and house, one morning I was very ill and not able to go out for holy Mass, He sent a priest to say holy Mass and give me holy Communion. I had had no wicks for the lamp and as I was afraid the b. Sacrament might be left without a light, I asked the Canon to send some, but this holy priest gave me some without me asking for any. I have enclosed Canon Daly's letter as proof of what I am saying. They made enquiries but could not find out who it could be. It seems to me such an incredible condescension on the part of our b. Lord. When I have been ill and unable to assist really at holy Mass, I have seen the sacred Mysteries actually performed in my room. I don't mean to say that a priest really said holy Mass in my room but in the same way as I see the awful bitter Passion and feel and offer myself a sacrifice with Him to His Eternal Father. The day I did not get to holy Communion was when I was at Burnley and I suffered more that day than I can tell, though I tried to make a cheerful offering of my holy Communion for a poor soul, I know not who it was exactly, who would have died without the Bread of Life, and I offered up all I might go through in consequence for the good of that soul, and I saw through the mercy of God it was saved.

"I think I have told you all now with the help of the God of all Wisdom, Knowledge, Power and Understanding. And in His holy Name I will conclude to the glory of the sacred Head and of the S. Heart.

"Your obedient, and devoted child

"TERESA HIGGINSON,

Enfant de Marie."[11]

Canon Daly in the letter referred to (dated November, 1876), says:

"I wonder who the old priest can be who said Mass on Thursday. Louie will have brought you plenty of wicks but the poor old priest has forestalled her."

The full story of the old priest's visit as she afterwards told it to Miss Ryland was as follows: Teresa had been left in charge of the church during the priest's absence. Her supply of wicks was running out and she wrote for more but they had not yet arrived. One morning there came a knock at the door and when she opened it she found there an old priest whom she had never seen before. He did not speak and she noticed with surprise that he seemed familiar with the house, for while she turned to shut the

---

[11] Letter 60.

door he walked straight through into the church. She followed him into the sacristy where he handed her a box of wicks. Though he still said nothing, she understood that he wished to say Mass and went to prepare the altar. When she returned, he had already put out the vestments and taken the chalice out of the safe. She served his Mass and received Communion. Afterwards she asked him if he would take tea or coffee, but as he did not reply she left him to finish his thanksgiving and went to prepare his breakfast. Just as it was ready, the milk boy arrived and she sent him to call the old priest. The boy came back saying he was not there. Teresa, much surprised, went to the sacristy which was indeed empty. In the evening a young father came to take the Sunday duty, and Teresa told him about her visitor. He supposed Canon Daly must have sent him, but when Teresa wrote to the Canon, he said he knew nothing about the matter, it must have been the Bishop. But the Bishop too pleaded ignorance and asked for further details as to the stranger's appearance. On hearing Teresa's description, he said it corresponded exactly with that of a former priest of the mission who had since died.

Father Powell was at first doubtful as to the nature of the mysterious Communions of which Teresa spoke and he told her to ask our Lord about them. A few days later she wrote:

"I asked our dear b. Lord (as you told me) whether I was to receive holy Communion again any time when He had given me It. I mean was I to receive from the hands of the priest after He Himself had administered It to me and if I did wrong in doing so. And this is what I understand. That I should not do so knowingly, that not even a priest can do so without special privilege and permission, I mean they must obtain faculties from the bishop to duplicate, but if, as it happened with me yesterday, that our divine Lord and Master should fill the whole heart and soul with such a desire and love for Him that we are as it were out of ourselves to possess Him and we are not conscious of anything but Himself, then there is no wrong. It is all His doing and we should not be uneasy about it as we have no power over ourselves. His desire is one with ours and we must humbly prostrate ourselves before Him confessing our unworthiness and thanking and praising Him and loving Him more and more. Oh my God how wonderful Thou art!"[12]

---

[12] Letter 68.

7

The Devotion to the Sacred Head

IT is during this stay at Neston that we first hear of a subject which was to be henceforth the all–absorbing interest of Teresa's life — the Devotion to the Sacred Head of Our Lord as the Seat of His Divine Wisdom. While awaiting the ruling of the Church on this important matter, we may venture to believe that the promotion of this devotion was the special mission for which Her Divine Spouse had designed her: that the singular graces and favours which He conferred upon her so freely were intended, not merely for her own sanctification, but with the further object of fitting her for this work. Our Lord Himself, she frequently assured her director, had taught her that this sublime devotion would sum up in itself all the worship due to His sacred Humanity, and be the great antidote to the pride of intellect and disbelief which are the crying evils of these latter times.

When, in the cold hard days of the seventeenth century, Our Lord wished to prove to the world the burning love of His Sacred Heart, He chose for His messenger a simple nun, and now, in our own age, He has sought a still more lowly soul to send forth as the herald of His Wisdom. Surely it is a point of no small significance that the instrument He had selected for this great work should be no renowned, world–famed professor, but an unknown teacher of a poor school! "I confess to Thee, oh Father, Lord of Heaven and earth because Thou hast hid these things from the wise and prudent and hast revealed them to little ones.

Yea, Father, for so it hath seemed good in Thy sight." Where indeed could He have found a littler one than this simple, humble, teacher whose life was devoted to the very poorest of His children?

Teresa's first reference to this subject is on the feast of the Sacred Heart, 1879 — about the very time when Father Powell, inspired no doubt by the Holy Ghost placed her under obedience to write out for him all the secrets of her soul. For the next few years she recurs to it again and again, showing how frequently Our Lord appeared to her, each time explaining more fully the hidden depths and beauty of the Devotion and impressing her with His ardent wish for its propagation. She burned with longing to carry out His Holy will, though, knowing her own helplessness, she constantly implored Him to commit the task to some more worthy soul, some wise and learned man whose words would carry weight. But God's ways are not man's ways and He made it clear to her that, weak and powerless as she was, it was to her that the work had been confided. She laboured incessantly for this end, and yet, in spite of all her prayers for light, He never showed her what it was exactly that she had to do. Much as she loved to hide herself away, she would have gone forth gladly to summon the whole world to honour the Sacred Head, "the house which Wisdom hath built for Herself", but this sacrifice was not required of her. She did what she could: she taught the Devotion to the children and spoke of it to all her friends. Many, to her joy, embraced it with enthusiasm. Among them were Father Wilberforce, the well-known Dominican, Father Humphrey, SJ, and Mons. Weld, who all examined into it most carefully and then adopted it. The matter was at length brought before Dr. O'Reilly, the Bishop of the diocese, and Teresa prayed much for some clear proof which might convince him and cause him, not merely to sanction the Devotion, but actively to promote it. But no such proof was forthcoming and, though he allowed a little book of prayers to be printed, he took no public action. Teresa herself never wavered in her faith and hope, looking always for some open manifestation of the Will of God, as did also her two confessors. Father Snow wrote: "Both Father Powell and I expected that important miracles would take place and that these would be of great help in furthering the Devotion to the Sacred Head and at the same time be useful if hereafter there was question of her canonisation. But I never mentioned this subject to Teresa, nor did Father Powell to the best of my belief. On the 30th of May, 1884, which would be shortly before Whit Sunday of that year, she spoke to me of her intense desire to have the Sacred Head honoured and the intense suffering it caused her. I told her to wait for Whit Sunday when perhaps our Lord would let her know what she could do. On June 6th, she told me that on Whit Sunday our Lord had made known very clearly to her that it was not by wonders and miracles that He would make known the Devotion to the Sacred Head. That it was the wisdom of the world to look for signs but not His way; that when He Himself promised the Blessed Sacrament, He might have convinced by wonders those who refused to believe, but it was not according to the ways of His Wisdom."

And so Teresa longed and prayed and waited, until at last she seemed to understand the special part assigned to her, when she wrote: "If it pleases Him that I should not do anything but be consumed with this desire, then His Holy Will be done."[1]

The explanation of the devotion must be given in Teresa's own words as she understood it from our Lord Himself. For the sake of clearness, the chief extracts from her letters dealing with the subject have been grouped together, though in point of fact they extend over several years. The first revelation seems to have been made to her in the little village school house at Neston, on the feast of the Sacred Heart, 1879, shortly after her return from Sabden. She described it to Father Powell, first explaining the way in which our Lord prepared her for this great vision:

"During Holy Mass on Friday our blessed Lord brought before me all my nothingness and miserable sins and filled me with

---

[1] Letter 136.

such great confusion that I felt that I should almost die. He has so often done the same of late and shown me at the same time His infinite Majesty that I have been almost annihilated. Ah my God who shall stand before Thee? It seems to me that this feeling must be the same, or something the same, that the poor soul feels when she stands before God to be judged. This great humiliation was succeeded by a sweet calm and holy joy after I heard these words again: "Fear not, it is I" (and such a torrent of sweet tears streamed down that seemed to refresh the soul wonderfully.) Not that I really heard the words spoken by the ears but they seemed impressed on the soul in such a manner that there is no doubt of what I heard, and these words are works, for, as at the Creation God said "Let there be light" and it was so, so I see in an instant verified the import of these words, for my poor soul that seemed so hard dry and cold, almost despairing enjoys at once that peace which the world cannot give.

"During the whole day I remained very recollected and al-though you told me to give myself entirely into the hands of God, I continually reminded our B. Lord that both you and Father Wells told me nothing was to be done in public, for our B. Lord made me feel that He wished to bestow some great favour upon me which covered me with such shame and confusion that I could hardly raise my head. For when I see our divine Lord giving His treasures to this vile traitor, I beg of Him to consider what He is about, for I fear that others might undervalue His great gifts seeing them given to so vile and wicked a wretch.

"When I retired to my room in the evening a deep recollection came upon me. Oh my God give me light and help that I may be able to express clearly to my director this which is entirely Thy work. Pity my weakness and by Thy obedience unto death, oh my God and by this same Wisdom which Thou hast shown me, instruct me, or do Thou oh Lord what Thy unworthy servant is unable to do...

"I was considering the excessive love of the Sacred Heart and offering to my Divine Spouse this same love to make amends for our coldness, and His constancy and infinite riches to make up for our poverty and misery, when our divine Lord suddenly represented to me the Divinity as a very large bright crystal stone in which all things are reflected or are, past, present and to come, in such a manner that all things are present in Him. This immense precious stone sent forth streams of richly coloured lights brighter beyond comparison than ten thousand suns, which I understood represented the Infinite Attributes of God. This great jewel also seemed to be covered with innumerable eyes which I understood represented the Wisdom and Knowledge of God... Our Blessed Lord showed me this Divine Wisdom, as I was saying, as the guiding power which regulated the motions and affections of the Sacred Heart, showing me that it had the same effect and power over its least action, and raising it, as the sun draws up the vapour from the ocean. He gave me to understand that an especial devotion and veneration should be paid to the Sacred Head of our Lord as the Seat of divine Wisdom and guiding power of the Sacred Heart, and so complete this heavenly devotion..."[2]

This vision occurred at Neston, but most of the subsequent revelations took place at Bootle, in the Church of St. Alexander which she foresaw would become a great place of pilgrimage, as she told Father Powell: "Our Lord has this morning shown me that your requests will be granted and that greater wonders than those at Knock. He will bring to pass in our very midst, that the eyes of all nations shall be turned towards us and pilgrims come from afar off."[3]

The right–hand corner seat of the front bench on the Epistle side is still pointed out as the place where Teresa knelt, and where the heavens were so often opened to her and she saw and heard many things which it is not given to man to utter.

In Easter Week, 1880, she wrote:

Ap. 9 80

---

[2]   Letter 4.
[3]   Letter 28. Knock is a popular place of pilgrimage in Ireland.

"When I went into the church a little after five on Easter Sunday morning, I had hardly knelt to adore Him present in the most holy Sacrament of His Love, when He drew me so entirely into Himself that I know not what I saw or heard for some time; but when the powers of the soul again began to act He represented Himself to me (I think) as we see Him in pictures of the Sacred Heart and His Sacred Head radiant as a sea of light and a glorious sun shining to its very depths and acting on the affections, motives, and entire workings of the Sacred Heart and raising them even as the sun draws up the vapours from the ocean. In this light, I saw distinctly formed the figure of a silvery dove which I understood was the Holy Ghost, and rolls of glory (I was going to say clouds but that is hardly correct) or pillars as a rainbow appeared above which I felt represented the Eternal Father. The whole formed an Eye which I knew was the Eye of God in unity. And from it I understood that our dear Blessed Lord wished His Sacred Head to be specially worshipped as the 'Seat of Divine Wisdom' and the powers of His Human Soul adored therein, as it is the seat of the intellectual powers of man.

"He has many times as I have before told you revealed to me His intention of crowning the devotion of the Sacred Heart in this point and I think when He spoke of the wonders He would work in our midst that He referred to some manifestation to this end."[4]

On April 27th, she wrote in a tone of triumph and in a trembling hand as though still half rapt in ecstasy:

"Our divine Lord says *the time is at hand* when the Wisdom of the Father shall be adored and the Love of God for man shall be revealed in the Light which shineth in darkness and enlighteneth every man that cometh into the world. It is the Will of our dear Blessed Lord that His Sacred Head be adored as the Seat of Divine Wisdom: not the Sacred Head alone, (I mean as we worship His sacred Hands and Feet) no, but the Head as the shrine of the powers of the Soul and the faculties of the Mind and

---

4   Letter 30.

in these the Wisdom which guided every affection of the Sacred Heart and motions of the whole Being of Jesus our Lord and our God. It is not His divine Will that the attributes or abstracts of the soul or mind, or that divine Wisdom which guided, governed and directed all in Him (the God Man) should have a distinct worship, but that they should all be specially honoured and His sacred Head adored as their Temple. And our dear Blessed Lord has shown me too how the head is also the centre of all the senses of the body, and that this devotion is the completion, not only of the devotion of the Sacred Heart, but the crowning and perfection of all devotions; and He showed me how the adorable Trinity at His baptism revealed to the world this special devotion, for His Sacred Humanity is the tabernacle of the thrice holy Trinity; and that St. John had specially spoken of this devotion for the Most High revealed to him that He should be thus worshipped before the end of the world, and he spoke of it as a magnificent city, etc. seeing the multitudes of variety and beauty and splendour of this Seat of divine Wisdom. It is a world of infinite magnitude, a sea of fathomless depths, a never setting sun of light inaccessible and immeasurable heights of untold mysteries of perfection and beauty. Our dear Blessed Lord did not positively state the precise time that this should be made a public devotion but He gave me to understand that whoever should venerate His sacred Head in this manner should draw down on themselves the choicest gifts of Heaven; and those who shall try by words or means to hinder or reject it shall be as glass that is cast down, or as an egg that is thrown to the wall, that is that they shall be shattered and become as naught, and shall be dried up and wither as grass on the housetop.

"Our beloved Spouse also let me know that it was in this church that He would manifest to the world the manner, etc. etc. that He wished to be honoured and the time, and all concerning this most wonderful Devotion. And I think it is *that soul* that is drooping as the vine under the weight of heavenly gifts and saturated through and through with the Precious Blood, that in

His infinite Wisdom He has ordained to make known His holy Will to the world. For He continually shows me this precious soul so dear to Him, and frequently before He makes known to me anything concerning this heavenly devotion (to His Sacred Head) He comforts me also with it. For when I feel my poor heart breaking with sorrow at the coldness with which He is treated and the way He is betrayed even by His priests, He shows me this soul as His consoler and refuge, this lily in which He delights, and the will of this holy one blending so completely with His that they seem as one, this understanding in which the light of God shines as the midday sun in the clear waters of a spring, and that memory that is always recollected in God, that heart that pants and languishes for Him and wastes itself away in longing desire to be dissolved and be one with Him for all eternity. Oh my God how much You have taught me in this soul which You drew from the same abyss of nothingness as myself, and yet, through her ready compliance with Thy adorable Will in all things, Thou hast raised her to a pinnacle of perfection which but very few saints have ever reached. Oh my God how wonderful are Thy works and how incomprehensible Thy judgements and unsearchable Thy ways. For this jewel of Thy house is a wonder to the angels and Thou Thyself hast shown me that (she) *this soul* is one of the centre pieces of Thy Sacred Heart. I know not whether *this soul* is a priest, or even a male or female saint, but I know you will join with me in thanking God for all He has done for it, and allowing us, unworthy as we are, to live and worship before this same tabernacle where in His Love He deigns to listen to us as well as to this great servant of His Sacred Heart. I think our dear Blessed Lord shows me this soul to humble me, for I always feel that I am sinking away in the abyss of my own nothingness whenever He allows me to see it, and yet my whole soul seems to overflow with gratitude to Him for raising this soul to such perfection, and love and admiration at His work and delight beyond utterance at His reserving her (I mean the soul) to comfort and console, to love and adore Him as she does. And this last week, after our beloved Lord has shown me the greatness of His gifts to this saint, He has made me feel what black ingratitude it would be if she refused to fulfil His designs. I understand that of course it will be a great humiliation for her to undertake the great work which I think He intends, and I pray for and compassionate her exceedingly, yet I burn with desire to see His holy Will accomplished and say with her and for her, 'Thy holy Will be done, for Thou art my light and strength, Thou art my Protector and Helper, what shall I fear.' Although I have no curiosity to know who this chosen one is, yet I feel an ardent desire to be near her and to render her some service, to go and meet her as St. Elizabeth went to meet our Blessed Lady, our dear Mother Mary, at the time of the Visitation."[5]

The above is the first allusion in Teresa's letters to this wonderful soul, though she seems to have known about it as far back as at Wigan, for Miss Ryland recalls her asking quite simply one day: "Do you know that Father Wells directs a saint ? I wonder who it is. If I knew I might do something for her, perhaps wash for her. Have you any idea who it is?"

After this she often writes of it to Father Powell, begging him to ask for prayers and longing to be allowed to do something for this chosen one.

"Oh my Father pray fervently for me and ask that soul so dear to His sacred Heart to pray for me also. And is it too much of me to ask of you to let me render some service to this soul that so I may imitate Him a little Who has lavished on her such wonderful gifts. It seems so strange to me that you should never mention this holy one to me (not by name) but by telling me of her, that feeling the influence of her presence I might love Him and glorify His holy Name more for all He has done for her. For surely she is a glory to His Name."[6]

Again she says:

---

[5] Letter 36.
[6] Letter 38.

"Oh my Father may I do something for this one so dear to Him? I will not offend their humility in any way. I would not thus beg of you dear Father but I feel it would be a great service to my poor soul and I would not breathe one word of it — but just as you wish. I do not think I should be disheartened at seeing them doing so much for Him. I think I should feel I could get them to love Him for me and I would really try to learn the lessons Jesus would show me in them."[7]

Father Snow wrote later: "Both Father Powell and myself were convinced that the soul was no other than her own, but, knowing that it was Our Lord's own secret, were silent when she spoke of it." And so it came about in the mysterious designs of Providence that Teresa learnt humility from the vision of her own sanctity, and that her mighty prayers, so pleasing in the sight of God, were offered, all unconsciously to herself, for the perfecting of her own soul.

Teresa had mentioned that St. John speaks of the Devotion to the Sacred Head as the Seat of Divine Wisdom, and Father Powell asked her for the reference. She replied:

May 9, 1880.

"In obedience to your wish I asked our dear Blessed Lord where St. John had said anything in reference to the Sacred Head as the 'Seat of Divine Wisdom', and He gave me to understand that it was the chapter to which you referred without telling which one it was in particular, and He said that as by the cunning and deceit of the devil man first fell from God in Paradise and incurred darkness of intellect and death — so in these later days of darkness, self-indulgence, intellectual pride and conceit, the brightness of eternal light into which no defiled thing cometh shall shine out more glorious and brilliant than ten thousand suns, and the image of God's goodness and majesty and power shall be seen in this unspotted mirror of truth, purity knowledge and love.

---

[7] Letter 63.

"Oh my father, do we not see the depth of that divine Wisdom in the time that He has reserved for the manifestation of His adorable Will in this respect? He each time also shows me the great blessings and graces He has in store for all who shall further His divine Will to this end, and makes me tremble with terror at the dread punishments He has in store for all who shall hinder, or try to hinder the furtherance of this heavenly devotion, for their jaws He says shall be locked as were those of the lions in the den into which Daniel was cast, they shall be shattered and become as naught. And the twelve Fruits of the Holy Ghost that sparkle so beautifully in this divine Wisdom are, as it were, the foundations to this city of the Lord which He has dug deep in humility. For He humbled Himself becoming obedient unto death, even to the death of the Cross."[8]

Again, a few days later she said:

May 23, 1880.

"After holy Communion this morning I asked our B. Lord in what particular place St. John referred to His Sacred Head as the Seat of Divine Wisdom and He did not tell me what text or words. He gave me to understand that it was spoken of in the two last chapters of the Revelations and with this mark were sealed the numbers of His elect."[9]

On Ascension Day, Our Lord once more appeared to her in glory and three times asked her: "What wilt thou?"

"Oh my Lord and my God, what will I but Thy holy Will in all things? Lord what wilt Thou have me to do? Teach me to do Thy holy Will for Thou art my God! Oh my Father I know not how I live. Who would not be annihilated in the presence of such awful majesty, such overpowering and unspeakable glory and power as I beheld in Him Who is the Wisdom of the Father our Lord and Saviour Jesus Christ. Who could tell the dread and fear that came upon me? For I cannot express what I felt, and if it

---

[8]   Letter 42.

[9]   Letter 47.

were not by a miracle of His power I should die as I sink into the abyss of my own nothingness and misery.

"What I have mentioned above happened on Thursday morning early and all my bodily strength seemed to leave me and I have been very weak ever since. I was going to say I saw our dear blessed Lord in His glorified humanity, but I suppose it is not right to say so, but I feel very certain of it which appeared in greater majesty and glory than I have ever before seen Him and He addressed me, saying, 'What wilt thou?' I was crushed and humbled as God only can humble and at first a great inexpressible fear came upon me, but our dear Lord seemed to behold me with such loving tenderness and compassion that by degrees the fear passed off and I felt amazed and astonished at the marvellous condescension of our dear B. Lord and lost in His mercy and love. Oh with what confidence those words inspired me, though I feel that in them too He was asking me to do some great thing for Him of which at present I have not the remotest idea, but my misery is such that it gives me greater confidence that whatever He wishes to do in me or through me He will do Himself. I give myself and all that I am or have (which is nothing) into His sacred Hands to do with me whatever He shall please, without thought of pain, humiliation or feelings. His holy Will is my only pleasure and if I can lose or suffer anything for Him, He knows I shall consider it as a great gain. Oh my God with Thee I make an oblation of my whole being to Thy Eternal Father, my character, etc. saying, 'Lord I am Thine, my love is all for Thee, do with me what Thou wilt now and forever more Amen.' Holy Mary be a Mother to me. St. Joseph and all the angels and saints of God pray for me."[10]

She again refers to this vision in a later letter where she says:

"Oh my God how shall I find words to express the glory the majesty and beauty of that countenance before which the Seraphim and cherubim fall in mute admiration and adoration and I, like the apostles on Tabor, cannot sustain this flush of glory, this

---

[10] Letter 40.

stream of the Divinity, and in amazement I prostrate myself to the ground and with trembling reverence adore what mortal eyes are not able to behold or human tongue able to describe. — Oh magic wand of obedience that changes all things into purest gold, oh Rod of Aaron which opens a passage into the depths and riches and knowledge of God; oh Key which unlocks the secrets of the Divinity and the world to come; oh flower which ever blooms in the Sacred Heart; oh power which lays mountains low and overcomes every obstacle and makes every way easy and straight — in you I will write what I am able to say of those things which I have beheld.

"It was very early on Ascension morning that I beheld our B. Lord in the way I have above described and I think as He is represented in pictures of the Sacred Heart, only that around His sacred Head shone a light of indescribable brilliancy and beauty: as it were a sun in which sparkled twelve magnificent crystal stones reflecting all the colours of the rainbow. And in the Head I saw as it were an ocean of fathomless depth, smooth and clear, and the brightness of the sun's rays penetrated to its very depths, and in it were reflected all the beauties of the sun and twelve stones like diamonds in which were reflected the green, yellowish green, purple, red etc. and all the colours that sparkled in the sunny rainbow, and nearly in the centre of this was an eye as I have drawn on the other side. The awful majesty which overpowered me left me unable to move for hours and, although it is now ten days since, I have not regained my natural strength and it is with difficulty that I go about at all. The human mind is too weak and the intellect too dull to understand, comprehend or describe the awful grandeur of the Divinity and I think it is a miracle we live after a glimpse of it.

Oh how terrible will be the lot of the reprobate at the sight of this overwhelming majesty, this crushing power – and here we see with what reason the devils trembled at the descent into Limbo –

But I am again wandering. Light streamed from every part of His Sacred Person, and I saw flames of fire bursting from His Sacred Heart which was surrounded with thorns and surmounted by a cross, and I saw a silvery light in the form of a Dove hovering over it as I have shown above and the sun's rays streamed into its very depths and our Lord addressed me in these words: 'What wilt thou?' as I have before told you."[11]

On May 27, 1880, our Lord again showed Himself to her in all His glory:

"This morning at holy Mass when the Sacred Host was raised at the elevation, I saw as it were the whole court of heaven in prostrate adoration; then all was lost in the excess of light which shone forth in effulgent splendour from the sacred Person of our Lord Jesus Christ Whom I beheld as I have before described, but with a sun of transcendent beauty and brilliancy shining around His sacred Head and lighting up the very depths of His Sacred Heart. And He made me very clearly see that the time is at hand when He will make known to the world the desire (which has been consuming Him as it were) which He has to have His sacred Head adored and worshipped as the Seat of Divine Wisdom."[12]

Later in the same day she wrote a further explanation of the words of St. John in the Apocalypse:

"While making a short visit to our dear Blessed Lord in the most holy Sacrament of His Love, those things which I asked you to read for me this morning were represented in the soul and impressed very clearly in my mind, and I saw how admirably they corresponded and how beautifully the comparisons described the Sacred Head as the 'Seat of Divine Wisdom', for, if you call to mind those things which I have written regarding what our dear B. Lord has shown me and helped to narrate respecting His sacred Head, you will see how He Himself represented to me in the S. Head (as the mind) a transparent sea of

---

[11] Letter 44.

[12] Letter 48.

light, in which were twelve beautiful precious stones in which sparkled and reflected all the splendour of that sun which overshadowed it and in which too were twelve other crystal stones all of unspeakable beauty and magnificence and in which gleamed all the colours of the rainbow. And I think I mentioned a resplendent light of greenish hue I see 'having the glory of God and the light thereof like unto a precious stone, as it were a jasper, as crystal.'

"And He gave me to understand that this Wisdom and Light was the seal that marked the number of His elect ('and they shall see His Face and His Name shall be on their foreheads'). And is not the Seat of Divine Wisdom 'as it were a new heaven and a new earth'? The soul and intellectual faculties and the dwelling place of the Most High, and the earth or human head the shrine and centre of the senses of the body by virtue of the hypostatic union a new earth. — And in another place it says: 'And I saw no temple in it, for the Lord God almighty is the Temple thereof and the Lamb', showing distinctly the union of the two natures in the one Person of Jesus Christ. And the glory of God enlightens it. He is the Beginning and the End, and His Knowledge and Wisdom are infinite as they are eternal. And the great and high wall are things in God which are beyond our understanding, and the twelve foundations are the virtues which come from the Fruits of the Holy Ghost (and also may be the Apostles as teachers of Divine Wisdom and Pillars of His Church). Solomon's prayer for Wisdom was most pleasing to God, and He promises to give to him that thirsteth of the fountains of the water of life gratis, and blessed are they that wash their robes in the Blood of the Lamb that they may have a right to the Tree of Life and may enter in by the gates into the city. And he that shall overcome shall possess these things and I will be His God and he shall be My Son."[13]

Our Lord next signified to her the day on which He wished this feast to be celebrated.

June 2, 1880.

---

[13] Letter 48a.

"As I told you, our dear B. Lord expressly asked me to tell you from Him that He wished His most Sacred Head to be publicly worshipped and honoured as the Seat of Divine Wisdom, and said too that the Friday, octave day of the feast of the Sacred Heart, should be dedicated as a festival day in its honour, and special reparation and atonement be then offered to Him. For He said, 'See oh my beloved daughter, I am clothed and mocked as a fool in the house of my friends; I am crowned in derision, I who am the God of Wisdom and all Knowledge, I the King of Kings, the Almighty and All–powerful One am presented with a sham sceptre, and if thou wouldst make some return, thou canst not do better than tell my servant E. from me that *I now wish* the Devotion made known which I have so often communicated to you, and I wish the first Friday after the feast of my Sacred Heart to be set apart as a festive day in honour of my Sacred Head as the Seat of Divine Wisdom, and that public adoration be offered to Me for all the outrages and sins which are continually being committed against Me.' He also said that you must not be disheartened at difficulties that may and will arise and crosses that will be numerous. He will be your support and your reward is great. 'And anyone who shall assist in furthering this Devotion shall be blessed a thousand fold, but woe to him that shall reject or go against my wish in this respect, for they shall be scattered in my wrath and shall know their place no more, but to them that honour Me I will give of my might, and I will be their God and they shall be my children and I will place my sign upon their foreheads and my seal upon their lips."[14]

Untold blessings are promised to those who shall try to further our Lord's wishes in spreading the Devotion.

"Our B. Lord said that all that He had promised to those who should worthily love and honour His Sacred Heart should be poured out upon those who honoured it themselves or were the means of others doing so. Oh Sacred Head, may Thy Wisdom ever guide us, and the sacred Tongue ever bless us and plead for

---

[14] Letter 49.

mercy and pardon, and may we never hear the curse pronounced against those who shall hinder or despise this Devotion."[15]

With each fresh revelation our Lord seems to have impressed upon her more and more His ardent longing to have His sacred Head honoured, and to have urged her to do all in her power to carry out His wish.

"Again our dear B. Lord has made me feel that excessive desire that seems to consume Him to have His sacred Head honoured as the "Seat of Divine Wisdom", the governing power which rules the sacred Heart, the Shrine of the powers of His holy Soul and the centre of the senses of the human body. Oh my Lord and my God, why dost Thou chose one so unable to do anything in furthering and accomplishing Thy holy Will? My poor heart is breaking because I cannot and still Thou urgest me more and more and Thou burnest me too with this unceasing flame that at times I know not what to do, I feel myself almost dying of desire to see His holy Will accomplished...

"I was making my usual visit on Friday morning when with the eyes of the soul I saw Jesus consumed as it were with a burning fire, and the light of that sun which is ever shining seemed to penetrate the most secret recesses of His sacred Heart. I felt that inexhaustible fire burn me as it were. Oh my God how can I find words to express what I would say: I mean that our B. Lord let me see and feel something of that desire which He has to have His sacred Head honoured, as I have before made known. I saw how the divine Wisdom governed, and the powers of the holy Soul of Jesus Christ cooperated in the redemption of man, and I was lost in wonder and admiration at what I beheld. — I know not at least half I saw, but I was impressed with the great desire of Jesus."[16]

"I know He is infinite Wisdom and His word is creative and I (marvel) how He can desire as He desires and yet delay so long.

---

[15] Letter 51.
[16] Letter 49b.

His ways are not the ways of men and His designs are in the depth of His eternity. As the dew falls silently and unobserved on the bosom of the earth and it sinks in and fertilises the barren soil, so even now. He made me experience on Sunday the very aching of His sacred Heart to make known this crowning Devotion to His sacred Humanity, and showed how the motions and love of His sacred Heart were swayed by the powers of His Soul and intellectual faculties, and how the heart without the mind of man is incapable of merit — if a man is unconscious what can His Heart do, or if wanting in reason at what account do we value his gifts or deeds? And I understand that even the devotion to His sacred Heart is incomplete without this devotion to His sacred Head... He brought before me all He has before taught me respecting the devotion to the Seat of Divine Wisdom and His desire to have It honoured and impressed upon me again all about the great mystery of the Incarnation and the inseparable union which existed between Himself, the Eternal Father, and the Holy Spirit, and showed me how jealous was the Blessed Trinity of the beauty of His House and the Place where His glory dwelleth...

"Oh infinite Wisdom, boundless Love, how unsearchable are Thy ways. Make known oh Lord Thy desires to have Thy sacred Head honoured as the 'Seat of divine Wisdom' and to have Thy holy Soul sorrowful unto death comforted. Breathe Thy complaints oh Lord my God into the soul of one who has power to act. Arise and show that Thou art the Almighty God. Make known the burning desire of Thy sacred Heart. Make haste oh Lord for Thy own dear sake. Do not thus delay I conjure Thee through Thy most Precious Blood and for Thy bitter Passion's sake. I ask Thee, oh ever Blessed Trinity in the holy Name of Jesus, in honour of this same Seat of divine Wisdom, and through the burning love of His sacred Heart, I ask it in the name of Mary and Joseph and for the salvation of souls that Thou wilt make known and spread this Devotion. Oh Lord Thou knowest the desire with which I desire to satisfy Thee yet how weak and helpless I am and how little is yet done. Speak Lord and say what Thou wouldst have us do...

"I understand too that in the devotion to the Seat of divine Wisdom the Holy Ghost will be unfolded to our understanding, or His attributes will shine forth in the Person of God the Son: that the more we practise devotion to the sacred Head, the more we must see of the working of the holy Spirit of God in the human soul, and the better we will know and love the Father, the Son, and the Holy Ghost who are ever in a unity of Essence though in a Trinity of Persons...

"Dear rev. Father I think if we began to ask our dear Lord three times a day, through His Precious Blood and cross and passion, to hasten the Devotion and spread it far and near, He must grant our request, when our desire is but as a small spark compared to the burning furnace of His desire. Oh, I cannot understand how He can so yearn to be thus honoured (He Who is almighty) and yet delay so long to accomplish His ardent wish. Yet I know His ways are unsearchable and His Wisdom infinite, and that which He wills must come to pass, is certain to be."[17]

At times our Lord would comfort her by allowing her to foresee the great glory He would gain from the practice of this Devotion, and the special rewards He held in store for those who furthered it.

June 15, 1880.

"Our dear B. Lord showed me the great glory that would be given to the adorable Trinity and to His sacred Humanity through this Devotion. And He told me not to be downcast because others did not accept and pay adoration to Him in the manner He wished at once, for those who appeared the most against it now would make up by future fervour; that His Will is omnipotent and that those things that man might and would use as stumbling blocks to this Devotion He would turn into the very means of advancing it."[18]

---

[17] Letter 51a.

[18] Letter 52.

September 10, 1880.

"You know how anxious I am that the Will of our dear B. Lord should be perfectly accomplished in respect to His sacred Head being honoured as the Seat of divine Wisdom, so I thought if our dear Mother Mary asked Him for some proof for us to show our beloved Bishop He would give it her as a birthday present, and so I petitioned Him and her also. When suddenly that dark thick cloud which had overshadowed me for so long a time disappeared, and the glory and radiance of the Sun of Justice seemed to inundate my poor soul and so overpowered me that I was completely out of myself, and I beheld and felt the delight and glory that filled the Sacred Heart of Jesus at the little homage we had already paid Him in the prayers we were saying and had said in honour of His sacred Head as the Seat of divine Wisdom, the Shrine of the powers of His Soul and intellectual faculties, the centre of the Senses of His adorable Body and the completion of the Devotion to His sacred Heart. And He gave me to understand that He would crown and clothe with a peculiar glory all those who furthered this Devotion. He would clothe with glory before angels and men in the courts of heaven those who clothed Him in glory on earth and would crown them in everlasting bliss. I saw the glory prepared for three or four concerned therein and I was amazed at the greatness of their reward for I felt that our B. Lord and His holy Mother considered this homage to wipe out the outrage offered to the most wise and holy God when He was crowned and mocked in derision and scorn and clothed as a fool. It would seem that now those thorns would blossom, I mean that He would wish now to be crowned and acknowledged as the Wisdom of the Father, the true King of Kings. And as the Star of old led the Wise Men to Jesus and Mary, so in these latter days the Sun of Justice must lead us to the throne of God in unity and Trinity. Our B. Lord made me again understand that proof shall not be wanting, but I felt that it was not the one we looked for, I mean that poor dear Maggie should be restored to sight. He did not and does not seem to wish to let us know what proof He intends, but I think it is to be something about that holy soul He has so often shown me as His delight and consolation. If you ask that one so dear to Him, I have no doubt but what we shall obtain our request. I thank Him and love Him more for all He has done for this one and I thought He was pleased for the honour you had shown them."[19]

---

[19] Letter 63.

8

The Devotion to the Sacred Head
(continued)

EVER since our Lord had first spoken to Teresa with regard to His Sacred Head as the Seat of Divine Wisdom, this devotion had been acting as a leaven on her whole spiritual life, until she came at last to view everything in its light. In November 1880, she wrote:

"It has been the good pleasure of our dear blessed Lord to allow me to participate more fully in His dreadful bitter Passion during the past week and He has impressed on my soul, more clearly than I ever before saw it, the 6th Station where St. Veronica presents the towel to wipe the Face of our Lord. And He has made me feel that He Himself commenced that devotion which is so near and dear to Him, the Devotion to the Seat of Divine Wisdom, by impressing the image of His sacred Head and Face upon the towel she offered Him. It rewarded her piety and He comforted Himself in the glory and love and compassion which should in after ages be rendered to Him and the adorable Trinity in it. Oh Seat of divine Wisdom and guiding power which regulates and governs all the motions and love of the sacred Heart, may all minds know Thee, and all hearts love, all tongues praise Thee now and forever. Thou art truly the Light that shineth in darkness, the height and depth of knowledge, for in Thee are all things present. Oh my Lord and my God, I conjure Thee by this Seat of divine Wisdom, by the love of Thy sacred Heart and by all the Precious Blood Thou didst shed and pain and anguish Thou didst take upon Thy sacred Humanity, to imprint now Thy seal upon this Devotion and give proof positive to His Lordship of Thy holy Will in this respect. Hasten oh Lord the day when, all gazing into the depth of Thy divine Wisdom and untold love, we may commence that immeasurable bliss here of gazing into that Face which is the joy of the saints and angels, and which we too hope to enjoy for all eternity. Oh Light and Love, come quickly and slake this raging fire which consumes my whole being, come and accomplish Thy Will and my only desire. Oh Lord, make no long delay. Oh Thou Who in the beginning didst say, 'Let there be light' and it was so, speak now oh Almighty God and will that this unfailing light shine forth and the re-splendent rays of this sun brighten up our minds and hearts; prove oh Lord, if such be Thy holy Will, that Thou art the living and the true God.

"Oh Mary, by all the love and homage thou hast bestowed on this Seat of divine Wisdom before which the cherubim and seraphim prostrate lie in awe and trembling fear and love, but which thou hast so often pressed to thy sacred Heart and pillow-ed on thy breast. Oh Mary and Joseph, all ye choirs of angels and gleaming rows of saints, raise now your minds hearts and hands to the adorable Trinity and beg of the Holy of holies to look on those warm red drops of priceless worth, the Precious Blood of Jesus which have obeyed the order of His divine Wisdom, and by His obedience unto death and all the Wisdom and Love He has shown towards His creatures to arise and spread this light over the whole face of the earth. Where would we all be if it were not for His infinite Wisdom and Love? In nothingness out of which He called all things. Then let all things acknowledge, praise, bless and love this Wisdom and adore the sacred Head of Jesus as its seat. Not my Will but Thine be done. I mean I am ready to wait Thy good pleasure, but oh Lord Thou knowest how this fire burns within me, Thou knowest all things, my love and my desires are not hidden from Thee.

"Oh dear rev. Father, I trust this is not anything wrong in me, I mean to wish so ardently to have this Devotion established when it does not seem to be His holy Will to give the proof the Bishop desires as yet. I try to wish to wait His time, but at times such a sea of fire, I mean such a burning desire comes upon me to have His holy Will accomplished, I mean to have the Seat of divine Wisdom honoured after the manner He has made known to me, that I am so weakened by its fury that I know not how I live. Then I know not what I wish, for I feel I could live for ever and endure with pleasure the very torments of Hell if it would gain one act of love and adoration to Him (in this form) Whom I know and love above all things. And at the same time such an impetuosity in the soul to escape from this earthly prison that no tongue can express and no one understand, but they to whom our dear Lord imparts it."[1]

The following was the reply to a question of Father Powell's:

Nov. 11, 1880.

"In honour of the Sacred Head as Seat of divine Wisdom and Shrine of the powers of the holy Soul and intellectual faculties and centre of the senses of the body, I write dear rev. Father in obedience to your wish. Oh my love and my Lord, my God and my All, help me to gather in short that which You have shown me in such abundance. Thou hast shown me the light of Thy countenance and let me taste how sweet Thou art, Thou hast taken me into Thy house and instructed my understanding, and knowledge Thou hast infused which no man could speak, but oh Jesus my beloved Spouse, in glory to Thy holy Name and in honour of Thy sacred Head and love of Thy sacred Heart, I write with certainty of doing what is required in obedience.

"I asked our dear B. Lord to let me know what you desired, and He opened to me such a flood of light and knowledge that it seems to me that all thoughts of men and words are as so many ciphers when we would try to express what He shows and makes us feel, but I am doing what you desire. The question you

[1] Letter 65.

113

asked me was (I think) why our dear B. Lord wished His sacred Head to be honoured as the 'Shrine of the powers of His holy Soul', when the soul was certainly all over the body and the head was not considered the acting seat of all the powers of the soul. And this is what I understand — that as the *Reason or Intellect* in us is that part of the soul that is nearest to God — is in a special manner the image of God, nay, is the very light of God in the soul, in which we see God as He is, and ourselves as we are, and are capable of judging right from wrong. And as the head is the seat of the reasoning powers, and the faculties of the mind repose therein, so from the sacred Head shine forth in a blaze of resplendent light all knowledge, wisdom, understanding and a guiding power to direct and govern the Will and Affections of the sacred Heart; and in this is seen the connection of the desired Devotion — the ruling powers of the sacred Heart are seated in the sacred Head. I will not enter further into detail for I think what you wish to know is clear. The soul pervades every part of the body, but as the reasoning powers are the highest faculties of the soul, and as the head is said to contain or be the Shrine of these faculties in a special way and the memory is said to exist in the brain, so the reason guides and directs the will and love or affections of the human heart. The head is the highest and noblest part of man but I do not mean that the soul is divided, no, these three powers though really distinct cannot be separated no more than the Persons of the adorable Trinity could be separated — they form together but one soul which is immortal and perfect in its powers when filled with sanctifying Grace as is the holy Soul of Jesus. And our dear B. Lord gave me to understand that though He was much offended by the sins committed through the weakness of the will and misled affections, yet the sins of the intellect far exceeded those in number and in magnitude. And as the sins of intellectual pride were now (more than ever) drawing away souls from the love and service of His holy church and filling Hell with souls, when this so called light of the nineteenth century (as a will o' the wisp) is leading men to think only of gaining painted shadows and empty bubbles, giving them in appearance what they are really taking from them in substance; when men are taught to eat poison and are fed with such and given to drink of a stream of (so called) knowledge, the waters of which are pestilential and deadly and as our Lord says 'By their fruits you shall know them', so we see at once that this knowledge is not of God, but of evil, this fruit is not from the Tree of Life. So when this light which men set up for themselves would lead away all (I mean the number that are guided by it are so numerous), Jesus the true Light will arise and shed true light and wisdom and heat over the face of the earth. He will give us to eat of the Tree of Knowledge, He will feed us with good fruit, the wheat of His elect, and from the wine which makes virgins He will give us to drink nectar and honey. He gives freely and we draw abundantly from the essence of sweetness and good things. The Sun of Justice shall arise and we shall see Him in the very light of His countenance, and if we allow ourselves to be guided by this light, He will open the eyes of the soul. He will instruct the understanding, He will recollect the memory, He will feed the imagination with real and profitable substance, He will guide and bend the will, He will fill the hearing with good things and the heart with all it can desire."[2]

She gained fresh light and saw more clearly into the meaning of the Devotion with each of the great feasts of the Church's year.

"The Annunciation, 1881.

"Almighty God has on several occasions instructed me regarding the great mystery of the Incarnation and I feel sure I have written on it before. I see more clearly now though why our dear Lord is called the Word, because He is produced by the Father's thought or contemplation of Himself, for St. John says: 'In the beginning was the Word and the Word was with God and the Word was God. etc. and the Word was made flesh.' I think that in all it pleases the Almighty One to show me He wishes to instruct me more and more fully concerning His infinite Wisdom

---

[2]   Letter 67.

and love. And although the Son and the Holy Ghost are equally powerful, yet the almighty power is attributed in a special manner to the Eternal Father, and as the three Divine Persons have the same *wisdom* and goodness, yet the *Wisdom* is particularly attributed to the Son and the Goodness to the Holy Ghost, and we render a great homage to the ever Blessed Trinity by adoring our dear B. Lord's sacred Head as the 'Seat of divine Wisdom'."[3]

"The Ascension, 1881.

"When I knelt to adore the thrice Blessed Trinity for all the glory of the sacred Humanity, I was caught up as it were and dissolved in the excessive heat and glory of the Sun of divine Justice, and I heard sounds of praise and songs of joy in the heavens which echoed and re–echoed from the earth, and they were hymns of thanksgiving and admiration of the Seat of divine Wisdom. Then I saw reflected in the large crystal the glory which the ever blessed Trinity would receive from the Devotion to the sacred Head and the numberless souls that would be guided by its light to the bosom of the true Church and eventually to the throne of God. I understand too that this should be the one great means of the conversion of poor dear England, and that it was not far distant when she would bow her understanding to the obedience of faith and repair in some manner through this Devotion the great evil of her apostasy, and that Mary's name and Mary's Son should be more honoured than ever they had been dishonoured by our people."[4]

"Whitsuntide, 1881.

"I saw how the sacred Head was in a special manner the dwelling place of the Holy Ghost, and as at the moment of Creation the Spirit of God moved upon the waters, so He is ever enshrined in the Sea of glass and His brightness is the light thereof, and His love the Sun that gives light and governs all things in this terrestrial and celestial Paradise as the sun rules the things of earth. I have understood from our dear B. Lord that He

---

[3]   Letter 87.

[4]   Letter 99.

wished the great mystery of the Incarnation to be made very clear (or taught very carefully) to the children."[5]

On Corpus Christi our Lord again appeared to her:

June 19, 1881.

"Then He really came and gave me holy Communion Himself and drew me entirely into Himself, even as a raindrop into the ocean, and there He represented to me the great desire He had to have the Seat of Divine Wisdom honoured, and He instructed me in this manner: that the uncreated Wisdom of God is God the Father, Son and Holy Ghost, and that God the Son, becoming man and being the Image of the uncreated Wisdom of God, built for Himself a House which is the sacred Head 'for Wisdom has built herself a house.' And as Jesus has promised to remain with us forever, so He and the Spirit of Truth etc. will guide and govern and enlighten His Church to the end of time. And I saw Him as a sun drawing up vapour from the earth, so will souls warmed by the heat of this Sun of divine Justice and guided by its light ascend to the great white throne to adore the ever blessed Trinity in Persons and Unity in Essence. — Then, when I went into church, He urged me more and more to make known His desire, and there seemed to be a crown of fire which consumed His sacred Head and ate into the very brain and He said: 'Behold the burning desire I have to have my sacred Head honoured as I have instructed you.'"[6]

July 16, 1881.

"Our divine Lord has made me feel that it is with this special Devotion as with the mustard seed, that, although so little known and less practised, it will be the great Devotion of the Church in time to come, for in it the whole of the sacred Humanity is honoured — the holy Soul and intellectual Faculties, which have not hitherto been specially venerated and which are nevertheless the noblest part of the human being, and the sacred Head–sacred Heart, in fact the whole of His sacred Body. I mean

---

[5]   Letter 100.
[6]   Letter 103.

that the members of His adorable Body and five senses were ruled and governed by the intellectual and spiritual powers, and we venerate each act they suggested and the Body performed; for if we move only our hands, we must use the powers of the soul if it be only the will to do *it* or anything else; but in each action of the God Man we see an infinite degree of wisdom, power, knowledge and love, and in the motive of each act we see the perfect fulfilment of the law, 'loving God above all things and our neighbour as ourselves'. In other words the honour and glory of His Eternal Father and love and zeal for the salvation of man. And who can speak of that Love? ...

"He urged me to pray for true light, faith and wisdom for all, especially heretics and all poor sinners, and made me feel that the people of our dear land should shine in the brightness of this true Light and bring back more souls through this Devotion than they had scattered through the darkness of their infidelity. And it seemed to me that Mary prayed with me and reminded Him her divine Son that this England is called her Dower and He filled her hands with graces and blessing for us and a new glory as it were shone around her the reflection of the glory that surrounds the Seat of divine Wisdom. And our B. Lord renewed all the promises He has made to bless etc. all who practise or further this devotion in any way."[7]

On the feast of the Epiphany, 1882, she was filled with consolation when our Lady came and placed the divine Infant in her arms.

"And as I beheld Him, the eternal Son of God and Mary's Son, our dear little Infant Jesus, that instant I perceived these words infused into the very centre of my soul: 'Take courage my loved One, for the Seat of divine Wisdom will be known, praised, and adored as I wish and I will glorify my Name in thee.'"[8]

And again He showed her the great things that would come to pass in the church of St. Alexander which she loved so well:

---

[7]   Letter 106.

[8]   Letter 117.

"He brought very clearly and distinctly before me how in this church He would be honoured and how it would be filled with worshippers from far and near and loving hearts will gather together and praise glorify and thank Him, making reparation to the Seat of divine Wisdom, and holy souls will comfort and condole with Him, honouring His divine Soul, and here souls will be drawn to His Soul and they will be instructed by Him in the Wisdom of His sacred Head and burnt with the fire of His loving Heart. Here in the sacrament of His Wisdom and Love they will see things as they really are, and He will bless them and all who truly adore Him and honour Him as He desires with an everlasting benediction."[9]

Ardently she longed to see that day and prayed incessantly that she might be allowed to know clearly what it was our Lord was asking of her, but still she was content to await His good pleasure in disclosing it.

May, 1883.

"On Saturday I was so overpowered and annihilated, crushed almost out of existence, and when I got to my room and was about to prepare my meditation a deep recollection came upon me and our dear B. Lord drew me entirely into Himself. The powers of the soul were not able to act. The eye of the soul was wide open in God drinking in knowledge and strength, love and confidence, yet the faculties of the mind I think are overpowered with God's infinite beauty, power and awful purity; and the love God has for Himself and the work of His hand which is felt and understood very forcibly in the soul is too great for the human heart to bear, and this I think causes a kind of death to the body while the soul reposes in God: a sweet though agonising death which gives a new life. — I felt (though I did not see any form of a dove or any sensible representation) that the Holy Spirit of God hovered over me, or rather saturated me through and through, and showed me that the gifts He had entrusted to me were for His glory and that of the Father and the Son. And He gave me a

---

9   Letter 134.

119

fortitude to act and instructed me that *I had to do His work* and that I must not shrink from the duties He would impose on me in reference to the Devotion to the Seat of Wisdom and His holy Soul, yet He did not tell me what that work was and I did not ask. I feel it is much more perfect to wait though it seems so long, yet I know what He says must be, and though He urges me earnestly yet I know all time is as nothing in His sight and, if it pleases Him that I should not do anything but be consumed with this desire, then His holy Will be done. I am all Thine do with me what Thou wilt! And when I find myself saying to Him: 'How long oh Lord wilt Thou delay?' I check myself and say, 'Not my will but Thine be done.'"[10]

During the month of June our Lord again impressed upon her the infinite love of His sacred Heart and how He suffered from the neglect and cruel ingratitude of His children.

"There is no pang like this loving in vain as it were which Jesus suffers so intensely. No spear can pierce so acutely as coldness from the souls He has loved unto death. Here He taught me a *little* of that by allowing me to enter as it were into that divine and loving Heart and so participate in some way in this pang of His sacred Heart. He gave me holy Communion twice on Friday, once before you and once after, towards two or three o'clock in the afternoon. It seems as though a sword of fire and light pierced me through and through my soul and body saturating me in its flame. Then on Sunday He seemed to bathe me in His most Precious Blood and showed me how the Devotion to His holy Soul sorrowful unto death and to the Seat of divine Wisdom was only another means which His love urged to draw us more closely to that sacred Heart. It is *not* in any way intended to take the place of the Devotion to His sacred Heart, only to complete and further it. And He again impressed upon me that all the promises that He made concerning the practice and devotions of love to His sacred Heart should be bestowed a hundred fold upon those who practise devotion to the Seat of divine

---

[10] Letter 135.

Wisdom. And I understand that His *time is as hand* and we *will not have* to wait so long as you have given me to understand."[11]

Although to the end of her life Teresa recurred again and again to this all–absorbing subject, and though she never ceased to pray and do all she could for the spread of the Devotion, the following letter, dated just before Dr. O'Reilly bade her cease writing, is the last in which she enters in any detail into its meaning. It gives a most striking diagnosis of the pride of intellect and the rebellion against authority which are the crying evils of the day, and in it she again describes the favoured soul which was once more shown to her, but now more beautiful than ever — so beautiful in fact that at first she mistook it for our Lady. How far was she in her humility from thinking that this glorious soul could by any possibility be her own!

June, 1883.

"He showed me how man outrages the divine Wisdom by the abuse of the three powers of His immortal soul and by his sins — stamps out as far as he can the image of the triune God in himself and by mad folly tries also to rob nature of its God, tries to prove that matter is eternal and creative in itself and that there is no God or need for a God; that when nature decays in one form it only assumes another, that for instance that decayed bodies evaporate into gasses of different kinds and are scattered in the air — that these atoms accumulate and adhere together forming different substances and reappear as a new creature, and that so matter and nature are creative of themselves and need no creative or providential power to call them into being or maintain them in existence. That man in his pride of intellect and perverseness of will tries to drag down the great eternal Three in One, the Beginning and End of all things, from heaven and blots Him out of earth; that infidelity is rife, and man denying God puts away from himself any law or restraint against his vile passions, for if there is no God there cannot be a divine law commanding this and forbidding that. Oh my God, my God, Look not upon our

---

[11] Letter 136.

sins but upon the Face of Thy Christ — Listen to His dying prayer, Father forgive them for they know not what they do — oh look on the gaping wounds and the warm flowing Blood and have pity upon us and save and pardon us for this same most Precious Blood.

"Man too darkens his understanding by his infidelity. Take away the sun and we cannot have light or heat. Take away faith which is the light of the soul and all is decay and desolation; if we have not faith we cannot love or serve God. If we do not believe there is a God, well may God in His wrath say that man is flesh that is quite corrupt. Now God must have some recompense for all these blasphemies and outrages against Himself as God. It is worldly wisdom which is folly that is drawing down souls into an abyss of darkness which is Hell, and as of old when the heart of man set his affections against God, the sacred Heart of Jesus really human yet divine, because (united to the Person of God the Son) belonging to God the Son made Man, was the atoning object and Jesus revealed the burning love of His sacred Heart and complained of man's coldness and demanded a reparation and condolence, and souls were warmed in that furnace of divine love and souls burnt again with charity towards the God of Love — now too when infidelity and pride of intellect and open rebellion against God and His revealed law, self will and self–conceit is filling the minds of men and drawing them away from the sweet yoke of Jesus and binding them with the cold heavy chains of self–seeking, private judgment, and abandoning all right to be governed and wishing to govern oneself, disobedience to God and His holy Church — that same Jesus the incarnate Word, the Wisdom of the Father who became obedient even unto the death of the Cross, again gives us an antidote, an object which can and does, and will in every way make up and repays a hundred fold the debt that is contracted to the infinite Justice of God.

> Oh what atonement could be made
> For guiltiness like this?

> Or who such ransom could have paid
> To save from the abyss?
> See there a victim nature scorns,
> The Head of Jesus crowned with thorns.

"Our dear B. Lord has again and again impressed upon me His great desire to have His sacred Head honoured as the 'Seat of divine Wisdom', and as it is the abuse of reasoning powers which is now working such devastation in souls, it is the faculties of the mind and the powers of the soul that are sinning against God, so He complains, ah so pitifully, that His Soul is sorrowful even unto death. And He impresses upon me more and more that *His Soul* is not known, *His Soul* is not loved, and tells me *not by actual words*, but He infuses this complaint and saturates the soul with this feeling, which is as it were the overflowing of His holy and adorable Soul and makes known in an unmistakable manner that He wishes His holy Soul to be comforted, and shows and makes me feel that sorrow and anguish that so wrung from Him that complaint to His Eternal Father.

"And as the angel of old told Abraham that God would find a Victim for the holocaust, and turning round he found a lamb, a male lamb of under one year old caught by its horns in the thorns of the hedge, so now God again provides a Victim, a peace offering, a sacrifice of propitiation, 'the Seat of created and uncreated Wisdom crowned with thorns'.

"And our obedience and faith, like Abraham's, must first be true and tried — we must bow our understanding to the *obedience* of faith and God will show us the Lamb caught in the thorns which He particularly and expressly wishes to be a sacrifice to His outraged Deity, to His infinite and Eternal Wisdom. Ah, how beautifully God shows me the likeness of this Lamb which He distinctly says through the mouth of His inspired writers was provided by God. It was caught in the thorns, then it was sacrificed, its blood was shed, its heart was pierced and it was consumed by the fire of sacrifice. So the sacred Head crowned with thorns and the dewdrops of Precious Blood are as damask roses telling of the Love that draws forth those streamlets of ruby red…

"I think it is the same soul that our divine Lord has before shown me and whom He loves with an especial love, whom He has lavished His choicest gifts and graces upon, whose whole being seems to rest in Him, in whose soul is reflected very perfectly the Triune God, Whose will is in all things one with His, who is burning with and in the flames that consume His sacred Heart, whose soul gives Him great adoration, who condoles with Him in His sorrows, who is as He gave me to understand an angel of consolation to Him. And He showed me very clearly how perfectly this soul adored the Seat of divine Wisdom and rendered comfort to His holy Soul. I think He wishes to teach me by this holy soul what gifts and graces He bestows on those who give themselves up entirely to Him. And if it were only to reflect one single ray of glory to God such as shines in such profusion from this one, oh it would be worth trying for, for all eternity, she gives such glory to her Creator, her Redeemer, her Spouse. Her love is all for Him and her zeal for souls and His glory is as the pillar of fire which went before the People of Israel. Our dear blessed Lord seems to me to love this soul so tenderly and He gave me to understand that He will reveal the brightness of His shining in her, that multitudes may be drawn to love Him, to praise and thank Him for the gifts He has given her. She is truly a Child of Mary, an ornament to the Church. Oh how He humbled me in this soul, and gave me, poor worm of the earth, confidence and love for Him and His work, for I love this soul on account of the glory she gives to our dear divine Spouse, and I thought I would ask you to let me offer our undertakings to Him through her to Mary. And I begged of Him through the love He has for Himself to show His work in her and thus glorify His name. I begged of Him through the Wisdom of His sacred Head etc, etc. and for Mary's sake, for I have heard Him by those words in the soul, show her to Mary and tell her that she is His Spouse, that she has risen early to meet Him and the dewdrops are on her feet etc. The dewdrops of His most Precious Blood and roses encircle her brow. I think He has given to her the marks of His Precious Wounds and she is sealed with His Seal, and Wisdom is on her lips. Oh how it makes me want to do something for Him, how puny we are and how little we see we have done when God shows us a generous soul like this. I have asked our dear Lord to show her to you and others, for I know you will glorify God in His wonderful work in Her soul. Is it presumption of me to wish to speak with this saint? To hear her say that sweet name of love, Jesus, for I feel that it would make me love Him more. Blessed be God in His angels and His saints, Amen.

"When I last saw this soul, at first I thought it was our dear b. Lady, for it seemed to me that the angels of God gazed at her in wondering admiration, and yet the glory which now ascends to the blessed Trinity from this soul and the graces that God showers down upon the earth through her is wonderfully increased. Ah how wonderful is God in Saints. Our dear b. Lord instructed me that the Devotion will be acknowledged and will rapidly spread and draw many souls to Him. I often find myself begging of Him to choose someone who is to reveal the longing wish of His sacred Heart to have the Seat of divine Wisdom honoured. I feel that everyone must think that our dear Lord could not throw such pearls to such swine as I am, but I check myself in obedience and say: 'Thy Will be done on earth as it is in Heaven'. I know I asked Him to let this favoured soul be the messenger of His love for she knows of and practises this Devotion. Will you ask our dear Lord to let this soul if it be His holy Will be an instrument instead of your obedient child,

"In the sacred Head and loving Heart,
   "TERESA HIGGINSON,
      "Enfant de Marie."[12]

---

[12] Letter 137.

9

St. Alexander's, Bootle

THE letters quoted in the last two chapters extend over the period from June 1879 to 1881, and are but a few from the wonderful series (about 125 in number) written in obedience to her confessor, which form so intimate an autobiography of Teresa's soul during these years. They deal with many and varied subjects, and most of them are in direct response to some question from Father Powell. At one time he told her to write of the Passion in which she so often accompanied our Lord; at another he asked her to describe the Dolours of our Lady. He bade her write of the mystery of the blessed Trinity, the Incarnation, Purgatory, the state of the soul after death. Others again of the letters deal with the history of her own soul and describe the various ways in which Almighty God revealed Himself to her and instructed her. Again and again she seems to have lost all control over herself and to have fallen into ecstasy as she wrote. The sentences are unfinished and the writing trails away illegibly. Sometimes, if human language seemed utterly inadequate to express the truths of God, she would wait till after Communion, when our Lord would tell her what to say, or our Lady herself would instruct her. "Thank our b. Lady for me", she once wrote, "for helping me to make you understand. I told the very same that I wrote and she told me you would understand, that that was the right way to express the state of my soul."[1]

---

[1]   Letter 215.

Important as these letters are to a true knowledge of their writer, it is impossible to give them all in a short account of her life. In order not to interrupt further the thread of the narrative, a number of them will be quoted in a later chapter, as showing the mystic height at which she dwelt, while her feet trod the crowded thoroughfares of one of our great modem cities. How little indeed could those with whom she lived guess at the inner history of the quiet, unobtrusive, little woman who came and went so humbly, to church or school, or on her errands to the poor! Now and then a ray of light would as it were, flash out, but her confessor alone knew the burning flame of divine love which consumed her soul. And truly it is almost bewildering to turn from the letters wherein, by the "magic wand of obedience", she reveals the inmost secrets of her heart to the simple, even commonplace story of her daily life.

In the autumn of 1879, Father Powell offered her a post in his own school, which she joyfully accepted. It was at St. Alexander's, Bootle, that she had first begun to teach, and she wrote to him, September 20, 1879:

"I shall be pleased to begin work on the first of October as you desire me, though naturally I would prefer you to be there when I commenced so that you could give us your special blessing, but that you will do wherever you are, I am sure. I feel sure that you know how unable I am to do anything and that is really the secret of my apparent success; for as a helpless child looks to its mother for all it wants, so I, the most miserable and helpless child of God, look to Him and my good Mother and depend on them for all and they always give me more than I could ever expect. So any good result is theirs and the glory thereof. Oh how grateful I am to Him for this inability to do anything, for what He undertakes is perfectly accomplished. He is infinite Wisdom and can and will open the heart and ears of His little ones. The only thing I fear is that I may be a stumbling block to them, but I know you will pray fervently for them and me."[2]

The spirit in which she entered on her new duties may be seen from the following letter:

"Which is the worst street in the parish? I have promised our b. Lady to say the 15 mysteries of the Rosary for 15 days (I mean an extra 15) and do all that you would allow me for their benefit, and I have asked her to receive them as a special gift for her divine Son and prove to all by the change she makes in them that she is the all–powerful Mother of God.

"When you have time, will you kindly make me out a fresh order of the day? Did you receive a letter from me the Sunday or Monday before you went away?

"I renew my entire obedience to you in all things and as far as you permit I will be a servant to the people, for it is my only wish to help to save their immortal souls."[3]

A few days later she wrote again:

"I have been through all the houses in Mordan St. and 27 of the people have promised to come to confession and many of those have been today and nearly all are entering or re–entering the Holy Family Confraternity. So you see we are now bound in another debt of gratitude to Mary our dear Mother and I know you will join with me in praising and thanking her and her divine Son for their goodness and mercy towards us... Our dear little ones are coming a little more regularly to school and are trying to be good pious children. Ask their guardian angels to let me know quickly each child's character and see his little faults that with his help I may correct them, and pray that I may do my duty to them in every respect and may never scandalise them in word, look or action."[4]

Teresa at first lodged for a few weeks with a Mrs. Carter, and then went to stay with Mrs. Nicholson, a convert who kept a little

---

[2] Letter 15.
[3] Letter 16.
[4] Letter 17.

shop almost adjoining St. Alexander's. The tiny back room which Teresa occupied looked on to the wall of the church and here it was, at a little table in the window, that she wrote most of her wonderful letters to Father Powell. Mrs. Nicholson was a widow and her daughter, Ellen, a girl of about fourteen was attending a training school, studying to become a teacher. This child was greatly attracted to Teresa and when at home loved to spend as much time with her as possible. Her quick eyes noted many strange occurrences, but they caused her little surprise for, as she explained later, being but a recent convert, she thought in her innocence that all Catholics were affected in such ways!

Teresa was often ailing and her mysterious illnesses were a sore puzzle to her friends. Strangers were sometimes inclined to attribute them to hysteria, but those who knew her best were all agreed that she exhibited none of the symptoms common to that complaint. Rather they were impressed by her calmness, her retiring disposition, her strength of will (none ever dared to take a liberty with her) and her tremendous self–control. She was never in any way excited or emotional and her whole conduct was distinguished by that utter sanity which is so marked a feature of her writings. And yet her friends could not but be surprised by her strange attacks of weakness — as at Wigan she would be quite prostrate in the mornings and only after receiving Communion would she recover and be able to carry out her duties for the day. Then too, her frequent ecstasies, her terrible sufferings, her excessive penances and fasts, the attacks of the Devil, etc. could not always be disguised, and when any of these things came to the notice of others, her humiliation was such, as she herself expressed it, as almost to annihilate her. Her letters show the intense longing she had to keep hidden the mighty gifts God showered down upon her. Indeed so overwhelming was this desire that she began to consider it a fault, showing a want of conformity to the Will of God. On one occasion she wrote:

"Perhaps it would be as well to have a bottle of medicine from Dr. Raverty, it might stop any further talk or unnecessary uneasiness. I always feel at these times that I would be glad to hide myself anywhere out of the way. I trust it is not a want of resignation, for I say continually:

"Jesus my true and only Good I wish for naught but Thee

Behold me all Thine own my God, do what Thou wilt with me."

I have asked our b. Lord not to let anyone notice anything different in me but He permits it, perhaps to humble me a little. May His holy Name be blessed for ever and ever."[5]

The blood was often seen to flow from her wounds at this time, especially from the thorn marks on her brow. Miss Catterall, one of her fellow–teachers, tells how she met her one day coming out of church. Drops of blood were trickling from her head and the white scarf she wore round her neck was stained with it. Miss Catterall quietly advised her to change before going into school and she has never forgotten the look Teresa gave when she realised what had occurred.

In July, 1880, Teresa wrote:

"Last Friday my head bled several times and was noticed by the children and Miss Shuttleworth also (and she said she thought I was doing something to my head because it was Friday), and today at holy Mass both my head and hands bled more than they have done since Good Friday, and my sister's little girl called the attention of others to the fact. I don't think they suspect anything. They thought I had cut my head and forehead, but I was inclined (and did for a few minutes) ask our b. Lord to give me extra pain and stay the outward flow, but in an instant I remembered what you said and bowed my head in obedience to His holy Will. May His holy Will be perfectly accomplished in me and all of us. I cannot express the dread I have of anything of the kind. It does not disturb the peace of the soul and yet I feel there is a want of confidence and over solicitude on my part. Do you give me penance according as you may judge fit. I wrote on Friday afternoon but the paper was soiled

[5]   Letter 24.

and stained with blood so I thought under the circumstances it would not be *wrong* to *rewrite* what I had to say."[6]

July, 1880.

"I must tell you that when I bathed in the holy well (St. Winefred's Well) I noticed that both my feet and hands bled and I was tempted not to go in any more after the first time, but I put on, or rather went in the second and third time in stockings and yet a person who was present said, 'You have cut your foot, see how it is bleeding!' And then I feared that I had done wrong and I humbly beg pardon if I have, for I love Him with a love which He Himself has given me, and I prefer any torments rather than slight or offend Him in anything whatever, and the excess of His love brings such a clear brightness into the soul that I see my ingratitude and selfishness so forcibly that at times it seems unbearable. I beg of Him to help me to overcome this feeling of repugnance and ask Him that I may lose all sight of self and see Him only and wish only what He desires, for it has pained me much to see myself trying to hide those things (which are all His pure gift) when it seems to be His holy Will that others should see and know them."[7]

Aug. 1881.

"Since Father Harrington warned me respecting these favours, I have been very full of fear and I have continually begged of Him to take away all rather than allow me to offend in them, though they are dearer to me than anything else save Himself. I conjure Him to take them back if I will cease to glorify Him therein. I have always had great fear respecting them but lately it has greatly increased. I have asked Him again and again how He, the God of Wisdom, can thus throw pearls of such price to swine. Oh Thou Who hast died for me have pity on me! And our dear b. Lord has instructed me to look not to myself but to Him alone. If I do as He instructs, I shall walk securely on the waters,

---

[6] Letter 84.

[7] Letter 59.

but if to my own misery, I shall, like St. Peter sink beneath the waves. Oh He has impressed His infinite power, wisdom and love so clearly in the soul it would seem as though I was inundated with it. You told me to say the 'Magnificat' for my penance and such a delight in the works which God has done for me and I have experienced such a light and glory therein that I have trembled with fear for myself. Oh that I could hide myself entirely in His sacred Heart, but if such be His holy Will that others are to know, may His holy Name be blessed and praised therein. I trust He will give me strength not to be cowardly now, who is my only support."[8]

Sept. 1881.

"I have at the same time such an overpowering dread and terrible fear of that which I *know* to be God's Will in my regard. I mean that I shrink from the very thought of others knowing and seeing that which our dear Lord has done for me, and when I know as well as you what I am before God, and see on the other hand the precious jewels which He has given to this wretched miserable worm, and seeing that others knowing may make little of these inestimable favours, and perhaps think that they are mine whereas they are all His and I have nothing to do with them, I tremble with fear. Oh Jesus, my beloved Jesus have mercy on me! Save me through Thy most Precious Blood and grant that these great helps that Thou hast given me to Heaven I turn not into stumbling blocks. You see oh my Father how ungenerous I am, for though Jesus my dear crucified Spouse has increased the pain which is customary for me to suffer, as if to remind me more and more that I am His and that He is near and mindful of me (for it is His pledge of love for me), yet I look to my own nothingness and wickedness instead of at His infinite power and strength. I have thought that I cared not what others thought and said so long as I did that which I considered right, but I have deceived myself in this respect, for I find to my sorrow that I *do*; and yet I would not, if it were in my power to, check one

---

[8]   Letter 108.

drop of blood from trickling, or hide anything intentionally, since you have told me not, though I must own I never felt anything half so hard to bear. I find myself really cowardly and selfish for I see now very clearly that I think first of self and God afterwards, for when anyone makes any remark about any one of these favours, I feel as though I should sink into nothingness and I get quite ill, and then such a joy and delight that God's great desire should be accomplished that I know not how properly to express myself."[9]

In the summer of 1880, when at home for the holidays, Teresa was very frequently in ecstasy and evidently her family were more than usually upset about her, for on her return to Bootle she wrote to Father Powell:

June, 1880.

"While I was at home most of the time, I had no control over myself at all and I think they are a little alarmed about me. At first they thought I went to sleep and then thought I was fainting, and dear Mama asked me this morning if the doctor told me that I had fits for she said, 'There is something very strange the matter with you.' She says I go quite stiff but I have asked our dear b. Lord not to let them be uneasy about me and I feel sure He will do as I ask Him, at least He always has done so before. Mama seems afraid that it should get out that I have fits but I have given myself entirely into His hands as you desired me — I care not what anyone thinks, in fact I am very pleased they do think so, but Ellen Nicholson notices things very quickly and asks questions which are rather difficult to answer.

"The holy Tabernacle has now for some time appeared as I may say like a burning bush — I mean that besides that brilliant sun of light it seems as though flames also burst forth from it, and our dear b. Lord no longer veils Himself as at times He does and it seems to me a continual miracle that I am able to do the things I do (I mean when I am not in church), for whether in

---

[9]   Letter 110.

school or in conversation with others, although I join in with them, it does not at all distract me."[10]

Teresa remained at Bootle for nearly eight years — from 1879 to 1887 — and in the course of this time the retiring, shabby little teacher became a very storm–centre of controversy and abuse! We have seen the trials and sufferings which preceded her Mystical Espousals at Wigan, and now this faithful "Spouse of the Crucified" found herself called upon to follow her Lord from the beloved shelter of Gethsemane to all the publicity and shame of the heights of Calvary. As Father Snow explains: "Each degree of union in the life a mystic has to be prepared for by new favours and new sufferings. The greater the perfection and the higher and closer the union to which God calls a soul, so much the greater will be the sufferings — purifications, the theologians call them — and the longer the period they must be endured... Her Mystical Espousals took place on the feast of the sacred Heart, 1874, the Mystical Marriage on the 24th October, 1887. Notwithstanding the wonderful graces our Lord had given her during her whole life, this long period of over thirteen years was a time of preparation and purification for the Mystical Marriage which is the highest degree of union which a soul can attain upon earth." He then quotes St. Teresa:

"St. Teresa, in Chapter I of the sixth Mansion of the 'Interior Castle' describes the many troubles, both interior and exterior, the soul has to endure in preparation for the Mystical Marriage. She says: 'I wish to begin with the least, and this comes from the clamour which certain persons make with whom she lives (and from some with whom she never spoke, though during the course of her life they may have heard something of her), for they exclaim that she pretends to be very holy, that she goes to extremes and does extravagant things in order to deceive the world and make others appear to be worse who are better Christians without these extravagances. Those whom she considers her friends withdraw themselves from her and are the very

---

[10] Letter 52.

persons who offend her most: they are confident that these things come from the Devil and that she will meet with the same end that such and such a one met with who was ruined; that through her virtue will decay and that she deceives her confessor. They accordingly go to them and advise them, placing before them the example of some who by this very means have been ruined. A thousand other such scoffs and examples of this kind they make use of.'"

"Everything here described by the first St. Teresa", continues Father Snow, "took place with regard to our St. Teresa, only more so. The 'clamour' was greater than that described and greater than St. Teresa herself had to endure. It would take me hours to write the whole history of those times. At present it will be enough for me to say that the number of those who regarded her as a holy woman were few, and the number who regarded her as a 'lying hypocrite' were many."[11]

There are but few references to all this clamour in Teresa's letters and these are generally in direct reply to some question from her director. Throughout it all the one sure anchor to which she clung was obedience, and in 1881, she made a formal renewal of her vows:

"I, Teresa Helena Higginson, call all heaven and earth to witness the solemn promises I renew in presence of the adorable Trinity, of Jesus Christ in His sacramental presence, of Mary my Queen and my Mother, St. Joseph and all the saints of Paradise, of my dear good holy Angel guardian and the nine choirs of angelical beings, and in the fulfilment of which I hope through His cross and passion to live and die.

1. — I renew the vow of perpetual chastity and consecrate my whole being to Thee, oh my beloved Jesus, even as Mary offered herself to the Eternal Father in the Temple, so do I.

2. — In union with Thy obedience unto death I give myself entirely into Thy sacred hands, oh my Lord and my God, that Thou mayest do with me what Thou wilt; and also to my spirit-

---

[11] Letter from Father Snow to Father O'Sullivan.

ual director to be governed by Him in all things and led by him to Thee. Moreover I promise never to express a wish for anything but to give up always my will to that of others even in the smallest things (without it is something against Thy glory and the greater good of souls).

3. — I promise firmly to detach myself from all earthly things, places and persons, and use them only so far as they give glory to Thy holy Name, my Spouse and my only Treasure. I am also determined never to purchase anything for the use of the body, only that which I am bound to do in obedience or what is absolutely necessary, and these necessaries to regard them as only lent for a while for my use and not alter or give them away as if they were mine to do as I liked with them, for Thou knowest oh Lord I have nothing but my sins and iniquities.

"And as a safeguard to these vows I propose to mortify every sense of my body and never allow myself to gratify curiosity, but that which I would naturally seek is that which I am determined not to take and if I have a dislike to anything (if it be not imperfection) that I will take in abundance. And when I am sick and worn out then I will strive to say nothing and wait upon others as cheerfully as I can. Then I am determined never to take a drink when thirsty without I am told. Never to eat or drink more than is absolutely necessary and then those things to which I have the greatest aversion. Never to express a like or dislike and never in any way to speak of myself without it be to condemn or in necessity. Then, if I should feel pleasure in a person's company, strive to meet them as little as possible and if I have the chance of a conversation, go instead and kneel before Thee in the most holy Sacrament of Thy infinite Wisdom and Love. Then, oh my Jesus my only Love, I am resolved to spend all the time I can in prayer and I am determined never to rest more than one and half hour each day (without I am very sick and am told to take more rest). I promise also to strive to choose that which I feel is most perfect; to keep the body in subjection in all things and the powers of the soul in good training and the affections centred in Thee, so that in all things I may see Thee and all things in Thee.

"Then, oh my God, I give Thee all the indulgences I might gain, all the good Thou dost in me, together with Masses, alms, prayers, and good works offered for me after death for the poor suffering souls in Purgatory. And now, oh my beloved Jesus, I offer myself to Thee wholly and entirely, do with me what Thou wilt for I am all Thine, oh my loving Jesus, even as Thou art all mine. And I promise firmly to do all in my power to make known the burning desire of Thy most sacred Heart to have Thy sacred Head honoured as the Seat of divine Wisdom, and I will do my very best to spread this devotion and I yearn to shed my blood in testimony of it and to Thy greater glory. And now, oh my beloved Jesus, Thou knowest all things, Thou knowest how I love Thee, and I renew all the promises I have ever made to Thee, those I have not mentioned with those that I have and I beg of Thee to draw all hearts to Thee by the Wisdom of Thy sacred Head and the Love of Thy sacred Heart.

"Jesus my true and only Good
 I wish for naught but Thee
 Behold me all Thine own my God,
 do what Thou wilt with me.

"In the holy Name of Jesus and in obedience to rev. Edward Powell my spiritual director I renew the above promises made in childhood and renewed continually since, though without permission from any one to do so.

"Renewed this 5th day of June (Whitsunday) in St. Alexander's Church, Bootle.

　　　　"T. HIGGINSON,
　　　　　"Enfant de Marie."
　　　　LDS et hon BVM et St. J.[12]

One of the things that caused Teresa the greatest pain in all her trials was the trouble in which they involved her friends,

---

[12] Letter 101.

more especially her directors. In July, 1880, she wrote to Miss Ryland:

"Pray very fervently for me just now that with open arms I may embrace all that it is His holy Will to send me, and even when bowed down and crushed beneath the cross I may with grateful heart repeat: 'Lord it is good for me to be here. Lord I am Thine, do with me what Thou wilt.' And do not forget one either who through me has to do a great many things that are most repulsive to human nature, the rev. E. Powell, who like a faithful follower of our divine Master braves all for duty's sake and love of God. You know I am always a source of trouble and a heavy cross to the poor priest whom Almighty God chooses for my director, but to none so heavy as to my present wise and good director."

For her own part, keenly as she felt it, she accepted all this persecution with gratitude and even joy, and continually asked prayers for her calumniators whom she sincerely regarded as her greatest benefactors. In fact, she recognised it as in some sense the answer to her own prayer, for she wrote in 1882 to Father Powell:

"I asked our dear Lord too when I found the opinion many formed of me that He would open their eyes that they might see me as I really was, and I think in this He has heard my prayer, not that I think anyone could ever imagine how ungrateful I have been to Him my Spouse and only Treasure, the Lord and Master of my house, Ah no ! but at least they see I am not what they or others had taken me for. May His holy Name be praised for ever!"[13]

And again she said:

"You asked me what were my feelings when I read the anonymous letter. Well I told you at what I was hurt, but I felt that our dear Lord was not content in giving me Himself but that He would also give me a little Christmas present to reassure me that He is a faithful Spouse. For He never forgets me on these days,

---

[13] Letter 130.

and even when He is carried round to scatter His favours and blessings upon us all in general, yet He always sends me a little token of His love as a message to tell of His constancy, at least so I regard the things which have always been done and said to me by His holy anointed Priest on the nights of the procession of the most holy Sacrament. I cherish those little things as a bouquet from Him and I know through His Precious Blood that they are everlasting flowers."[14]

[14] Letter 131.

10

The Attacks of the Devil

THE Devil all this time was continually tormenting Teresa and one of his favourite temptations was to try and make her doubt the truth of her revelations regarding the Devotion to the Sacred Head.

"He says also that it did not look to be very great wisdom on the part of the Allwise God to choose one so base and wicked as I am to make known to the universe His desire of the sacred Head being worshipped as the Seat of divine Wisdom etc. Did I not think it more likely for Him to chose a great theologian and *a man known to be holy and wise in the things of God* instead of a worthless and ignorant thing like me? Who did I think would ever believe me? Besides, he said, in the written word it is said that false prophets should arise, and he told me to be on my guard and not lead astray any who would believe me.

"I know all he says about me is perfectly true, but though I feel even now that I would be glad to die in defence of anything I have told you I am very uneasy, and fear and dread seem to encompass me on every side. I try to take no notice of what he says to me, but then he told me that as a sign that what I was doing (to spread the Devotion to the Seat of divine Wisdom etc.) was not from God, he said I should be abandoned by God and left to the darkness of my own folly and ignorance. And he said, 'See how much light you will get from this supposed devotion and how wise you will be in a few days following and honouring that which you call divine Wisdom.' I try not to notice what he has said: I take the fear and disquietude as a sign that it was the Devil who then appeared to me, for I notice, and I think you have often told me, that in real visions (coming from God I mean) the fear passes away shortly and a holy peace, joy and confidence fill the soul; but in others, as in this, we are startled a little at first at what appears glory, but we begin to feel doubts and we become uneasy and fear grows and peace seems for a while to leave us on account of the many doubts with which we are filled, and we know not what to do. And if we gave way, we should be afraid to undertake anything for the love of God, for he would give us a false humility; but real ones fill us with a heavenly calm, fill us with great desires and a burning love which must act or our poor hearts would burst, show us our utter nothingness yet fill us with confidence when we see how mighty and rich and powerful our dear good God is. We look not to ourselves, but we forget ourself; we are lost as it were in His immensity; we feel He will and can give us great help to do or accomplish those desires with which He inspires us, or He will do all as we are nothing and can do nothing. I think we cannot be deceived by the Devil, at least I think it is our own fault if we are, especially if we tell all to our directors, besides I detected him (through the mercy of God) by his saying not to tell you, and although I felt it was him I was afraid for fear it was not, so I made up my mind to write at once. May the Wisdom of the sacred Head guide us in all our ways and the love of the sacred Heart consume us with its fire."[1]

AMDG et in hon BVM et St J.

Feb. 6, 1881.

"Oh Wisdom of the sacred Head guide us in all our ways,
Oh Love of the sacred Heart, consume us with Thy fire!

"DEAR REV. FATHER,

"I really do not know which night it was, but it was the one on which you gave me permission to take the punishment of a poor man's sins, so that our dear good God would give him the grace to make a good confession. Well, for some time past I have

---

[1] Letter 59.

felt at times that I cannot bear up under the excessive pains of soul and body which in pity He has graciously given me to endure for Him, and so it was on this night. I felt worn out and exhausted, faint and weary, and yet I love these pains more than all the world besides. I could hardly drag myself into the church for holy Rosary etc. I think it must have been Saturday night, but during the litany a poor man came and knelt near me, of course I do not know his name. May Jesus Christ through His precious Blood and Cross and Passion have mercy on him and all poor sinners. But when he came near me, I really think I should have fainted if I had not reminded our dear b. Lord that you said I *was not to faint in church*, but the stifling stench that proceeded from him I thought was that of the dreadful sin of sacrilege and the horrible cancer of impurity. Oh my Lord and my God, how wonderful Thou art! Though the soul of this man was so deeply dyed in sin, while it had Thy most Precious Blood to answer for, yet Thou urgest me so earnestly to plead for him by allowing me to know his state, etc. that uniting my poor voice with Mary's, and Thine in death I cried with Thee: 'Oh Father, forgive him for he knows not what he does!' And I told my Lord that with your permission I would take the punishment of his sins upon me, if He would grant him pardon and forgiveness, and the grace to make a good confession. And so I think He granted my poor prayer. And when I left the church I became overwhelmed with sorrow for these sins with which I had clothed myself — and yet I cannot say 'with sin', but I mean the punishment of those sins, for the guilt was forgiven. And oh my God, how I trembled with unutterable fear as I gazed into Thy dread and awful purity and strict Justice, when I beheld Thy tremendous power and majesty. Oh how can I express all the soul suffers when God draws her into the attributes of His divine and infinite justice, when she would sink into Hell itself more willingly than stand in the brightness of the all searching Eye of God: the flames of Hell would be cool in comparison with this. For the flames of Hell are but creatures made to punish, but this is the Creator. This is a little of what Jesus endured on the cross, and merciful Jesus have mercy on us. And so I was bent down in agony and anguish and I begged for forgiveness, when numerous devils came and mocked me and laughed at my presumption as they called it. They said all these miracles I asked so bounteously for myself were purchased at a high price, the Blood of the Holy One of God, God Himself. They showed me how justly God had punished one sin of thought in them — that He had already lavished on me ten thousand times ten more graces than He had given them, and What had I to offer in return? That I must be mad with pride and presumption to dare to ask such a thing. They tried to show me how blind I had become, and then they yelled most frightfully and told me now they had me properly in their power and I should pay for all. And then I besought my beloved Jesus and Mary to allow the Devil to torment me and I said the little invocations to the sacred Head and Heart. They rushed upon me and said they would burn me with a fire, a liquid fire, a fire that would burn and burn for ever and never consume. Then I felt every part of my body cringe and curl as it were with a scalding burn which seemed to saturate through the bones to the very marrow; then grasping hold of the throat they nearly strangled me, and I perceived again the horrible stench of those sins the punishment of which you had given me leave to suffer. Of course you know I know full well the Devil is a liar and I fear him not in legions any more than alone — not that I do not know his power and experience, or that I am weakness itself, but I know that my Lord is the Almighty God and my Mother, Mary, and she has ever had his head beneath her heel. He has been very quiet for some time, but every now and then he breaks out in fury like a mad beast without power to control himself. For the last week too, when I have gone to make a little offering of my children's work to my loving Lord in the blessed Sacrament of His wisdom and love after school, he has laughed aloud at my little nosegay of faded flowers, as they seemed to me, and he has claimed most, but I heed him not. I say, 'Lord perhaps they are faded and withered, perhaps many of them dead, but Thou art the Lord of Life, refresh them with Thy most precious Blood, breathe upon them the Breath of Life and they will bloom for Thee. Oh my Lord and my God, teach these Thy little ones to love Thee, draw them close to Thee. Mary our dear Mother, lay them fondly on thy breast, hide them deeply in the sacred Heart. Send me all kinds of sorrow and suffering, but spare them, for Thy mercy's sake. Oh holy St. Joseph and all the saints of God, pray for them. St. Michael etc. all ye angels of the Lord watch them in every place, guard and protect them from all danger of body and soul.'

"I forgot to say that my tongue remained much swollen all night and next day.

"Begging your prayers and blessing for my little ones and self
"I remain dear rev. Father
"Your obedient and devoted child in the S. Head and S. Heart.
    "TERESA HIGGINSON,
        "Enfant de Marie."[2]
            LDS et hon BVM et St. J.

(Ellen Nicholson recollects that one Lent Teresa suffered intensely from the terrible swelling of her mouth and tongue.)

Another time, when suffering from terrible spiritual desolation and darkness, she wrote:

Ap. 1882.

"In honour of the sacred Head and in obedience, I write of the trials it has pleased our divine Lord my beloved Spouse Jesus to send me. May His holy Name be blessed for ever for all His goodness to me. Besides I am determined to tell you everything as minutely as I can, first because I know the wicked One is anxious that I should not, and secondly that so you may judge whether these things are of God or otherwise.

"Oh how dark and dreary is everything! There is not the slightest glimmer of light to guide me I really feel that God is worn out with me, that He has cast me off on account of my

---

[2] Letter 81.

many sins and wickedness and I fear that He is punishing me with blindness of heart. Then I see the dark mountain before me of a most fearful passion and I prostrate myself before God, imploring mercy through the passion and death of His beloved Son. Besides having that fearful dread of that which I know God in His merciful love has ordained me to suffer, there is an unspeakable doubt and uncertainty overshadowing me and saturating me through and through, on account of my not being able to do as you tell me. I always have felt so sure and safe under your direction and always found myself able to obey you, besides our dear Lord has always told me so positively to obey you in all things, but now (although I have told our dear Lord after holy Communion that I am to go in school always till Holy Week and that you will give me Friday afternoons after three for Him to do with me as He pleases[3]) yet I really find myself unable to go in school. Oh I really do not know what to do. I beg of Him by His obedience unto death to enable me to do as I am told, and when I find that I am still unable to go, I fear that I must be under the influence of some wicked spirit and I doubt everything and think perhaps I am deceiving myself and *you*. Oh what sort of sorrow this is to me Thou knowest oh Lord Who sees all things, Thou knowest how I love Thee and how I suffer. I am ready for all sorts of tortures, one thing only do I fear and that is that I offend Thee, oh God of my heart. I know I deserve to be abandoned by Thee, but Lord, see, is not my soul saturated with Thy Precious Blood which I receive daily and for the sake of It spare me from sin, stay near me Lord or I will betray Thee. I am all Thine oh my beloved Jesus, do with me what Thou wilt. I trust in Thy wisdom and love that Thou wilt lead me aright: if it be Thy holy Will to leave me in darkness and doubt, then I will close

---

[3] One of the accusations made against Teresa later on was that she absented herself from school without leave, but she had permission from her director to do so at certain times.

my eyes to all things and try to follow Thee in darkness as in light. I will praise Thee oh Lord in all places and at all times.

"The Devil too, like all cowards, now that he sees how worn out I am, attacks me most violently in such a variety of ways that I have not known at first what kind of visitation they are. But as rev. F. Snow told me because I had tried to honour the s. Head, our dear Lord would enable me to discern him at once, I have not felt so fearful about this. I always do know him and I fear him not, only that he takes time. He has tried me with every kind of temptation and when the temptation has been at its height he has come as an angel to comfort and console me, and on the Thursday night before the feast of our b. Lady's Dolours, I was a very long time as it seemed to me between life and death. I had gone through the Passion, and the Devil abused me by throwing me about and a fearful thirst consumed both soul and body, and I begged through the wisdom of His s. Head and love of His s. Heart for one little drop of Precious Blood (oh it seems to me that words cannot describe these desires, this thirst that eats up the very soul), when the Devil came pretending to be our Lord with the b. Sacrament and he said that, God as he was, he could not resist this prayer in honour of the Seat of divine Wisdom and he said, 'Eat of the Bread of Life and drink of the refreshing fountain of my sacred Heart.' Numerous devils were with him as angels too, but the glaring splendour of his glory is so different from that of our Lord's that I wondered at it and said: 'Lord if it be Thyself, I humbly adore Thee, yet, as such I know Thee not. I know Thee best as my crucified Spouse.' For an instant I was in doubt, I hardly knew what to do, I could not get any holy water, I was too weak, but I raised my left hand to remind Him, my Lord and my God, if it were He that I was all His for ever, and when I did at once that sham glory was turned into a cloud of sulphur or brimstone which almost suffocated me, and he howled most fearfully and retired."[4]

---

4 Letter 121.

These attacks of the devil continued the whole time of Teresa's stay at Bootle and her own account is confirmed by Father Powell and those who lived with her at the time. Ellen Nicholson often noticed strange sounds and smells, but never guessed their significance, until one day Teresa lent her the life of the Curé d'Ars who suffered so much from the assaults of the Devil. Her curiosity aroused, Ellen innocently asked Teresa: 'Does the Devil torment you?' Teresa looked at her but said nothing and the child knew she must ask no more. Next day Father Powell sent for her and told her to ask no questions, but that she need have no fear of the Devil for he could not do her any harm.

After Mrs. Nicholson's death when Teresa went to share the lodgings of her fellow–teachers in Ariel Street, these diabolical attacks seemed to increase in violence, and the following statements were written by the other inmates of the house at Father Powell's desire:

"15 Ariel Street, Bootle, August 26, 83.

"On Sunday night the 19th Aug. I noticed a knocking which seemed to come from the next house, but remembering that no one was living there at the time I thought it must be someone knocking at one of the houses near and took no more notice of it. Presently the window opposite the bed was shaken but not loudly, a noise was made on the landing and rustling through our room past the wall and up to the second window which was shaken so violently that I felt it would either fall out or be shaken to pieces: this seemed very singular to us as the night was as calm as it could be and there was no wind.

"The following night I heard no sound of anything unusual but Miss Roberts turned round towards me and asked me what I was laughing at. I was surprised at her asking me, as I had neither laughed myself nor yet heard anyone else do it.

"On Tuesday night the 21st inst. shortly after eleven o'clock I heard a terrible noise against the wall of Miss Higginson's room nearest the landing which sounded like a loud clap of thunder and seemed as if it would shake the wall down, then a loud knocking as of furniture being broken to pieces on the floor in one corner of her room. We were all three so terrified that I called out loudly for Miss Higginson and after a short time she came to us looking deeply troubled. She told us not to be frightened, that it was the Devil who had terrified us, that he had told her that he would let us know that he was there but she did not think we should have heard him. We tried to persuade her to remain with us for the rest of the night but could not succeed. I do not remember hearing any more noise during the night.

"The next night (Wednesday) whilst kneeling saying my night prayers, I distinctly heard blows given with great force, striking Miss Higginson first on one side of the face and then on the other. I stood up and listened for a few seconds, when her head was knocked several times on the floor of her room. I thought it would be almost broken from the force of the knocks. Then most terrible and piercing screams and sounds of someone being dragged across the room towards the door and struggling and pushing at it as if to get out, the screams continuing all the time and ending with a fiendish yell. Then everything seemed quiet and settled.

"During the afternoon of the 23rd, the blackboards in the room over the one I was teaching in seemed as if being continually dragged about. I went upstairs wondering why there was so much noise and asked about the blackboards but was assured by both teachers that they had not been moved at all. I felt certain they had as the effect of the moving about shook the partition against which I was sitting twice over. The noise was heard continually during the afternoon even when the children from the room overhead (standard 4 room) were out in the playground. Sometimes it sounded like the low growl of some wild animal or a rumbling of thunder. I asked one of the boys in the room if he heard any noise and what it was like. He said, 'Yes, they are rolling something on the floor upstairs.' In the evening there was a fearful smell in the kitchen as of sulphur and something else, I cannot describe what, but it was quite sickening.

"One night whilst staying in the house with Miss Higginson, I heard knocks given continually but could not find anything or give any account of what caused it or who did it. Just after getting into bed, I was quite frightened with one knock I heard but did not speak for a bit until I saw Miss H. looking at me and I asked her if she had heard it. She said Yes, but told me not to mind anything but to get to sleep soon.

"I heard nothing more after that. The night I heard these knocks was I believe the 2nd July, 83.

"KATE CATTERALL,
"Aug. 26, 83."

"15, Ariel Street, Bootle, Aug. 26, 83.
"Sunday night, Aug. 19, 83.

"I was falling asleep when a loud shaking of the window near my bed awakened me. The night was calm.

"Aug. 20. On Monday night I heard a laugh which seemed to be in the room. I thought it came from Miss Catterall, found no one in the room had laughed and only Miss Flynn and myself had heard it.

"Aug. 21. I heard loud knocking and shaking of furniture in Miss Higginson's room. The noise was so violent that it frightened us very much. We called Miss Higginson who in a short time came to us. She told us not to fear as it was only the Devil who had tried to terrify us.

"Aug 22nd. After being in bed for a short time I was disturbed by a loud noise as of someone being slapped on the face. (The noise came from Miss Higginson's room). Then followed loud knocks as if someone was being shaken and banged about the room, then Miss Higginson's room door was shaken very violently and terrible unearthly screams were heard. The noises and especially the screams terrified us so much that we did not sleep at all during that night.

"Elizabeth Roberts.
    "Aug. 26, 83."

        "15, Ariel Street, Bootle, Aug. 26, 83.
    "On Sunday night Aug. 19th, after I had been in bed a few minutes, I heard a noise on the landing as if someone was shaking Miss Higginson's bedroom door very determinedly, then there was a slight rustling noise past the bed in our room and both the windows shook very violently. I thought it very strange as the night was so calm.

    "Shortly after eleven o'clock on Tuesday night, Aug. 21st, I was greatly alarmed by one knock at Miss Higginson's room door then a confused noise almost like thunder. It seemed as if someone was kicking the door and flinging furniture about in her room. It was so terrible and we were all so afraid that my sister called at once for Miss Higginson who came to us in a few minutes and told us not to be afraid, that it was the Devil who came to torment her. She tried to assure us that he could not harm us, that he was only frightening us in order to torment her the more and to let us know he was there. But in spite of all she said, I was so frightened when I thought of the noise I had heard that I could not sleep at all during the night.

    "The next night Aug. 23, I was more terrified than ever. We had not been more than a few minutes in bed when I heard a noise in Miss Higginson's room as if someone gave her five heavy blows on the side of her head, then as if she was taken and banged violently against the room floor three or four times. Two or three minutes afterwards, I heard a terrible noise at her door as if someone was kicking it and at the same time screeching and yelling most frightfully. This frightened me most of all, it seemed altogether so unearthly and so unnatural. I was again unable to sleep that night.

    "On Monday, Aug. 20th, before I got to sleep I noticed all at once an awful bad smell which seemed to come from the door. It was very disagreeable for a few minutes.

"Again on Wednesday night, as I was passing through the kitchen, I noticed something like sulphur, it seemed to get in my throat and made me cough. I could not account for it in any way.
"MINNIE CATTERALL, Aug. 26, 83."

"15, Ariel Street, Bootle, Aug. 26, 83.

"When sleeping with Miss Higginson one night during the last mid–summer holiday, I had just been talking with her and she had said good night when I felt myself raised up from the bed and almost suffocated. As soon as I could, I called for Miss Higginson and she asked me if I felt ill. I said, 'Yes'. She told me to make the sign of the cross and say a Hail Mary and I should be all right. I did so and fell asleep.

"On the night of the 20th of Aug. I heard distinctly a scornful laugh which seemed to come from the door of the room in which I was at the time. The next night I was disturbed in my sleep by a noise as of knocking which awakened me and then I heard someone call out. I was confused and when my own name was called and someone knocked at my bedroom door, I thought something must be the matter. When I opened the door and saw Miss Higginson standing and heard the other young ladies up, I was really frightened. She asked me if I was afraid and said the others wanted me to go into their room and stay with them, they were so frightened.

"The night after there was a noise as of somebody being struck on the head and face, and soon a noise as if some person was talking, then loud screeching and yelling. We were all very much frightened although we knew what it was.
"JOANNA FLYNN, Aug. 26, 83."[5]

"On Thursday night Sept. 20th", writes Father Powell, "I was called by Miss Catterall to come to the house where Miss Higginson is staying with them because they heard several noises and were much terrified. They said they heard a noise as if a person

---

[5] Miss Flynn was the landlady of the lodging.

was sawing in their bedroom and soon afterwards in the parlour underneath. They all rose and ran down stairs; as they were descending, they heard as if from the top of the stairs a long mocking laugh like descending the musical scale. They ran out, Miss Roberts without her slippers, and sent for me. After I had been in the kitchen some time with them all, I heard as if in the room above where Miss Higginson was as if a body had been dashed to the ground, worse than if a person had fallen. It shook the ceiling, the windows and the kitchen. After some minutes I heard as if a person was dragged across the room and her head bumped two or three times against the floor. I stayed some time after but all was quiet.

"ED. POWELL."

11

Rumours and Investigations

ONE of the sure tests of the saints of God is that they should pass through the searching fires of opposition and persecution, not only from the world and the Devil but more especially from the good and well–meaning. This proof was not wanting to Teresa. In spite of her efforts to remain hidden and unknown, as the rumours of her wonderful life began to get abroad, friends and foes arose and sides were taken both for and against her. The "clamour" of which Father Snow speaks at length reached such a pitch that it came to the ears of the Bishop of Liverpool, Dr. O'Reilly, who expressed the wish that her case should be submitted to the judgment of various learned priests and theologians. This was accordingly done, and the following letter from Father Powell to Father Fisher is of great interest, both as an account of his personal experiences and as showing his own unshaken belief in her.

"Bootle,
"Aug. 17, 1882.

"MY DEAR FATHER FISHER,

"The Bishop desired me to ask you kindly to enquire into the following case, and to give your opinion whether it comes from God or not. I may mention in the first place that Miss Teresa Higginson is one of my teachers in the boys' school, that I have known her for about seven years or more, that she has given me full permission to make use of any information derived in the confessional and that she does not know about her letters having been copied. When first she came under my direction, perhaps nine or ten years since, though perhaps only seven, I found she had the prayer of union, and after some time, I gave her permission to communicate daily. This was the reason why she so loved St. Alexander's. Once I found out she had obtained the church key from my housekeeper, and spent from four a.m to Mass at 8 in the church. At the Quarant'ore she stayed there from ten o'clock Mass until 8 p.m. without ever leaving. She had received communion at the 8 Mass.

"I did not at first know about her extraordinary life, as she kept all to herself, thinking, as she said, our b. Lord wished all to be kept secret of His extraordinary favours. I found it most difficult for her to explain anything by word of mouth, so it struck me to put her under obedience to write something I could *not* understand. I then made her explain other matters in the same way, and though it was a terrible struggle and trial to her to write all about her mortifications etc. Her life has been a most innocent one, very few even venial sins, she mentions most of them in her letters — from when she was four years old Our blessed Lord seems to have called her in an especial manner, and I never read in the lives of the saints of anything equal to her austerities. A wire belt of some instrument used at Neston to clean something or other, which, when ordered to stop any mortification as she was ill, it took her three months to extract from her flesh, boring holes with a hot iron and putting in vinegar and salt. I tried the truth of this once, granting at her request leave to touch the arm just above the wrist with a hot iron, asking next day to see it, and finding a ghastly wound. She did not know I would ask to see it. Eating putrid dripping, rotten eggs and the water in which herrings had been cleaned etc. For three weeks I tried to make her eat and found everything was vomited: at last I asked her, as she was very ill and the doctor could make nothing of her, if she knew what was the matter. She replied when asked but never a word before: 'I think our blessed

Lord does not want me to take anything.' I gave her leave to take nothing and next day she was quite well again. I got one to watch her for a week. She — Miss Higginson — pretended to eat, but Ellen Nicholson who lives in the house, watched her closely and noticed she never swallowed anything. She saw she was watched and when urged to eat used to pretend to eat by chewing india rubber, etc. In answer to my enquiries she told me she never eats now, except when at home at Neston, and then very seldom. She never sleeps either, I really believe, but for that I have to take her word. It is now over three years that I began to know of her extraordinary life. I have known her to find out a boy who stole a sovereign in another part of the school and tell him exactly how he took it. Once she was wrong about a person whom I asked her to pray that he might live: she said he would recover but he died. She has often been totally insensible, always unconscious to all else after holy communion. I once sent a pin into her arm, but she evinced no feeling. But whenever in that state she always obeys her confessor. I have known her to be most outrageously abused by a priest here, and others who overheard the abuse told me she never said a word. When I had a chance (in her desire to protect another teacher, believing too readily what others said and speaking unfairly of another — that she gave the dullest boys to her fellow–teacher, etc.) of finding fault with her before the other teachers, she took it most humbly and I found apologised at once. Once when accused of theft in another place, her parents, when they heard of it a year afterwards, wished to prosecute the calumniators, she was miserable until she got them to give it up. She got me to say Mass for this enemy of hers, though I did not know then the accusation.

"For a long time I was in doubt, but her inspirations are not, or very seldom, external appearances. She speaks of them as 'Seeing with the eyes of the soul: knowledge impressed upon the soul: infused into the soul.' I believe there is no instance of deception with such revelations, that such is beyond the power of the Devil. I was told how St. Gertrude had been under delusion for thirty years, that the deception was at length discovered by her confessor forbidding her to have any extraordinary communications with our blessed Lord, yet they continued. I forbade Miss H. to have any communication until I gave her leave. I did not then advert that she was going to Neston that week, where they have not always Mass. On other occasions similar our blessed Lord brought her holy Communion; on this occasion two angels brought it. Thinking this was also forbidden, she refused it, and there was no communication until I withdrew the prohibition. I am sorry to give you so much trouble, yet I think you will find it a pleasure as well. Father Snow of Aughton and Father Bertrand Wilberforce said they never read anything so beautiful as many of her letters. The narration of the Passion will, I think, well repay perusal. It taught me a very great deal indeed.

"If this is all the work of God, our blessed Lord wishes His sacred Head to receive special adoration, and that, as with the devotion to the sacred Heart, He chooses one most insignificant and plain in appearance to make His holy Will known.

"In these days of pride, self–will, rebellion against His Church and intellectual pride, He wishes that sacred Head, treated with such mockery and crowned with thorns, to be publicly and specially adored as the special Seat of Eternal Wisdom, the Shrine of the Will — so tortured (as man sins especially with the will) by His taking upon Himself all the sins of the world, so awful for the will of an all–pure God to do; of the memory clearly cognisant of every sin of every individual; of the understanding grasping iniquity by the full knowledge of God's Justice and Holiness. These powers of the Soul of our blessed Lord being specially dwelt upon complete the devotion to the sacred Heart, thus revealing the springs so to say of His love.

"Lately He has let her participate in the sufferings of His divine Soul. Unspeakable as were the sufferings of His Body, yet they are but like a drop in the ocean compared with what His Soul endured. As man's soul is the seat of guilt, our blessed Lord through all His Passion, but particularly in the Agony in the garden, took upon Himself the punishment due to every sin that would ever be forgiven — in fact equal to an eternity of Hell for each mortal sin. Her letters, I certainly think, give a most wonderful completion to the whole of the Incarnation.

"I send you some prayers composed by her, and my first request is that, if you find nothing objectionable in them, I may get the Bishop's leave to have them printed.

"Finally, if there is anything further you wish to have explained, I shall be most happy to do so. It may give you great trouble, but if it is from God, the promises are that all that aid in promoting this devotion shall receive the choicest blessings m return from our divine Lord,

"Yours very sincerely,

"ED. POWELL."

Among those who were asked to examine Teresa's writings was Bishop Ullathorne who refused, saying he was much engaged and did not think a perusal of the letters would be of much avail without a knowledge of the writer, adding a word urging "extremest caution with respect to females who are liable to mistake imagination for revelations!"

Bishop Knight was also cautious. He read the letters and wrote: "The impression they convey to me is first of all that they are the outcome of a mind deeply impressed with religious feeling and sincere in believing what she writes. So much of it is purely subjective that the evidence is intrinsic only, or else dependent on the character of the writer, and while this is known to *you*, others would be without it in forming a judgment. The devotion she is especially drawn to is of course unexceptionable as being one aspect among the many of the cultus of our Lord's Humanity."

Father Bertrand Wilberforce, OP, was another of those to whom Teresa's case was referred. He was deeply impressed with the devotion to the sacred Head and not only adopted it himself but did all he could to spread it. He sent Father Powell a long memorandum[1], including a careful analysis of the devotion and his opinion as to Teresa's own sanctity and reliability, and in a separate letter he says:

"I think much of what she writes is, especially for a person of her education and little reading, very wonderful and that it shows great illumination of mind. Her humility, obedience and mortification are wonderful, and, on reading the letters, my mind seems to feel they are true."

Another of those consulted was Mons. Weld who carried on a long correspondence with Father Powell, bearing chiefly on a little book of prayers to the Sacred Head which they were anxious to publish. Mons. Weld also wrote to the Bishop himself, saying:

"If all the information I have received is correct (a matter which would have to be tested with very great rigour if circumstances, which do not at present present themselves, rendered a juridical examination on the part of your Lordship necessary), she presents a case of extraordinary love of God and zeal for the salvation of souls, profound humility, unhesitating obedience, love of mortification and suffering only to be paralleled by that of some of the greatest saints. This seems to date from her infancy. If all this is true, we should not be surprised if our Lord bestowed upon her some of the favours which He usually bestows on such souls. He seems to have been prodigal to her in this way and what she relates with great reluctance by order of her director to whom she is bound by vows of obedience, is beyond the power of invention of one who has not made a deep study of the writings of the more mystic saints, and at the same time is so varied that only a profound knowledge of theology could enable one who was not exceptionally enlightened by our Lord Himself to vary what she has copied to such an extent as to oblige the reader to admit that all that can be said is that the favours are analogous to those of the saints, but not identical with them. She fulfils faithfully the duties of her state as a

---

[1]   See Appendix A.

teacher, she influences all the other teachers, etc. with whom she is brought in contact, unostentatiously for great good and piety, she strips herself of everything and gives all her earnings away. As far as I have read of her extraordinary favours, I have seen nothing to which I could take exception."

There is one point which seems to have struck most of those interested in Teresa's case as very extraordinary, and that is the absence of any striking supernatural proof. They were in constant expectation of some great sign or miracle which should, as it were, guarantee both Teresa herself and the truth of her revelations. But God's ways are not our ways, and no such proof was given. Mons. Weld wrote to Father Powell: "I am struck by the absence of the more tangible signs by which our Lord generally confirms the truth of a great work when He entrusts it to the charge of a soul." And Father Snow writes: "As to miracles, I have to say that both Father Powell and I quite expected that important miracles would take place and that these would be of great help in furthering the Devotion to the Sacred Head, and at the same time be useful if, hereafter, there was question of her canonisation. But I never mentioned this subject to Teresa, nor did Father Powell to the best of my belief."

Father Hall, OSB, was asked to make a careful study of Teresa's writings and report on them to the Bishop. At first he was apparently very favourably impressed, for he wrote in November, 1882, to Father Powell: "You will be glad to hear that after having read all Miss T. H.'s letters and thought over her case, I shall have to report to our good Bishop that T. H. has been, and is, supernaturally favoured and illuminated. As regards the Devotion to the sacred Head, the arguments pro and contra are similar to those advanced and answered in connection with the Devotion to the sacred Heart."

What happened to change his opinion is not evident, but, in a letter written a week later, he questions her statements regarding her bilocations, which he compares with similar experiences of Ven. M. Agreda. He then adds: "From her letters I had concluded that T. H. was exceedingly clever (seeing that she teaches in your school), had had a good education in a convent, possessed a lively imagination, etc. Our mishap the other evening enabled Father Snow to undeceive me somewhat." (He missed his train and so was able to have a long talk with Father Snow.)

From this time his belief in her began to wane. In December, 1882, he wrote: "We cannot question T.H.'s truthfulness, but it seems clear to me that her vivid and strong imagination accounts, and is accountable for, several statements in her letters." It was not until the following August that he completed his report, which seems to have been unfavourable, to the no small surprise and disappointment of Father Powell, who wrote to him:

"Bootle, Sept., 1883.

"MY DEAR FATHER HALL,

"On Monday last week the Bishop told me he was satisfied I was duped by Miss T. H., that in your report you ascribed something to hysteria, some to delusion; and that "*assuming* certain things narrated to be true", that there was something supernatural or preternatural. His Lordship further added that in a conversation he had with you, you were stronger against this being the work of God than even in your report.

"I thought this was very different from what you led me to understand. I have not seen your report. I think you often said all rested on her individual testimony. Before I saw the Bishop, three other of my teachers and Miss Flynn with whom they lodge, as well as Miss H. heard such yells, blows, unearthly noises, that they could not sleep at all for three nights; that they sent one of their number to me at Bunter to give orders to Miss H. to tell the Devil — to whom they ascribed these disturbances — that he was not to frighten them any more, or to let them hear anything. The four were really very ill with terror. I send you what they wrote, describing what they each heard. Please return the book to me.[2]

---

[2]   These reports have been quoted in Chapter 10.

"I have to thank you for all your trouble in the matter, though, of course, I grieve for your decision.

"Yours very truly,

"EDWARD POWELL."

The result of all this was that the Bishop told Father Powell he wished Teresa to change her confessor and that she must write no more. True to herself, she obeyed without a murmur and of course her letters cease. The following, dated at the end of August, 1883, is the last of that wonderful series, written in obedience to Father Powell, and it shows how keenly she was suffering at the time.

"AMDG et in hon BVM et St. J.

"Bootle, Aug. 1883.

"DEAR REV. FATHER,

"In the holy Name of Jesus and in obedience I write of the trial which it pleases our dear divine Lord to give me at present. I have often written of the complete eclipse which from time to time takes place in my poor soul, but I have always felt some mitigation of it when I knelt before Jesus in the most holy Sacrament of His Wisdom and love I have been able at any rate to feel that I could throw myself upon His pity and compassion on account of my helplessness and misery and expect help and victory in His Name and through His most precious Blood. But now I feel to suffer an inexpressible agony when I kneel before Him; I feel and know I am in Him as the fish is in the water and His infinite attributes weigh upon me as it were to crush me out of existence (if it were possible) and after holy Communion I feel as if His precious Blood, which saturated the soul at that time, cried to heaven for vengeance. And oh how heavily does His infinite power press upon me in His justice, and how clearly I understand the wrath which He hurls against the sinner, the hatred He has for sin and how opposed it is to His awful purity and dread sanctity. Oh I cannot express the fear and dread that fills my whole being and I dare not even ask for mercy. I cannot say that all–powerful name of Jesus and Mary, I feel that the good God has cast me off, or rather holds me in His wine press and searches me through and through; and I think it is His dread presence which He makes me feel and understand so forcibly that is the actual cause of this bitter agony of soul, mind and body. I try to fix the eye of the soul upon Him and look at Him as if I existed not, for, if I could hide myself from myself, I feel I could rest on Him. Oh well He knows how to afflict the soul. When I say that I have not experienced this before I mean that it has never before reached such an extreme as now. Then the Devil too is very noisy, and those in the house are very terrified, for the whole house shakes and the windows *they say* rattle as though they would come out, and I know I am the cause of their sufferings, for they seem to me to be quite ill with it at times. I have tried to do as you told me and be quite indifferent, and I have actually told Miss Flynn what it is, as though it was nothing, and now I think she is worse afraid than ever; and I fear too I had a selfish motive in doing so: I thought she would pass it off, so I think perhaps I did it more to screen myself than to overcome myself. May His holy Will be done in all things. I really will not try to interfere or prevent the accomplishment of His all wise designs whatever they may be. I am sure you are ashamed of my cowardice and disgusted with promises I make so often and the fear I am in all the time that our dear blessed Lord would accept the offering I make Him. He knows though how I wish *to do all that* I say to Him, and I wonder often how it is that I shrink so fearfully from it. I do not mind what I tell Him people say or think and at the same time I am tempted to run away, and if it were not that I should be disobedient, I would have gone away long since. Of course I am firmly resolved with His help *never* to do anything without your consent but I have heard so much lately, in fact every day I hear something fresh I think. I really try to be like a dead person who neither notices abuse or praise, and yet oh how I fear and dread. Pray earnestly for me.

"Will you dear rev. Father if you know that soul (so dear to our dear crucified Spouse) ask them to pray for me that I may do the little I can (*well*) to forward the Devotion in which they are to play so prominent a part.

"Begging God to grant us the grace and help we need and asking your prayers and blessing I remain dear rev. Father

"Your obedient and devoted child

"In the sacred Head and loving Heart.

"TERESA HIGGINSON

"Enfant de Marie."[3]

"DEAR REV. FATHER,

"Since I wrote the enclosed, I have been obliged to tell all who it was that was making all the noise. They were really terror–stricken and I am sure you would have stopped it if you had been here, so I stopped it so that they might go to sleep, but I am afraid they could not rest till near six in the morning. Oh they were so frightened and are quite nervous and ill.

"I am just the same as ever; only I think worse of the two."[4]

It must have tried her sorely in the midst of all these trials to find herself cut off from the director who knew her so well and in whose hands she had found such peace. But our Lord had not deserted His faithful Spouse, and if He was depriving her of her trusted advisor, it was only to place her in the hands of another wise and holy director who should guide her soul safely to its journey's end. This was the Rev. Alfred Snow whose words have been so often quoted, and Teresa came in time to praise Almighty God for the wisdom of His choice. She wrote many years later in reply to a letter from Father Powell:

"As you say, 'God does arrange everything beautifully', and He often allows us to see how better able He is to judge for us than we are to judge for ourselves for things that are a great cross, or would be if we had not implicit confidence in His tender

---

3   Letter 140.
4   Letter 141.

care; He lets us presently see how it was the very best thing that could happen to us. May His holy Will be the only aim of our life. In the case you refer to I tried in every way to hide what I felt and I don't think I said more than He knows what is best and in obeying his Lordship we are certainly obeying and pleasing Him. Yet no one but Himself knows what a trial it was for me, His poor weak cowardly child. I remembered at once all the doubts and troubles I had experienced before He, in His infinite Wisdom and love, had given you to me for a director, and I thought no one else could ever be able to understand me because I was so stupid in explaining what I wanted to express."[5]

Father Snow had originally trained for the legal profession and had then become a priest. He had for some time been curate at St. Alexander's, under Father Powell, and was now in charge of the mission of St. Mary's, Aughton.

In September, 1883, he received a letter from Father Powell saying: "The Bishop also wishes Miss T. H. to have another confessor. This I have told her and I certainly wish you to undertake that little responsibility. It is very little because our Lord teaches her. The Bishop does not want her to write any more either. The Bishop did not ask me to change my opinion. He only stated his own conviction. He added, however: 'If it is the work of God, it will prosper in spite of opposition.'"

Father Snow did not give an immediate answer. He notes in his diary:

"September 10, 1883. Letter from Father Ed. Powell saying the Bishop desired Miss Teresa Higginson to have another confessor, asking me to undertake that responsibility.

"September 14, Saw Father Powell and told him I felt great diffidence in accepting it and would not give a positive answer till after my retreat. Stated all my objections and asked him to consider them and then say if I ought to consent. Also saw Miss T. H. and told her I would give certain answer after my retreat, and urged her that the one thing she was to consider in choosing

---

5   Letter 270.

a confessor was the good of her own soul. I afterwards heard her confession for the first time."

He finally agreed to accept the responsibility and from that time to the day of his death he remained her director, and she was under vow of obedience to him. She certainly had no occasion to repent of the decision, for never for a moment did he falter in his belief in her; and for her own part she came to look on him as her true father to whom she could turn for advice and help in all her needs both spiritual and temporal. Having undertaken the direction of one already so far advanced in the ways of God, Father Snow set himself to make a special study of the mystical life, and, when later on he became Chancellor of the diocese, few guessed how saintly and spiritual a soul lay hidden under the calm exterior of this most successful and business–like administrator. It was a revelation even to his closest friends, long years after Teresa's death to find the old man, now nearing his own end, sitting with the tears streaming down his face lost in contemplation of the days when he had been in such fatherly relations with one whom he venerated as among the great saints of God.

12

The Clamour of Tongues

AFTER the death of Mrs. Nicholson in 1882, Teresa went to live with her fellow–teachers, the Misses Kate and Minnie Catterall, at 15, Ariel Street. Here again she occupied a back room looking on to the sanctuary of the church, and her fellow–lodgers well knew that once her door was closed she must never be disturbed. Her daily life continued as before but many strange happenings took place in that little commonplace brick house. The assaults of the Devil have already been described and the terror–stricken girls would often rush across to Father Powell, when the tumult became more than usually alarming. At other times Teresa would be lost in ecstasy, in fact this was of such frequent occurrence that it ceased to cause them any surprise. "She is off again", was their only comment. When in this state nothing could rouse her unless, as sometimes happened, they called in Father Powell, when at his command she would immediately come to herself and try to appear as though nothing unusual had occurred. One day some friends came in to see her and, after tea, she asked one of them to read aloud from some pious book. In a few minutes she was in ecstasy. This was about seven o'clock and she was still in the same state when the friend's husband came in about 9.30. The landlady said: "Oh, nothing you can do will rouse her", and to prove her words she seized Teresa's chair and proceeded to bump it round the room, Teresa remaining all the time serenely unconscious.

Miss Catterall describes her appearance on these occasions: "At times her face quite suddenly looked as of the finest alabaster; then her heavenly look and serene smile directed as I thought to something far distant amazed me in spite of myself. Numberless times I saw her in her unconscious state as if dead to the world. I ventured to raise her arms but they fell as if lifeless. In the same way I tried to raise her head and shoulders from the back of the chair but with the same result. I often and often watched her very closely on these occasions. Sometimes she appeared very calm and intensely happy, at others pleading with her very heart and soul, then as if prostrate with grief, while at others she gave the impression of being as it were saturated with pain. I remember in Holy Week in one of these states her face and mouth were distorted in a most unearthly manner, as if in the excruciating pain of being pressed or crushed by some terrific pressure. No one knows the feelings of horror and sadness I felt at these times with the sight of it all. Then on coming to her normal self how weak she was and how she appeared as the most abject of creatures. Numberless times at night she appeared too weak to walk upstairs, then I have helped her and got her safely to her bedroom but how I managed it I did not know as her whole body seemed a dead weight and I was not at all strong at that time. I concluded of course it was her good angel who did it. If I happened to be out on any of these evenings she would say she would wait till I returned as I seemed to know just how to handle her. I can just fancy I see her serene smile of thanks."

Often when in these conditions she was favoured with visions of Our Lady and the Holy Child, or her guardian angel or one of the saints. This was evident from the expressions of joy and wonder that fell from her lips. "How beautiful she is!" she would exclaim again and again, or "Oh the lovely Little Child."

As at Wigan, she was often in a state of complete prostration in the mornings. Someone writes: "She did not court attention and the only thing in church that made me notice her was that she would suddenly collapse and disappear from view. She did not faint but it seemed to me that her spirit was so much occupied with higher things that it forgot the body. She was the most grateful of beings, yet she never once thanked me for lifting her up. I don't think she ever knew."

On one such occasion when she fell she struck her head with great violence against the heating apparatus. A lady who was kneeling behind ran to pick her up, expecting to find her half dead. She replaced her on the seat and found that she was unhurt but quite unconscious of her surroundings. At that moment Father Powell came out of the sacristy and, seeing what had occurred, went up to her and touched her on the shoulder, saying: "Kneel down, my dear child." She at once came to herself and obeyed.

With all this it must be remembered that Teresa was first and foremost a school teacher. This was her vocation and her duty to the children always came first, and none of these things was allowed to interfere with it. It was a constant source of astonishment to her companions that, even during the times of her utmost prostration, school–hour always found her active, full of life and perfectly able to carry out her duties. One of the charges brought against her was that she absented herself from class in order to say her prayers. This was explained by the fact that one Lent when she was in terrible suffering Father Powell gave her leave to go to the church on Friday afternoons, but when she found her work was being affected at other times also she remonstrated with our Lord, reminding Him of this permission. "I have told our dear Lord after Holy Communion that I am to go in school always till Holy Week and that you give me Friday afternoon after three for him to do with me what He pleases."

All her free time was spent in visiting the poor and sick. One who knew her at Bootle writes: "I have a vision of her now in my mind coming along the road in her dinner hour — she did not seem to need any dinner herself — carrying a wooden bucket of pea soup in either hand, on her way to the poor." Another time

Miss Catterall met her coming home from seeing a poor mother who was very ill with quinsy. "I felt quite heart–broken to see her weak, haggard look and the evidence of a bad throat. I discovered she had asked to have the malady herself instead of the woman who was better next day. I believe she often did similar things."

Although the striking miracles for which her directors still looked as proof of her mission were withheld, here, as at Wigan, she worked many, what Father Snow calls "minor miracles". The children often came to her to be cured of their little ailments. Toothache and earache would vanish at the touch of her crucifix, and drawers would open when she made the sign of the cross. One of the teachers once lost her temper and thrashed a boy severely. There were red marks on his back and the indignant mother brought him to the school to lodge her complaint. The girl turned imploringly to Teresa who quietly laid her hand on the child's shoulder and, when his shirt was taken off, all signs of injury had disappeared.

Meanwhile, despite all the efforts of those in authority, tongues could not be silenced. Stories and rumours flew from mouth to mouth, causing her increasing trouble and humiliation, and naturally her friends came in for their full share of the storms that raged around her, though they loyally maintained the silence urged upon them by Father Snow and Father Powell. There are no longer any writings to tell us of her inner life, but a little diary kept by Father Snow throws many sidelights on these years, and shows that the "Spouse of the Crucified" still journeyed with our Lord to Calvary and was being further purified for the great union which had yet to be accomplished.

October 19th, 1883.

"At Father Powell's request I went to see Miss Catterall who was ill. Miss H. came in, and before I left was in a rapture. Miss C. told me she had been that way nearly all the week, while she was in the house."

November 2nd.

"I questioned her about her ecstasies and the nature of her visions and the mode by which she was taught divine truths. She found it difficult to explain but told me the truths were placed in the very centre of the soul without the succession of words and not through the medium of either senses or imagination."

November 23rd.

"Heard her confession and saw her afterwards in the house. She told me she had again this week been participating in the sufferings of the Passion having made an offering of herself for Father —. I spoke to her about devotion to Our Lady (Grignion de Montfort.) She told me of a boy who had broken a slate pencil in his ear, a small piece remaining in the organ. In trying to get the piece out he put it in still further. He was taken to the chemist opposite who tried to get it out, but was unable to do so and told those with him to take him at once to the hospital. They took him instead to Miss H. who was in bed suffering. She made the sign of the cross over his ear, and though neither she nor the boy perceived the piece coming out she found it afterwards on the sheet. I have the piece of pencil."

November 30th.

"Heard her confession. Told me our blessed Lord was still urging her to have His sacred Head honoured but He did not tell her what she was to do."

January 18th, 84.

"Again heard her in the house. Told me she was still participating in the Passion. I asked her the object and she told me it was now in reparation for the sins of bad priests."

February 1st.

"She had been accustomed very frequently to get into ecstasy towards night and be unable to go upstairs at bedtime until one of the teachers brought Father Powell and in obedience to him she would come to herself and go upstairs with help. Last Friday I told her that she must always go up not later than nine o'clock. She was able to do so and Father Powell was not sent for once."

March 26th, April 4th and April 10th.
"Was in bed each time motionless, speechless and evidently enduring great suffering but was conscious when I gave her absolution."

April 18th, (Easter Week)
"Our Blessed Lord told her not to fear about the devotion to the Sacred Head. It would be established but He did not say the time.

"I had been reading about bilocation etc., and spoke to her about it. In her case she was perfectly conscious of her own identity in both places. She was teaching in school and at the same time speaking to a savage in a savage country.[1]

"Her sufferings in Holy Week were greater than ever. Described them as though the very image of God in the soul were being effaced."

May 2nd.
"The Holy Name. While at Sabden she used to call the sheep and they came in great numbers to hear the Holy Name."

May 30th.
"Spoke of her intense and consuming desire to have the Sacred Head honoured and the suffering it caused her. Told her to wait for Whit–Sunday when perhaps our Lord would tell her what she could do."

---

[1] See Appendix B.

June 6th.

"She told me that on Whit–Sunday our Lord made known very clearly to her that it was not by wonders and miracles that He would make known the Devotion to the sacred Head. That it was the wisdom of the world to look for signs but not His way. That when He Himself promised the Blessed Sacrament He might have convinced by wonders those who refused to believe, but it was not according to the ways of His Wisdom."

"During the midsummer holidays she went to her home at Neston so I did not hear her. Her Mother died on September 28th."

"Teresa was with her Mother at the end. She died very peace-fully after receiving all the rites of the Church. The priest who attended her said he had never seen a last illness and death which had edified him so much. She was fully conscious, joining in all the prayers for the dying and her last words were : 'Oh Jesus, have mercy on me. Jesus Mary Joseph!'"[2]

Although her dear mother's death must have been a great grief to Teresa, she said afterwards that she could not really feel unhappy about it, she knew what a welcome Our Lord had given her.

One of the entries in Father Snow's diary relates to a matter which became one of the most fruitful sources of scandal and controversy in her regard — her extraordinary fasts.

"I told her not to appear to eat at home and to tell her sisters that her confessor had commanded her not to appear to eat without really eating and that she had taken no food but the Blessed Sacrament for a long time. She told me she had said to her sisters what I had instructed her to say but they paid no attention to her and appeared not in the least to understand what she was talking about. When they dined she remained upstairs, but afterwards her sisters spoke to her as though she had been at table all the time with them and from this she felt sure that her

---

[2] Letter 145.

guardian angel had taken her place. I told her that for the future she might at home appear to eat as formerly."

"All those with whom she lived bear witness to her long and severe fasts, and many of them declare that to the best of their knowledge they never actually saw her swallow anything. Father Snow in a letter says: "I asked her how long she had taken no food. She said she began after her first Communion and thenceforth never took food on the day she received, and then got in the way of doing without altogether."[3]

At times her confessor would order her to eat and she at once obeyed, but she never could retain anything and the physical pain it caused her was intense. The thing she shrank from most was attracting the attention of others, and so she would come to meals and pretend to eat, even going so far as to chew a piece of indiarubber, and very often Our Lord would hear her fervent prayers and help to preserve her secret. But in spite of all her efforts it was, of course, impossible that this long–continued miracle should remain altogether hidden. She explains why it was she felt called on to fast so rigorously in a letter to Father Snow:

"As to me abstaining from food etc. I do not think our dear Lord intends that as any proof of the revelation (of the devotion to the S. Head), I think it is only that I might be enabled to suffer and undergo certain things that I could not learn or endure otherwise. I mean that I could not have that other sense, or knowledge, or spiritual sensitiveness that gives us an abiding knowledge of God and spiritual things and which is more than all the senses of the body united into one, like the angels know and see without eyes to see (not beholding things in the eternal Mind of God) but a clear sight and hearing which make soul and body participate far more than feeling, etc. in whatever God wishes to teach."[4]

---

[3] Letter to Fr. O'Sullivan.
[4] Letter 160.

The "clamour" was all this time growing worse and worse. Many who had been her friends now turned away from her, and the greater had been their former devotion, so much the more intense was their indignation against one whom they had come to look upon as a "lying hypocrite". Some of the priests were among the most active of her opponents. Miss Catterall met her one evening walking away from the church just as the service was about to begin. She asked what had happened, and Teresa gently answered that two of the curates were standing at the door and had refused her admittance. She returned meekly to the house, but her indignant friend accosted the curates who replied that Teresa was not fit to be in church, she was mentally deficient. Miss Catterall reported the matter to Father Powell who at once summoned Teresa back to the church.

It was on the head of this devoted and loyal friend that the brunt of the storm first fell, and to her intense distress, in October, 1885, he was moved from St. Alexander's and went to Lydiate, where he remained until his death. After his departure Teresa's troubles reached their climax. His successors did not believe in her, and as Father Snow says: "They appear to have agreed together to snub and humble her as much as possible... On the last occasion Miss H. was with me, I told her that she must tell me the harsh things anyone might say to her. There was no time then but she must tell me the next time she came. Tonight under obedience she told me that she went to the priest's house to sell some tickets. Father — received her at the door and spoke to her very severely asking what she was doing prowling about there — that if she came again he would give her in charge of the police as a suspicious character and more in the same style... I asked her what she did and she said she went into the church and begged Our Lord to give Father — some special blessing."

During all this time of persecution her interior sufferings were becoming ever more and more intense. In Lent, 1886, she wrote a most pathetic appeal for prayers to her two devoted friends,

Father Powell and Father Snow, the writing so weak and trembling as to be almost illegible.

AMDG et in hon BVM et St. J

"Bootle, Eve of the Annunciation, 1886.

"DEAR REV. FATHER,

"Oh do pray hard for me tomorrow. I am so bad tonight.

"Begging your prayers and blessing

"I remain dear rev. Father

"Your obedient and devoted child

"In the s. Head and loving Heart

"TERESA HIGGINSON, Enfant de Marie."[5]

And a week later she wrote again to Father Snow:

"I hardly know in what words to express the urgency I feel is necessary to implore the help I need just now but I feel I cannot ask in better words than those used for the poor souls: 'Have pity on me, have pity' etc etc. Oh my Father, I know you will often offer me to Him as a willing sacrifice and whisper to Him in the blessed Sacrament that I only wish His adorable Will to be accomplished. I feel the awful time I have so long dreaded is upon me, and I feel too that I am as it were entirely alone and every source of light and consolation is shut out, for I cannot look now for holy Communion when I am not able to get out; and judging from past experience our dear b. Lord will not I think give Himself to me, yet may His holy Will be done; with Him or without Him I trust in His precious Blood, and through the agony of His holy Soul I hope that He will save me from offending Him. I offer Him my life and death for I feel as though I should not get over this Lent, for that which He has already given me to understand is so terrible that death is as naught before it — yet I feel too all that I have as yet undergone in His Name is only a shadow of that which He will now reveal to me, and I am awaiting His time and holy Will."[6]

---

[5] Letter 156.

[6] Letter 157

This is the last letter Teresa wrote from Bootle, and in it she refers to the greatest of all her trials — the persistent refusal of her parish priest to bring her Holy Communion when she was unable to get to the church. Her friends, who were very anxious at her state, did all they could to persuade him but without success. On April 4th, Miss Catterall wrote to Father Snow:

"Miss Higginson still continues much the same as yesterday. Father X has not as yet brought her Holy Communion neither has he called to see her (that I know of).

"Yesterday while we were out Mrs. Archer called and told Miss Higginson that she would ask herself and try to get Holy Communion brought to her, but if she did so, no one came.

"Last night Dr. Raverty called and said she seemed a little better. When we asked him if he had seen Father X, he said he had seen him that evening (Saturday). Perhaps I may be wrong in my surmises, but I fancy that when Mrs. Archer asked Father X he saw the doctor and asked him to call so as to see if there was any danger of death, so as to necessitate his bringing the Blessed Sacrament as holy Viaticum. She seems very much distressed at being unable to receive Holy Communion and today she asked me if anyone would bring It, and I told her that a priest in another parish could not bring it to her from his own church. She seemed very much grieved, but said: 'Our blessed Lord knows what is best', and her eyes filled with tears. She also said she did not know how she should get through the Lent. Today is, I believe, the first time she has been unable to get to Mass on a Sunday."

A week later Miss Minnie Catterall wrote:

"BOOTLE 11 Ap. 86.

"She has been in bed since last Thursday week and seemed to have been suffering very much particularly in her throat, tongue, mouth, etc. Dr. Raverty has been almost every day to see her, but does not say much. He sent her medicine which she took about twice; it made her fearfully sick; she had scarcely swallowed it when it came right back again.

"Yesterday morning she knocked for me about a quarter past seven, and I was rather astonished to see her almost ready for Mass. I knew that she was going to be able to go out because she told me (I think it was on Thursday) that she was going to be bad on Friday, but then she would be better until the following Thursday, and perhaps able to go into school.

"After next Thursday she expects to be worse than ever she has been — to use her expression, 'properly launched out into the deep'."

Holy Week was now approaching and Fr. Snow evidently felt that she could not be left without her one support and advised her friends to try and find her lodgings elsewhere. Miss Minnie wrote again:

"Ap. 14. 86.

"We did not go to Mrs. Lancaster's after all, as Miss Higginson thought if she was anywhere in Bootle she would be sure not to get Holy Communion. We went off to Fr. Smith's Walton and he went out and arranged with one of his people for Miss Higginson to stay until Easter Sunday. It is quite close to his church and he says he will be very glad to take her Holy Communion whenever she can't get out. I am going to stay with her at nights so as to look after her in the mornings. Kate and I will be with her all the time except during school hours, and I think she will be all right. There is only one person in the house where she is staying and Fr. Smith says she is very good."

Teresa remained in this lodging until after Easter, when she went to her sisters at Neston and wrote to Father Snow:

"I have not been so well as I usually am in Easter Week, and I think it is our dear b. Lord's holy Will that I shall know greater sorrow and sufferings than I have hitherto. May He be loved praised and blessed for ever."[7]

---

[7]   Letter 158.

Truly her soul was being led through the refining fires! She did not return to Bootle. She received a curt note from her former landlady:

"DEAR MISS HIGGINSON,

"You are not to come to 15 Ariel St. any more except to take your things. I think home is the best place for you. If you like, I will send your things to Birkenhead. Rev. Fr. says you need not come back and whether or no I could not do with you any longer."

Doubtless the reverend Father had already himself informed Teresa that her services were no longer required, for he was re–organising his staff and introducing masters into the boys' school, and about this time the Misses Catterall also left St. Alexander's. But even her absence could not silence the busy tongues, and tales of every kind were spread abroad. Some reported having seen her carrying food into a hidden corner and there devouring it. Others declared they had met her in the street the worse for drink. More definite charges were also brought against her, as is clear from the following letter from Father Snow:

"Ap. 17 1886.

"MY DEAR CHILD,

"Another little cross for you. Almighty God has been pleased to allow someone to enquire into certain things concerning you with a view to trying your truthfulness, more especially with regard to your not eating or drinking. You must therefore give me an explanation of the three following things.

"1. It has been said that there has been found a piece of something that appeared to be masticated meat in the vessel that contained the gargle you used recently for your throat.

"2. Some bread and meat was seen in your box. Tell me how it came there and what became of it.

"3. Miss Flynn has said that in the mornings to gargle your throat there was provided for you a quantity of tea equal to two cups full and that after you had finished there remained a quantity equal to one cup full.

181

"Write me an explanation of these things and send this letter back along with your own.

"I hope you found your sisters very well. How is my little friend Percy? My kind regards to all. Praying God to bless you

"I remain my dear Child

"Yrs. affecly. in Christ.

"ALFRED SNOW."

To this Teresa replied:

"DEAR REV. FATHER,

"I duly received yours of yesterday and in obedience and in the holy Name of Jesus and Mary I answer as far as I can.

"1. With regards to something looking like meat. I remember Miss Flynn passing the remark about it appearing like a piece of flesh, but I think it was a piece of clotted blood. I have often got up something like it before. I know positively it was not meat.

"2. The bread and meat you mention was in my box but I did not know that anyone saw it. I got a barm cake buttered and a quarter of meat from Miss Smith's shop one Saturday night for a poor lad who promised me to go to confession. He was begging and I found out he was a Catholic and had not been to the Sacraments for a long time. I got him to go and thought to give him the bread and meat afterwards. I saw him go into Fr. Rigby and then went to Miss Smith's and bought the above telling her about him, either her or Mrs. O'Hara, and asking them to say a little prayer for him. Then I went to wait for him coming out but I missed him and I put the cake etc. inside my jacket and left it there. On Sunday morning I put it inside my little tin box intending to give it to some child but I forgot it and left it till Tuesday morning. I then took it to school and gave it to one of the boys to give to someone who had hens. I think it was T. Macmanus who took it.

"3. As for the missing cup of tea, I really do not know what became of that without it was the day I upset the basin, or that one of the Miss Catteralls emptied it away before I gargled my throat a second time, for Miss Flynn would bring me some tea in a jug and leave it so that she need not come up more than about twice a day, and Miss Catterall was very kind sometimes bringing warm fresh tea and throwing out the cold and always helping me by raising me and holding the cup for me.

"Many thanks for your kind enquiries for my sisters and Percy whom I found pretty well.

"I am not surprised about the questions you have asked me and I have answered as far as I can. I expected more a great deal to have been said and I know the Devil will do his best and Almighty God will permit a great many things to be sifted and I am only waiting His divine pleasure. You need not mind my feelings — do what you think is best, but I feel convinced that our dear Lord will not gratify vain curiosity and He has continually made me feel in a most singular manner that I am all His and that I must as it were keep myself more to myself, or I should say more to Him, than ever. Begging your prayers and say blessing

"I remain dear rev. Father

"Your obedient and devoted child

"In the s.H. and l.H.

"TERESA HIGGINSON."[8]

Many similar accusations were brought against her of which she could sometimes give no explanation. One of her most active opponents was Father — who had formerly been her devoted admirer and done all he could to promote the Devotion. In May, 1886, she wrote to Father Snow:

"I went to Liverpool yesterday and saw rev. — and he told me he felt very dissatisfied about all he had heard. I need not tell you how hurt I was, although I am truly grateful for it. I did not think I could care so much but when our dear Lord sends a cross of course He knows how to make us feel... He is going on his retreat tomorrow, so please say a little prayer for him, and when he returns he says he is going to devote some time in thoroughly investigating things, that he wanted to be quiet now. I know he is doing it all for our dear Lord's sake."[9]

---

[8]   Letter 159.

The rev. Father duly carried out his enquiries, with the result that a little later on he wrote to Father Snow: "I have just sent into the Bishop at his own command a full report of the investigations I lately made into the case of Miss Higginson. He told me to write down all I knew about her and all that I have lately found out about her. This I have done at considerable length and I think that the case I have handed in to him is most damaging to her unless you and Fr. Powell can prove that the statements in it are untrustworthy. For this purpose, namely to give her every opportunity of clearing herself from the accusations made, I have petitioned his Lordship to place what I have written in your hands that you may show it up or confirm its statements.

"I am sure that, from what you know about her, you will easily be able to bring the truth to light and I have no fear in abiding by your decision, after you have examined into the facts that I have had to state to his Lordship.

"Above all I trust that you won't be angry with me for not previously stating to you what I was preparing to send to the Bishop, for I was afraid that you would perhaps wish me to make omissions which my conscience would scarcely permit me to make.

"At any rate I have every belief that her case will now appear in its true light, for you can easily prove the matter."

But in fact the matter was not so easy to prove. Teresa herself, who suffered keenly from this notoriety, refused to make any attempt to clear herself except to her confessor, and indeed many of the accusations brought against her seemed impossible of solution at the time. Stories went from mouth to mouth and lost nothing in the telling. Misunderstandings arose and strange events occurred for which no other explanation can be given than that Almighty God allowed them for her sanctification. Her own suggestion as to the Devil's impersonation of her is supported by some of her friends, who are convinced that this did actually happen on more than one occasion.

---

[9]   Letter 162.

The following incident, related by Father Snow, shows the sort of mystery that arose for which no explanation could be given and which was eagerly seized upon by those who sought occasions against her.

"A Mrs. Banks, a lady in the parish, presented Fr. Powell with a surplice. It so happened that Miss Higginson made one for him of exactly the same pattern. Not wishing Fr. Powell to know from whom it came, she took it into Cook and Townsend's of Liverpool and asked a young woman at a counter to add some little detail to it and to have it got up at the laundry and send it to Fr. Powell without any word as to whence it came. Some time after the housekeeper, Mary Kelly, was getting up the surplice Mrs. Banks sent and called Miss Higginson's attention to some alteration or repair that was needed, and Miss Higginson, having no other thought than that she had made that very surplice, referred to some difficulty she had had in making it, in short she said she had made it and had it sent to Fr. Powell. Mary Kelly, knowing that Mrs. Banks had presented it, considered that Miss Higginson was lying and taking credit to herself for the gift. Miss Higginson could not explain the mystery, nor did she try to solve it, but left the matter in the hands of God.

"Eleven years later the following letter was sent under cover to the Bishop 'to be forwarded to the Rev. Mr. Powell, late of Bootle.

" 'REV. SIR.

" 'About eleven years since I was forewoman in a Liverpool drapery establishment and while there I undertook to send off by our delivery van a box to you given in by a lady customer, but yielding to a strong temptation I kept it and sold contents which was a linen surplice with deep crochetted lace in Marie monogram for 30/–. I was then a Protestant but have since become a Roman Catholic and wish to make restitution and beg your Reverence to pray for me and to forgive me. I am heartily sorry and beg God to forgive me and I wish to atone for this and my many other sins and ask you holy Sir to pray for me. I enclose p.o. for 30/–."

"In all probability Mrs. Banks was the person to whom the surplice was sold for 30/–."[10]

This incident of the surplice was one of the charges brought against Teresa by Father — in his report to the Bishop. When it was cleared up, Father Snow at once wrote to tell him, saying: "I send you a copy of a letter received last week by Fr. Powell. It was sent under cover to the Bishop 'to be forwarded to the Rev. Mr. Powell late of Bootle.'

"The matter concerns you more than me. I had at the time such overwhelming proof of her sanctity and high gifts that I paid little regard to the many wicked things said about her. All the saints have had to suffer such things and Benedict 14th says they are 'essential to a saint that has to be canonised.'

"I will only add that all that has happened since that time (1886) has confirmed me in the conviction I then had that she is not only a great saint but one of the greatest saints Almighty God has ever raised up in His Church.

"On the last page I have copied your remarks on the surplice contained in your letter to me in June, 1886. You see you as it were give the Almighty five years in which to clear this matter up. He has taken eleven. Mirabilis in sanctis Suis."

(This priest towards the end of his days wrote a letter to Canon Snow humbly retracting anything he had ever said against Teresa. The Canon sent to Miss Catterall telling her the good news and asking her to come and see the letter, but before she could go he was taken ill and died. Neither the letter nor the report to the Bishop have been found and the probability is that both were destroyed.)

---

[10] Note by Father Snow in his correspondence with Father —.

13

Final Purification

DEEPLY as Teresa suffered, neither the loss of friends and reputation, nor her many other trials, troubled her so much as the fear lest all this talk and scandal should prejudice the Devotion which she had so much at heart. On June 1st, 1886, she wrote to Father Snow:

"Never before has it pleased our dear b. Lord to try me half so severely. It seems as though my poor soul was in extreme agony and my heart was bursting with anguish. Then I suffer more, far more than I can express, in those things that are going on lest they may in any way injure the Devotion, for I know the rev. X tried to do all he could to spread it and now he seems to think little of it, though he said he would rather favour it than otherwise, but under the present circumstances what could he do? Then on the other hand I feel that our dear Lord is able to look after His own glory and will do that which He pleases in His own good time, yet if through my imprudence or unworthiness it should be delayed, how sorry I am. Oh how often I ask him to have pity and mercy on me, for I feel I am too cowardly to bear that which in His love He gives me and I feel crushed down to the ground by the weight of this cross, and feel how grateful I should be if it pleased Him to take me to Himself; and on the other hand I ardently wish for more even and fear to appear in His sacred presence. I know you do and will continue to pray for me. Then I am weary of having no settled thing to do and no proper time for to do things in."[1]

Father Snow replied to her as follows:

"Our dear Lord has been pleased to multiply your crosses for your good and His own wise ends. But still you must certainly not lose heart. You know He has said the Devotion will be established in spite of all difficulties and opposition, and we may well suppose that He is allowing these evil things to be said in order that everyone may see in due time that the work is entirely His own. I daresay we have all made mistakes, but our dear Lord loves us in spite of our mistakes and if we humble ourselves before Him and ask Him to pardon us, He in His love will make use of these very mistakes to make the truth more certain. So trust in Him and do not be too anxious.

"I have not yet heard of any school that would suit you but I am going to Preston on Sunday evening and may hear of something there."

She was longing to get another post for it was a terrible trial to her to be idle, but she fully realised the difficulty under the circumstances of finding anything in the Liverpool diocese.

"I do not think that any Liverpool priest would have me in their school for I know many reports are circulated among them, so in charity to their children they could not permit me to go in among them, much less teach them."[2]

Father Snow himself says that the "clamour" was so great that it would have been most imprudent, if it had been possible, to find any situation for her in the whole diocese, for the clamour would certainly have followed her. It even appeared at one time as though the Bishop would forbid anyone to have any dealings with her, and in her distress she wrote to Father Snow:

"I have been expecting a line from you by every post and as I have not yet received one, I begin to think his Lordship has desired you not to have anything to do with me. If so, may

---

[1] Letter 164.
[2] Letter 171.

almighty God's Will be done, but if so, to whom shall I go? It seems as if everything is coming at once. I would not care very much if all the things I have heard are being said only concerned my own reputation, but I feel they are doing material damage to the Devotion at present, yet I feel certain that, as God is Truth and Justice, He will bring things right in the end.

"It seems to me that the Devil has certainly been allowed to personate me in several cases for there are things being said that I never knew or thought of, much less said. Then about dear —, I am sure I never had an unkind thought towards her; she was always very kind to me, much kinder than ever I deserved. Then I only trust that those who consider me guilty of such fearful sacrileges etc. will try to make reparation to His outraged love in the Blessed Sacrament. And if He is better loved and more reparation given to Him, He only knows how willingly I would lose a thousand characters at such a gain.

"I have thought that perhaps it may please our dear b. Lord to allow people to really consider me guilty of the different sins I have offered myself to expiate and let me feel the shame and confusion that the persons would feel at these things being known, and if I could save one from shame on the last dreadful day, how willingly will I submit to more, for I did not think these things could affect me so keenly.

"I do not intend to contradict one of the accusations, only to you as you are answerable to God for my poor soul, and I protest in His adorable presence that I have tried to lay open my poor heart and soul to you and have not hidden anything purposely from you."[3]

Teresa's suggestion as to the Devil's impersonation does appear to be the only solution to many of the charges which were brought against her. There are like instances in the life of St. Margaret Mary, when the nuns were scandalised by seeing her, as they thought, devouring food in the pantry! Be that as it may, the evil One certainly allowed Teresa no peace.

<hr>

[3]   Letter 165.

"The Devil was very boisterous last night. He told me that he had got parties to say that I had taken meals with them and if persons would not say what he wanted, he would do so himself, he would not be thwarted this time. He could do as he liked with me and he would take care to do it."[4]

So the summer months passed by. Her enforced idleness was a constant trial to her and, worse than all, in the little country church she found so few of the consolations of religion which meant all the world to her. She wrote to Father Snow:

"I would be so grateful if I could get settled in a school. I suppose you did not hear of any that would suit me. Well God's holy Will be done. He knows what is best. We never have exposition here; how I would like to be at Walton this next week. We always went several times during the octave of Corpus Christi. Here the church is only open for about an hour and a half in the morning for Mass, so I cannot spend much time with Him in the b. Sacrament of His love. Oh what beautiful feasts there are just now. Corpus Christi, Sacred Heart, and holy Soul and sacred Head. How I wish I could do something to further the Devotion to His sacred Head I offer up every action for that end... Dear St. Alexander's, I did not think I cared half so much about it as I really do. It has been a very good cross for me and I try to be really grateful for it and all the others. In spite of all our dear Lord's love and goodness to me, sometimes I feel so weary I hardly know what to do. I know the more we are crushed down by crosses the nearer we are to Him and the more we should love and thank Him."[5]

With all her heroic virtue Teresa had a very tender heart and, despite her utter conquest of herself, there is a pathetic human note in her letters at this time which seems to bring us into closer touch with one whose feet were set so high upon the mountain-tops of God. Little as she says, it is easy to see how deeply she felt the desertion of her former friends.

---

[4]   Letter 173.

[5]   Letter 166.

"I have heard a great many things that have been said but it does not change my feelings in any way towards any of them. I know it is God's holy Will that these things should be and I would not feel them the same from the hands of others. I do not think one word has been said that I have not heard yet. I thank our dear Lord for it and love them more who say these things. I have heard that rev. Fr. — has said I said a great many things, but I know there is a mistake somewhere and if it pleased our dear Lord that they should be proved false, then it will be so; if not, I am willing to bear it."[6]

At last, in August, 1886, she succeeded in getting a temporary post at Eccleshall in the diocese of Birmingham.

"It is close to Stone so I can go to the convent there. I am so pleased about that, though I feel it more than I can very well say, leaving all that has been so dear to me, but I am glad of a chance of a little self denial. We do not know how much attachment we have for persons and places until we are obliged to leave them."[7]

But a terrible disappointment awaited her at Eccleshall — the mission was not yet properly established and there was no daily Mass. Whenever possible she went to Stone, where her friendship with Father Wilberforce assured her a cordial welcome. "I am quite at home in Stone but it is a long way for me — 3 miles to Norton Bridge Station and then 4½ in the train, but each morning I got a ride down at 6¼ so our dear Lord has been very good to me."[8] She was not always so fortunate and it seems almost incredible that the frail, suffering, little woman should actually have tried to walk the distance!

"I had to walk five miles to holy Mass though I got a ride home again. I am very done up." But our Lord had not deserted her, for even when depriving her of Mass, He seems always to have come to her Himself.[9]

---

6   Letter 177.
7   Letter 178.
8   Letter 181.
9   Letter 185.

"I don't know what I am to do about holy Mass on weekdays. I miss it very much, though our dear Lord has been so good to me I have never yet missed Holy Communion. May His holy Name be blessed for ever and ever."[10]

At the end of September, the school at Eccleshall was temporarily closed and Teresa returned to Neston, but a month later she took a post at Osbaldistone near Blackburn. Here once more she was disappointed in the matter of daily Mass, though she was nearer the church and was able to visit the Blessed Sacrament.

"We don't have the holy Sacrifice every morning here, four times this week and three times last. However, I must try and be very resigned. I do really want to wish only that which our dear good God sends me. I can get into the church now, morning, dinner time and night, as I asked and rev. E. Tunstall said the church should be left open, so I am far better off than when I was at Eccleshall. I feel it a long way to church and school from here; it is a good mile I think."[11]

She had one great joy in being able to spread the Devotion. "They are such good pious people with whom I live and say some of the prayers from the little book each night after prayers. I do ask our dear Lord every morning and often during the day to grant you all that is for your good and His glory. Our dear Lord does seem slow in convincing his Lordship (about the Devotion), but His ways are best and we must wait even as Mary did. I often think she must have felt it so hard to have the divinity of her divine Jesus hidden so long and wondered how it was the whole creation did not fall in adoration at His sacred feet. He knows how willingly I would suffer or do anything in my power to further the desire of His Sacred Heart."[12]

As Lent drew near a terrible dread overcame her: "Just a line to remind you to say a special prayer for me this week. I am

---

[10] Letter 184.
[11] Letter 197.
[12] Letter 197.

suffering such a fearful agony of dread and fear that I don't know how I exist."[13]

Meanwhile, her friends were growing anxious about her. Miss Catterall and Miss Ellen Nicholson had taken charge of St. Peter's school at Newchurch and their one wish was to have Teresa with them. Knowing she would do nothing without Father Snow's consent, they applied to him for permission to invite her there, and to their great delight he agreed to the proposal. She arrived on the 24th of March and, as was always the case towards the end of Lent, she was in a very suffering state.

"She has been in bed all day today", writes Miss Catterall to Father Snow, "and can scarcely articulate a word. Her throat seems to be in a fearful condition and I cannot persuade her to gargle it. She has not done it once since she came. She has been bad more or less every day, I think. She is worse this year than she has ever been before." Teresa herself afterwards referred to this as the "very hardest Lent I have yet known."

She remained at Newchurch for about four months. It seems as though our Lord had brought her to this sheltered spot, far from the tumult of the world, and surrounded her with tender loving friends, in order to perfect his Spouse for the final ceremony of her mystic union with Him which was now so shortly to be accomplished. As at Wigan, He had sent Miss Ryland to be with her in her hour of need, so now Miss Catterall and Miss Nicholson lavished every care upon her, and she here came in touch with two new and lasting friends, Father Musseley and his housekeeper, Margaret Murphy. Father Musseley was the priest of the mission at Rawtonstall to which the school at Newchurch (some 3½ miles distant) was attached. He was a practical minded Belgian and a very holy priest. From the first he was much impressed by Teresa, struck chiefly by her wonderful eyes which seemed to see so far. He questioned Miss Catterall about her, saying he felt sure she was holy in some special way. Miss Catterall, faithful to her obedience would tell him nothing but

---

[13] Letter 206.

referred him to Father Snow. However, he soon had opportunity of learning more for himself and he quickly came to regard her as a saint. Margaret, his housekeeper, had been a factory girl. She was a simple soul who possessed the golden gift of silence, and it is doubtless for this reason that she became one of Teresa's greatest friends. She loved to go over to Newchurch and used to sit for hours with her while the teachers were busy in the school. One day she said that though she knocked loudly at the door she could get no answer. She knew Teresa must be in and next time she saw her she asked why she had not been admitted. "Oh", said Teresa simply, "my guardian angel never told me you were there! He must have been busy getting the tea!" It was her custom to have the tea ready for her friends when they returned from school.

Another day when Miss Catterall came in, Teresa told her she had had a visit from a lady with a most beautiful child, and the whole evening she could speak of nothing but the beauty of this little child. Miss Catterall was puzzled as she knew of no such person in the neighbourhood. A few days later Teresa told her the lady had been again and this time she had been allowed to take the child in her arms. Then Miss Catterall understood that it must have been Our Lady, especially when Margaret said that Teresa had told her Our Lady had been to visit her and showed her the chair on which she sat.

It seems that during these four months, Teresa's life, thus hidden from the rude gaze of men, was one of almost continual miracle. As in Wigan, in the days preceding her mystical Espousals, she was in such constant ecstasy that her friends came scarcely even to notice it. Miss Catterall was in close communication with Father Snow and a few extracts from her letters will give a more vivid picture than any mere description of their daily life. On May 18, 1887, she wrote:

"I scarcely know what to make of her, she seems to be popping off either one way or another. On Monday evening she seemed very weak (a little before six) and said she did so wish to receive Holy Communion. In a few minutes she popped off; about five minutes after, I saw her open her mouth and I distinctly saw the Sacred Host alight on her tongue. She seemed all anxious to get it and at once closed her mouth. Then she seemed as though she was dead except that she seemed to have a most beautiful smile upon her face. On Tuesday at dinner time she popped off and you would almost have thought she was doing arithmetic, she would first put up one finger, then three fingers, then one again. I guessed she would be teaching someone about the mystery of the Blessed Trinity.

A week later she wrote again: "Since I wrote to you I have three times seen her receive the sacred Host. On last Friday evening, Father Musseley's housekeeper came to see Teresa. While she was here, she (Teresa) got ill, as it were, and both Margaret and myself saw distinctly the sacred Host alight on her tongue, but neither of us could see where it came from. I look upon Margaret as a very good person and she has become extremely fond of Teresa. She knew of course when she saw that Teresa was receiving Holy Communion."

Another letter gives a further account of Teresa's state at this time: "We were out almost all day and Miss Higginson was left all alone. She had told me during the week that she was going to be ill and I think she was not sorry to be left alone. Father Musseley brought her Holy Communion in the morning and she told me it was about four o'clock in the afternoon when she got all right. After we returned in the evening, she seemed all right for about half an hour and then she popped off. I must admit I have been greatly afraid twice, on Wednesday evening and last evening I was really afraid of her dying, she seems to suffer so acutely with her heart, it is most pitiable to see her, I never saw any human being suffer in such a manner. She is three times worse than she has ever been. She swells so very much and seems nearly choking. Last night I quite expected seeing her heart leap out of its place. Can you account for it being so bad? I don't know whether I am right or not but I think that her great love for our blessed Lord causes her heart to expand. No one has said it to me. It is only what I myself think. You can have no idea how bad she gets, I wish you could see her. I am sorry you could not come. I have several times seen her receive Holy Communion. On Thursday, I saw her receive the sacred Host twice within two hours. I forgot to tell you that last night when she was bad after receiving Holy Communion, she was speaking to someone (I am certain it was our b. Lord), pleading most earnestly for some persons but principally for some priests.[14] I don't know who they are, but it was most touching to see and hear her with tears streaming down her face and her heart beating so very hard. She was begging of Him to spare them and to strike her instead. I really could not help crying myself. It is fearful to see her and to feel the presence of God. I never used to have such feelings as I have now she gets bad. I am not afraid of her in any way, for I stay by her side all the time waiting to see if I can do anything for her. Do you think there is any fear of her dying? I have heard her exclaim several times: 'Let it break!' and it seems to me that her heart is really going to break.

"Do you think there is any fear of her dying? I do get so frightened sometimes, though I love to be near her to do anything for her, and I assure you I don't lose any opportunities of being by her side. I pity those poor priests whoever they may be. She has to plead so very hard for them. Last night she was pleading for someone who was dying, because she said to me when she got a little better, 'the Devil said he would have that soul in spite of the prayers of Our Lady and the Precious Blood of Jesus, but he is conquered again.' I cannot tell you how grateful I am that she is with me, she certainly is not the slightest bit able to go about and teach, she is always popping off many times in a day. Do you know, I have seen her receive Holy Communion thirteen times; I have plainly seen the sacred Host."

---

[14] Father Snow told Miss Catterall he believed the priests for whom Teresa was pleading in this touching way were some of those who had most violently opposed her.

It might well be thought that with all these strange occurrences Teresa could hardly have been an altogether welcome guest, and there is no greater proof of her strong and winning personality than the unfailing desire of her friends to have her with them. Despite her trials and sufferings, she was so far from being self–absorbed or gloomy, and they one and all declare that they never felt such happiness as in her presence. They describe her as bright and cheerful, "so merry", full of fun, telling little stories and entering into all the details of their daily life. She certainly was no spoil–sport and, though she took no food herself, she loved to prepare their meals, cooking most dainty dishes with careful attention to their special tastes. She seldom left the house and was never seen to open book or paper, and yet she was always ready to enter into conversation on any topic of the day, though where she got her knowledge remained a constant source of astonishment.

While such were the impressions of her friends, what was the secret history of her soul? Father Snow was anxiously awaiting tidings of the great event which, from his close study of mysticism, he was sure must be near at hand, but Teresa herself had no such suspicion and merely thought she was being prepared for further suffering in union with her beloved Spouse. Father Snow points out that one of the purifications preparatory to the mystical Marriage is the mortification of spiritual desires, and this was still Teresa's greatest trial. She had not strength to walk the three and a half miles to the church at Rawtonstall and, though our Lord so often gave Himself to her, she could seldom get to Mass. Her friends would occasionally club together and hire a cab, but, for the first time in her life she sometimes failed to get even to Sunday Mass, and the thought that she was disobeying one of the Commandments of the Church was more than she could bear. The following beautiful letter clearly shows her state of mind:

"Newchurch, June 3 87

"How can I attempt to speak of the love and condescension of our dear blessed Lord towards this poor worm of the earth, for you know what I am, and yet, in spite of all my misery and wretchedness, when I get very weak and these great desires come upon me, so much so that I feel I must really die if He does not come to me, He has satisfied the craving desire of my poor heart and soul and has given Himself to me several times in a day, and it has pleased our dear b. Lord to allow others to see me receive Him. May His Holy Name be forever blessed and His Holy Will done in all things. It is well said that love has no laws, and surely it is so when we think of the love of Jesus for His poor little ones. Oh my Father, these things seem quite incredible, yet it really is so. It seems as though He forgets Himself and thinks only of the littleness and weakness of His poor child. Oh was ever love like unto His love, the love of His sacred Heart.

"It has pleased our dear Lord that I should suffer a little more for Him this week and I was not able to get to Holy Mass last Sunday, (Whitsunday.) I do really wish to be resigned, yet I cannot tell you what a longing I have to get to Mass. Then there is that same feeling I always have about people knowing things about me and I seem unable to overcome it, for when I heard that dear Minnie and Nellie had seen, I felt for sometime as though I could never look at them again, yet I thanked our dear b. Lord for it.

"Rev. J. C. Musseley brings me Holy Communion and hears my confession every week. Is it not kind of him to come on purpose so far? I know you will ask our dear Lord to bless him for his kindness to me.

"Did you get the book you were expecting? and if so, did I make it clear enough about the way in which our dear Lord now deals with my poor soul? In the way I think I wrote about, it would seem as though God was in the very centre of the soul and the flames, if I may so speak, rose very high and those of the higher part of the soul particularly so, and God was in the soul as we might drop wine on sponge cake and it would be saturated with it. Yet in the one I would explain the soul is in God and learns things in a more perfect manner by looking as it were in the mind of God (as we might look at a thing in a bright glass) and the soul is more refined in feeling, her enjoyment is very great or her suffering excessive according as God may wish to teach her. All is peace and a great calm is always in the soul and this enables her to understand and see things very clearly, and she knows that all the things of this earth are only like so many bubbles that must sooner or later burst, and she understands what value and how to use those things of earth. And to me, because I am so impatient and covetous, I feel that I really cannot bear to stay here, and it seems as though my poor soul really left the poor body and would fly to Him with impatient desire, and if He did not increase the suffering in my soul, I do not think I could remain, and what a suffering there is continually in the soul on this account. It feels that as yet it cannot go, and yet on the other hand it knows that it could not suffer the same for Him in dying, so the poor heart is breaking because it cannot break. And then I feel as though I should have asked you to allow it to break, for that pain seems more than I can at times bear, yet it is so sweet in all that I cannot live without it, and yet I feel as I am dying through it at other times. And there is a knowledge of that which God teaches her so perfect that to see is to feel and be saturated with whatever it shall please our divine Lord to instruct her, and yet there is ever a longing desire that cannot be satisfied and will not be, until the soul possesses Him, never to be separated from Him.

"This may all seem contradictory one to another, yet this is the way it appears to me and I have asked the Holy Spirit of God to help me to make it clear to you. I could say a great deal more but I think you will now understand, and if it has pleased our dear Lord to let you be the same, I think you will understand very clearly, and now, while I am writing, I feel these desires again rising within me. I say the pain is great and so to me it is expressive, for it would seem as though God did not hear the prayer that went up to Him with each beating of the heart, and there is nothing to look at here and Holy Communion only makes it worse, and so the pang is very great, yet so sweet that it fills the soul with joy at being allowed to suffer it for Him."[15]

On July 18, she wrote to Father Powell.

"The three weeks holiday have been like a retreat to me and our dear b. Lord has given Himself to me so often of late that I feel sure He is preparing my poor soul for greater sorrow and suffering. And the way in which our dear b. Lord is now teaching and allowing me to suffer renders the soul most capable of understanding excess of joy or extremity of suffering, for we realise it in God Himself. May His Holy Name be forever blessed. I wish only His divine Will, though I am such a poor coward, yet suffering has I think become essentially necessary for me, for I do not think I could exist now without it."[16]

Our Lord still impressed her with the urgency of the mission He had confided to her in regard to the Devotion to His Sacred Head: "He seems to crave of me so earnestly to fulfil His desire and I feel so helpless that it causes me such a pang and at times I feel that I cannot endure it, for He seems to urge me on so tenderly and so piteously He implores, and yet I don't see what we can do."[17]

Towards the end of July, Teresa went on a visit to Elizabeth Dawson, her friend at Clitheroe, and she wrote in tones of joy: "Since I came to Clitheroe, I feel as if I had all I could desire on this earth. Two Masses every morning and a visit to our dear blessed Lord whenever I like to go in church, and I go in school every day and I can see the tabernacle from my bedroom window. I shall feel as if I were going into Purgatory out of Heaven when I have to return."[18]

---

15 Letter 212.
16 Letter 214.
17 Letter 218.
18 Letter 224.

It was in a tiny bedroom hardly better than a box–room that Teresa found her heaven and, little as she knew it, Heaven was in very truth about to stoop to earth in a most wonderful manner in this lowly spot. She remained here for three months, her life continuing much the same. Miss Dawson saw her receive Communion on at least one occasion, when she described the sacred Host as seeming to come through the roof. She also testified to having seen Teresa's brow perforated with holes as from thorns.

Miss Catterall was all this time doing her best to get Teresa back to Newchurch, and when Father Musseley offered her a post in his school, urged her to accept it. Teresa, suffering though she was, longed to be again at work, but all the same her heart failed her at the prospect of returning to the spiritual desolation of Newchurch. So strong was this feeling that she wrote to Father Snow:

"Seeing this uncontrollable feeling taking such possession of me that I really begin to think that there may be some wrong in it, or some attachment to my own will or way, I thought I had better let you know, for whenever I consider or speak about returning to Newchurch, such a loathing feeling comes over me that I can hardly endure it, and such a longing to be where I can visit Him in His sacramental presence. These things may seem very small to you or to anyone who is any way advanced in the way of perfection, but to me, poor wretched worm it is great, and it is the first time I think I ever thought twice of a thing after you had told me what you wished and yet I am led to consider these feelings coming from our Lord Himself, for when these great desires and love of Him come upon me that I find myself dying as it were through the desire of seeing Him and being united to Him inseparably; when it seems as though my whole being goes out to Him (as though the soul were tom from the body); when I am getting all right again, I find myself telling Him that I can never rest away from the Sacrament of His love, and I do not wonder at it for when He burns us with this fire, who but He can satisfy?"[19]

And satisfy He did, for she wrote a few days later: "Our dear b. Lord knows what is best for me and I do thank Him and wish to be as soft wax in His sacred hands. I can only tell Him I am all His and wish Him to do as He wills with me. Though I am in such terrible straits, at times I cannot say anything, only in my heart. And I really do not know how I feel and at other times it would seem as though God poured into me such excesses of divine Love that I feel dying as it were with very love… Our dear Lord continues to give Himself to me several times a day, and oh how He teaches me by His love what He is and what I am, and such extremities come upon me that I know not how I exist. May He be praised for ever and ever."[20]

Both Father Powell and Father Snow were at first in favour of her accepting Father Musseley's offer and she wrote to Father Powell: "Since Father Snow wrote and told me about your decision, I have not I think commented upon it, though none but our dear b. Lord can tell what it will be for me to go, for besides missing visits and morning Mass, it will cost 5s. for Sundays, then there are the holidays of obligation, and if I should run short, then I put myself in the way of breaking the commandments of the Church. I do not in any way wish to run away from the cross or seek to get my own way, though I should never take a school knowingly where I could not get holy Mass and I do not like to put myself in the way of forcing our dear b. Lord to work miracles of love for such a vile wretch as I am. Though I know in obedience I cannot err, and I have every confidence in my directors, yet I feel I should do wrong not to speak when I think you do not understand things, and I have missed Sunday Mass there so often that I could never like Newchurch."[21]

---

[19] Letter 227.

[20] Letter 229.

[21] Letter 280. Father Snow writes: "With regard to this letter, the reader should bear in mind that Teresa was at this time suffering

But after all the sacrifice was not required of her. On September 20th, she wrote again to Father Powell: "I daresay rev. A. Snow will have written to tell you that I am not going to Newchurch for which I am most grateful... I think it is very good of our dear b. Lord to have allowed things to turn out so favourably for me, for it would have been like penal servitude for me and though I made the sacrifice I still hoped it would be Abraham's sacrifice, and so it has proved Deo Gratias."[22]

Great as was her relief at this reprieve, her soul was still held in the purifying flames and she sent another urgent call for help to Father Snow:

Sept. 1887.

"I never have before experienced such terrible sufferings as I underwent last night. Oh my Father do pray for me, for I feel I really could not go through the same again. May His Holy Name be forever blessed. One five minutes of such agony I am sure far outweighs all united pains and sufferings of my life, and such an awful fear and dread I have of its recurrence that I wonder how I live. I feel that you understand something about it, but no one could I am sure frame words to express the overwhelming sorrows and extremities of the soul. Oh do ask our dear sorrowful Mother to protect and intercede for me her poor miserable child. It is post–time so I cannot say more tonight but I do wish I was nearer to you. I cannot say a word to rev. J.H. and I am in such a plight. I suppose I may give the satisfactions of Sunday to rev. Powell as it is his birthday.

"Thanking you again and again for all your care and kindness and begging your prayers and blessing I remain dear rev. Father

"Your obedient and devoted child in the S. Head and loving Heart

---

from the purifications preparatory for receiving the Mystical Marriage, and part of these sufferings is the mortification in spiritual desires and things. St. Peter of Alcantara taught St. Teresa this truth."

[22] Letter 232.

"TERESA HIGGINSON,
"Enfant de Marie."
"Oh do pray for me."[23]

---

[23] Letter 234.

14

The Mystical Marriage

THE long, long preparation was completed and the time had come at last when our Lord would clasp His beloved Spouse in the closest union possible to a soul on earth.

The wonderful ceremony of her Mystical Marriage took place during the night of the 23rd of October, 1887, between the feast of the Holy Redeemer and that of St. Raphael. She wrote at once to Father Snow and a few days later sent a somewhat fuller account in reply to a request from Father Powell. Her eyes had beheld that which it is not given to man to utter and she speaks as one still dazed from the glory of that vision. Her very writing, wavering and almost illegible, betrays that she was trembling on the verge of ecstasy as she wrote. The following is what she wrote to Father Powell:

AMDG et in hon BVM et St J

"In the Name of the most august and blessed Trinity and in holy obedience I write of the unspeakable favours which Jesus Christ true God and true Man, my divine Spouse and only Treasure through the excess of His infinite Love has bestowed on me, the very least of His little ones. Oh my Father, how can I find words to express this wonderful mystery, this excess of His mercy and love which is more astounding to me than the great mystery of the Incarnation. Oh my Love, my Love, my beautiful One, My Jesus, my Own, my All, my God, my (the writing becomes illegible).

"Oh my Father it seems to me almost impossible to continue, or rather I should say I am unable to begin and describe what I would. This is the third paper I have spoiled; I am carried away at the recollection of His wonderful condescension. I have twice before written the four pages and when I read them over I found it full of little prayers, and now again I find myself like one only half awake, for my whole being seems lost in His infinite immensity, His wonderful Attributes, the unspeakable dignity to which He has raised this little nothing. And so prostrating myself before the thrice holy Trinity and before Jesus, my own Jesus, my spouse and my Treasure, I beg of Him to guide my hand and my understanding that I may write without these little wanderings and make clear to you all that you would wish to know, to the praise and glory of His Holy Name. Oh my soul bless the Lord and magnify, for He has regarded the nothingness of His handmaid and has had compassion on my weakness and misery. He has drawn up this little drop of water from the earth into the ocean of His infinity, into the Essence of the Unity and Trinity of the Almighty God of Wisdom and Love, the all–pure and uncreated One, and made me one with Himself in the most holy and solemn bond of marriage. He has really and truly united Himself to me in the presence of the whole court of heaven, presenting me as His beloved Spouse to the Eternal Father and the Holy Spirit, and His Blessed Mother, St. Joseph, the Cherubim and Seraphim, etc. etc. and making me feel and understand how this sacred alliance was as real and as true as the union of His divine and human Nature in the one Person of Himself, Jesus Christ the Coeternal Son and the Son of Mary since the moment of the Incarnation.[1] And in His Name and with His help, I will tell the way as far as I can that all has been accomplished.

"Remember oh my Love and my Lord that I am all Thine and Thou art the God of Truth, the Word that is God, and that now I am one with Thee as the body and soul of man are one person, so my words must be a reflection of Thine, must be, as Thou hast

---

[1]   For further explanation of these words see p. 225 below.

said to me they shall be, Wisdom and Truth, as the honey that drips from the hive, pure and sweet, and all men may confess that these things are the works of Thy Wisdom and Love.

"Since the feast of our holy Father St. Francis[2], when my divine Spouse gave me the general absolution (as I complained to Him that I had not been able to receive it from the hands of a priest and we had no Franciscans here), He caressed my soul as it were and told me that He would give me the absolution, not to take away sins from which He had preserved me, but to saturate me with His most Precious Blood and make me more like Himself. And He let me feel that my soul (through His presence and the holy Sacraments) gave great glory to the adorable Trinity and was a reflection of Themselves in the powers in which He had and they had taken up their abode and which was glistening and saturated with His adorable precious Blood. He told me frequently that, as I had given myself wholly to Him to be His entirely, so He would be all mine, and that He would glorify me in the sight of the angels and saints, because I had emptied myself and become as naught to myself and had gladly clothed myself with the sins of others for the price they had cost Him and for the love of His image and likeness. And because I desired Him with a longing nigh unto death, He would unite Himself to me in the closest union possible and clothe me with the brightness of His glory, and because I had rejoiced and united myself to Him when I was reviled by men and had clothed myself in the fool's garment (as it were), as He was during His bitter Passion, so He was about to clothe me with the wedding garment of Purity, Charity and Truth. He also shot those fiery darts of love from His Sacred Heart into the very centre of my poor soul so frequently that I felt as though my breast was a liquid fire: a boiling seemed to be going on in and through my entire being, and the pain it caused was so excessive that I continually cried aloud to Him for pity and told Him again and again that He knew how I loved and desired Him and begged of Him to burn

---

[2] She had become a Franciscan Tertiary in October, 1885.

away all that was not Himself and so unite me and make me all His own, though never for one moment dreaming of the unutterable favour which His love has accomplished. In this fire which burns very clearly for there is no smoke or wet fuel — in this consuming flame all is brightness, and the light thereof is very pure so that the soul sees very clearly what God is and what He has done for her and that she has nothing of her own, all being the gift of her great and wise Creator and Redeemer, and she knows and understands how the Holy Spirit has sanctified her, and seeing what she is and what God is, she is as it were annihilated in His sacred presence. Oh how He has taught me what I am and what I owe Him and His excessive love!

"Well, on Sunday the 23rd, the feast of our Holy Redeemer, I thought of the holy Sacrifice being offered for me, I tried to make the same act of oblation to God of myself as my divine Spouse made to His Eternal Father during His most bitter Passion, and I felt that He graciously accepted the offering I made. Then in the evening I begged of the angel Raphael to guide me to my divine Spouse as he did of old the young Tobias, and I sent the angel of the Incarnation to present my soul to Him with all its affections, my body with all its senses to be all His forever, and I begged him to present me through the hands of Mary His Queen and my Mother as a clean oblation in His sight. Then I repeated several times: 'Oh Wisdom of the Sacred Head, guide me in all my ways, oh love of the Sacred Heart consume me with Thy fire', when I found my soul fluttering on my lips almost and my spirit softly stealing through the gates of death and I was fainting away with desire, and yet such a calm sweet peace was in my soul that it seemed to check the throbbing of my poor heart that tried to break, because it was overwhelmed with His goodness and love and yearned to be united with Him whom it loves with all its affections. Oh how I hunger and thirst after Him for He alone can satisfy! And as I was thus literally dying I think of desire of Him, He appeared holding the b. Sacrament before me and I thought He had come as He so frequently does to feed me with His adorable Body and refresh me with His most precious Blood, but refrained for some time (it seemed an age to me) and stood gazing into the very centre of my poor trembling soul, which would have left this poor prison of the flesh if it could to fly to and rest in Him, her only Good. Then He gave me Himself in Holy Communion and the Sacred Host liquefied and I seemed to drink of the Precious Blood till I was saturated through and through. And it changed all into Itself, and my divine Spouse spoke to my soul and said He would now fulfil the promise He had made to me so often and present me to the adorable Trinity, and unite Himself to me in presence of the whole court of heaven. I felt annihilated at these words, for I felt my nothingness and unworthiness and I think I would really have died if He had not supported me by a new miracle of power and love. Then He said, 'Arise my Beloved that I may glorify the triune God in Unity and espouse thee in Their adorable presence.' And turning then to His blessed Mother, He gave me to her as her daughter, and Mary taking hold of my hand gave it to Jesus and He withdrew the ring that He had before placed upon it and then replaced it on the same finger, saying: 'I espouse thee in the Name and in the presence of the uncreated Trinity and in presence of My Immaculate Mother, and I give you to her as a daughter and my Spouse for ever.'

"I was wrapped in the Essence of the Eternal Godhead and I heard and saw things which it is not given to man to utter, and when I began to come to myself I beheld the ring (which encircled the finger next the little finger of my left hand) which was a circle of thorns as it were, set with seven beautiful crystals more beautiful than diamonds which looked like liquid gems, the centre representing the Holy Soul of my divine Spouse in which the adorable Trinity is represented by the three powers, and are as it were a reflecting glass in which They behold their Unity in Essence. Then to the right is represented the Sacred Head as the Seat of divine Wisdom, and on the other side the Sacred Heart is represented, and the other four are to represent the Wounds in

His sacred Hands and Feet. Oh what brightness and beauty issues from this little ring; what glory it gives, that I could not behold it I think and live if it were not that He who gave it sustains me with His power. Then He allowed me to see the soul I have often seen before but now more beautiful than ever[3], and He told me, as I sang with the angels hymns of praise, that was the soul of His beloved Spouse, that that glory was my nuptial robe and that He with the Father and Holy Spirit were glorified in me and that I should dwell with them and His Blessed Mother and St. Joseph for ever. He also told me to remember that I was His, that He was Almighty God and I like Him must be about my Father's business. I understand I have a great deal to do for souls and many difficulties will surround me, but I must take courage and have great confidence in Him. Since then it seems to me that so many saints are with me, and the angels as a guard of honour watch in admiring wonder the mercies of the adorable Trinity to this very least of His little ones, and I could and do continually unite with my dear Mother Mary in singing the Magnificat and singing praises to the Father, the Holy Spirit and Jesus Christ my Divine Spouse.

"DEAR REV. FATHER,

"I could not describe what God has taught me while held in His infinite and divine Essence, for it seems to me that no form is represented to the understanding, but that the soul is in God's Immensity, and she sees and knows mysteries which are hidden in God and which it is not given to her to utter, and she enjoys without actually knowing what she enjoys. The secrets of God are made known, but the understanding, being lost in God, cannot comprehend what He has taught her.

"But when I see you I will try and tell you more.

"Begging your prayers and blessing and promising to do all I can for you and yours, I remain dear rev. Father

---

[3]   It was thus revealed to her (as Father Snow had all along believed) that this soul was none other than her own, and from this time in her humility she never once again alludes to it.

"Your obedient and devoted child
"In the S. Head and loving Heart
"TERESA HIGGINSON
"Enfant de Marie."[4]

The following is a letter to Father Snow:

"In the name of the Adorable and undivided Trinity, and to
the glory of Jesus my divine Spouse and only Treasure, in honour of Mary my Immaculate Queen and Mother, and in obedience, I will try and write something of those things which He has
vouchsafed to me the very least of His little ones. I have written
an account of the unspeakable favour which Jesus Christ the Son
of God and the ever blessed Virgin Mary has granted to me, and
when I read it over it seemed in no way to convey what He really
has accomplished, for the change that has come over my soul is
so astounding that I cannot express it or convey by any comparison what has really been done. I feel and realise those wondrous
words of our dear Lord, 'My peace I give you' etc. and it brings
such a sweet bright light in the soul that they only can understand who experience it, and our dear Lord has taught me the
hidden things of God with such excessive delights that all the
senses enjoy such an immense degree of sweetness that nothing
here could in any way describe. And if you wish me to tell you
what I have seen or what He has taught me, I can only say He has
taught me great truths hidden in His immensity. He has laid
open His secret and I have drunk to excess, and yet, as there is
no image of any sort represented to the understanding, the soul
learns and enjoys without knowing what she learns and enjoys.
These things may seem to you to be folly on my part, but perhaps
it is on account of my nothingness and misery that I am not able
to give you a better idea of what passes now or how my soul is
contained or held in God and how He acts with her. But even if
it is so, oh how I thank Him for knowing nothing and having
nothing but Himself, oh how rich I am in His possession! And
though the soul may be astounded at first at His condescension,

---

[4]   Letter 245.

yet afterwards when she considers His immense love, she lies as it were in peace without in any way considering herself. Yet she knows and understands how He is all hers and she is all His, but she has no thought but of Him. I mean she forgets her own misery and sins and does not wish to do this or that but only His adorable Will, and this she hungers and thirsts for as He makes her understand like Him she 'must be about her Father's business' and testify to the world the love and goodness of Jesus, her divine Spouse. Oh that I had the tongue of men and angels that I might proclaim to the whole world what He is and His wonderful love, that I could tell or give them to taste how sweet is the Lord and what they lose who run after the empty bubbles of the world. Oh all we could do or suffer for ages would be nothing to purchase so great a good. Oh that I could tell what I experience in Him who is all good, all powerful, all Wisdom. My soul doth magnify the Lord and my spirit hath rejoiced in God my Saviour because He hath regarded the humility of His handmaid.

"Oh my Father, you must pardon me. I do really wish and desire to make all clear to you, and I beg of Him, whom I know will not refuse my request, to teach you by experience and show you my soul as He sees it, that so you may know how to guide and take me with you to His eternal possession.

"Ah what a foretaste I have already of that eternal bliss, for the soul seems to have become one with God in such a close bond of union that all fear of losing Him seems out of the question, for it seems that the soul as a little drop of vapour is drawn up into the immeasurable ocean of God's infinity. Here she feels to possess all and she cares not whether she lives or dies.

"I don't know but what those great impetuosities may return, but at present I feel as though I had not to run after God as it were, but that I possessed Him and was more closely united to Him than my soul is to my body, that He is the soul of my existence and that I feel and live in Him, that He does all and that I do nothing.

"He has taught me oh so clearly too, all that He has done for me and how miserable a wretch I should have been without Him, and when He shows me the beauty with which He has clothed me and the wonderful works He has accomplished in me, I am forced as it were to sink in the abyss of my own nothingness and praise Him for His mighty acts. And instead of trying to run away as it were at telling you, I feel as though I were robbing Him of that which is His if I did not try to tell you as I know things myself, for all is His and I am and have nothing, and it would seem to be a false humility that I have hitherto had — wishing to hide His favours, as though I considered they were in some way mine, or that I had anything to do with them.

"I seem to have become as a powerful eagle that can soar to and gaze on the midday sun, and as those who look at the sun can see nothing but it for some time, so now I see nothing but Him in all things and all things in Him. That great fear of death and desire of it are gone and I feel such a real disengagement from all created objects, and I feel to have gained such a great dominion over myself that I don't think anyone can understand but those to whom our dear Lord my Spouse and only Love has given it, for I know too so well that I never could have acquired it no matter how I worked or exerted myself. It is all His work and I feel myself so freed out of this prison of death that I lie basking in peace in the light of His Truth. He has dug deep in the trench that so He might fill me with Himself. He has filled up the valleys on a level with the hills, and the mountains He has lowered that I may view their tops and look down on all things beneath. Oh my Father, I could never tell you all that in His goodness and mercy He has done for me, and it seems to take away from it rather than anything else when I try to express them in such cyphers as is the language of men, when trying to describe the truths and favours of Almighty God.

"Begging of you again and again to bless the Lord for all He has done for me, and offering His adorable Precious Blood in thanksgiving, I unite my voice with His, with Mary's and the whole court of Heaven in praising and blessing our God who sitteth upon the throne, and the Lamb who redeemed us by His blood and made us to reign with Him for ever and ever. Amen.

"TERESA HIGGINSON
"Enfant de Marie"[5]

CLITHEROE, FEAST OF ST. WINIFRED, 1887.

"Oh my Father it seems presumption almost on my part to attempt to describe the wonderful things our dear b. Lord has done for my poor soul, and yet I know I must endeavour that you may thoroughly understand His workings in me. Though it seems as if I could not comprehend at once all that His infinite goodness accomplishes, oh how clearly He has taught me in very truth the true estimate of all things here and to judge rightly of His gifts and graces. Here the soul becomes as it were a very queen of liberty, she has bound up all for Jesus and He sets His little captive free, she has sunk in the abyss of her own nothingness and He raises her to a most intimate union with Himself and the adorable Trinity. She has stripped herself of all things for His sake and He clothes her in His glory. She has tasted of the bitterness of life for His sake and He fills her with unutterable sweetness; and now she who was so afraid and weak is made strong and desires to fly to the heights and gaze on and bury herself in the centre of that sun at which sometimes she felt unable to look, for the light was too strong for her weakness. Now she desires to plunge deeper and deeper into that eternal Essence, to gaze into that sparkling crystal and there drink the waters of life and eat the food of the strong. Here she is taught that she is nothing and has nothing, that all is her divine Spouse's, and she feels as though she could go to the tops of the mountains and proclaim His greatness, His wisdom, His love, and His goodness aloud to the whole world, that all might acknowledge that He is the Lord and praise and magnify His Holy Name.

---

[5] Letter 246a.

"I feel as though I had no heart or soul but that God Himself is my soul and there He shines and rules all in such wonderful wisdom and peace. Oh my soul, bless the Lord and let all that is in thee praise His Holy Name. It would seem to me as though our dear Lord my divine Spouse and Mary my dear queen and my mother were keeping high court within my poor soul and allowing me to understand the glory that so many angels and saints are enjoying in His presence, for they are present with and seem to accompany me. Oh my Father, if it were only to witness the beauty of the stones in this circle of our union, to behold the gems that represent His sacred Wounds, I think it is more than human nature could endure, and it seems to fill my poor body even with a spiritual life and brightness that it seems buoyed up so to speak; but I do not now care what becomes of it, whether it is raised up before others or not. His glory and Holy Will are all I desire. I feel as though I could sing the Magnificat aloud with my more than Mother Mary.

"T. HIGGINSON.

"Enfant de Marie."[6]

Canon Snow, who had so long been looking for this great development in her soul, wrote at once to congratulate her:

"OCT. 28 87.

"MY DEAR CHILD,

"I praise and thank our dear Lord exceedingly for His great goodness m bestowing this unspeakable favour upon you and I rejoice with you and congratulate you with all my heart upon your marriage with the Lamb, for that is the name of the degree of union to which in His goodness He has now raised you, and it is the highest union to which any soul can attain upon earth. You are now, more than ever, His. You must now have but one thought — how you can please so good a Spouse. You must think only of His interests and He will take good care of yours. By all our dear Lord's dealings with you I knew He was preparing you for this union and I referred to it sometimes in speaking

---

6   Letter 246.

to you, and told you of the change it would make in your soul —
how you would have more courage and think less of yourself
(when people praised you etc.) and only of Him and His honour.

"I was away Wednesday and Thursday, and only read what
you wrote last night, but I have had great joy and consolation
ever since. But I feel like Lazarus in the presence of Dives and I
beg of you and your divine Spouse that I may have some of the
crumbs that fall from the rich man's table...

"With every good wish to you and your friends

"I remain my dear child yours affecly. in Christ

"ALFRED SNOW."

The very greatness of the favour conferred upon her did but
cause her to sink more deeply into the abyss of her humility
which henceforth could find its only adequate expression in the
words of Our Lady's own 'magnificat'. It confirmed her too in
her obedience, for she wrote to Father Snow:

"I think I told you nearly everything and I shall now be
looking out for a letter from you telling me exactly how to act, as
I do not wish to delay in giving Him the best fruit from the
garden, rendering to Him in the most perfect and suitable manner all that is in my power."[7]

Nor does this stupendous event seem to have carried her out
of herself or blinded her to the ordinary course of life, as is seen
from the following perfectly simple and matter–of–fact letter,
written only two days after it had taken place.

AMDG et in hon BVM et St J

"53 LOWERGATE, CLITHEROE, OCT. 26. 87.

"DEAR REV. FATHER,

"I received yours this morning and I am really grateful to you
for all your kindness. I should be most pleased to go to Edinburgh but I think it is too much to expect, though I have a feeling
which is more than a fancy that I have to go to Scotland and do
something there for the furthering of the Devotion or the good of
souls. May His Holy Will be fully accomplished in me and by

---

[7]   Letter 247.

me. Oh I do really wish to begin and do something for the glory of His Holy Name who does for me such unheard of wonders; at least I have never heard or read of the marvellous prodigies He works in me. May His adorable Name be forever blessed!

"I am sorry that I have been so careless and I will try and be more careful for the future, but it only shows how miserable I am and how unable to do anything of myself, when I cannot put two pieces of paper in their proper places" (she had enclosed only half her letter), "but I shall be most grateful to you if you will give me some penance for these acts of carelessness — small straws show which way the wind blows. I should like you also to set me certain things to perform, anything that you think would give glory to our dear b. Lord and do good to this miserably wretched sinner.

"Dear — has never written since the beginning of the month. I wonder why she does not write. I wrote last but I suppose I shall have to write again if I want a letter. Miss Roberts has been troubled very much with toothache, but she has had two extracted and she is somewhat better. The rest of my good friends here are pretty well and all unite with me in best wishes.

"Thanking you again and again, and begging your prayers and blessing, I remain dear rev. Father

"Your obedient and devoted child

"In the S. Head and loving Heart

"TERESA HIGGINSON

"Enfant de Marie

"Ever since Sunday night I am buoyed up as it were and if I did not know that I must do something for souls here, I should not be able to live."[8]

---

[8]   Letter 243.

15

Perfect Union

TERESA was now 43 years of age and she seemed to have reached the very heights of sanctity, but her work on earth was not yet accomplished. Father Snow says: "Although the Mystic Marriage is the highest state of union a soul can attain in this life, still God is able to communicate Himself more and more to the soul and the soul can more and more advance in holiness and merit. Now Teresa lived seventeen years and nearly four months after the Mystic Marriage. During this long period of closest union with her divine Spouse she lived the same life of constant prayer, suffering, participation in the Passion, and work for God. Who shall put a limit to her perfection and her holiness?"

The mighty favour which had been bestowed upon her brought no outward change: indeed to the eyes of men her life appeared only to become daily more and more "hidden with Christ in God". The terrible time of trial, when she had been called upon, as it were, to face the shame of Calvary was at an end and henceforth it seemed as though our Lord were once more withdrawing her from the public gaze to watch and pray with Him in the shelter of Gethsemane. There is comparatively little to record of the remaining seventeen years of her life. Their outward course was calm and uneventful, and of her true and inner life she rarely spoke. She was fully conscious of the great transformation which had taken place within her soul. Her perfect union with God had brought her an absolute peace and certainty which no assault could ruffle. His holy Will was hers and nothing could any more disturb her. St. Alphonsus compares those in this state to a man above the clouds who sees the storm raging below him without being touched by it. Even though the passions may appear, he says, the soul sees them without being either saddened or tormented by them. And St. Teresa speaks of the soul as appearing to be divided, the lower part may be full of troubles and occupations, while the higher part remains in utter peace. This seems also to have been the experience of Teresa (see letter 264, p. 230). She wrote frequently to Father Snow and Father Powell and tried at first to explain to them the change she felt to have come over her, but as the years drew on she spoke less and less of the inner life of her soul: it was too deep for sound! "Oh the more God teaches us, the less we can say", she exclaimed. "That is why Mary was so silent. Her soul and heart were too full to speak, and I think she would not have lived if she had tried to speak."

Her letters become more and more simple and even commonplace. She does indeed implore for help in times of darkness and desolation. She calls upon them to join with her in thanksgiving when our Lord once more turns His face towards her, she refers continually to His urgent desire to have His sacred Head honoured, but, for the rest, she writes mostly of the details of her daily life, asking prayers for special intentions, inquiring about events in Liverpool, sending messages to her friends, or a "pat to Donna", Father Snow's dog, etc.

Father Snow had arranged for her to go to Edinburgh, to the Convent of Mercy, of which his sister was at that time Reverend Mother. Here he knew she would find peace, and he asked specially that she should be left as far as possible alone and in no way made much of or brought forward, and his wishes were most loyally carried out.

St. Catherine's was a large and flourishing convent, and for the next twelve years Teresa found it a very happy home. She went once for a few weeks at the request of Father Forbes Leith, S.J., to help in the school at Selkirk; stayed several times at the branch houses of the convent at Dalkeith and Linlithgow; paid three visits to her sisters at Neston; and went once to stay with a friend at Clacton–on–sea, but for the most part her life was one of hidden prayer and service. She taught for the Sisters in the schools, gave instructions, visited the poor, waited on visitors, helped in the house, and made herself of use in any way she could. Several times she made application for a post as mistress, but these all fell through, so she waited on, content to carry out from day to day the Will of God. She had full opportunity of exercising her vow of poverty, for, earning no salary, she was utterly dependent on the charity of others. She often acknowledged with gratitude presents of clothing from her friends in Liverpool or Clitheroe, but good Father Snow seems to have been her main support, and she never tired of thanking him, turning to him in all her needs with the simplicity of a child.

She arrived at the convent in November, 1887, and was received most cordially by Rev. Mother and all the nuns. Soon after her arrival, Rev. Mother wrote to her brother: "I am delighted with her and so are the community, and we are most grateful to you for sending her and allowing her to stay. She is so nice and homely that we quite take her into our confidence and she lives with us almost as one of ourselves. One feels at once as if she could be so thoroughly trusted and as if she sees everything in such a right light. Her judgment seems so sound and her ideas and views so large and she is very free from all those little narrownesses and cranky views which some pious people seem to have. I think that is the great difference between 'pious people' and saints or real sanctity."

Teresa usually occupied a little room partitioned off the organ gallery overlooking the chapel, where, to her delight, she could pass the night in secret commune with our Lord in the tabernacle. Much of her time was spent in a pantry in which meals were constantly being prepared for visitors, and in this way her continual abstinence from food passed unobserved. St. Teresa says that after the Mystical Marriage ecstasies and other such phenomena tend to grow less frequent, and this was so with Teresa, though at times (especially during Lent and Advent) she would often be as of old, so weak that she used literally to have to be carried in and out of the chapel. Most of Holy Week she lay motionless on her bed like one dead, but it was only the sister who attended her on these occasions who knew the true meaning of her condition. She bore witness to the bleeding from her head and body. When she washed Teresa's feet, she saw wounds which she described as purple swellings like small plums on the instep. Teresa would never allow her to see her side, though she sometimes gave her pieces of cloth to burn which were stained with blood and had a most sweet perfume. She saw no marks upon the hands. Once when Teresa was unwell and sister brushed her hair, she noticed that she winced a little and, looking closer, saw that there were marks like thorns upon her head and that they were bleeding. One day she went into Teresa's room and found her lying back in her chair quite unconscious, her eyes cast up and her mouth open. On her tongue lay the sacred Host. This happened more than once and Rev. Mother wrote to Father Snow: "One of our sisters saw her receive Communion the other night just before ten o'clock. I told her not to talk of it, but stamped it on her mind so that she *could* tell it if required to do so at any time. She, Miss H., is much the same as when you saw her, suffering a good deal at times but always bright and not ill, though often suffering... She is always suffering for someone or something."

And so the hidden life went on. In one of her earlier letters from Edinburgh, after describing her various activities, she says:

"None of these things seem to distract me in the slightest. Our dear Lord makes me feel so clearly the abiding presence of the thrice adorable Trinity, and our dear Lord draws me so completely into Himself that *He only seems real* to me, and other things which I feel and see and touch are as though they were only empty shadows. I don't know if you will be able to understand from my description what I mean to impart, yet I don't know how to explain myself more clearly or thoroughly. Then there is also in the soul a feeling to give to God a love and homage that is in some way proportionate to the love and favours which He has given to the soul, and our dear Lord makes me feel as though I could pay that debt, for I feel as though my love was His love, yet this does not explain what I mean. I will say that His sacred Heart and mine were as it were one heart. I hope you will see what I mean. It is something real, not a feeling or a fancy. If you understand me, please write and say so, and tell me also what I can do more to return thanks to Him who has done so much for me, the Almighty God to such a worm as I am."[1]

Again she wrote:

"I feel that our dear Lord wishes me to work for him awhile in Scotland and I am so much stronger in myself and He helps me so wonderfully in all I do, or rather He does it all. Oh, how good He is to me His poor little worm. When I consider what He has done for me, I am struck dumb as it were with wonder, admiration, and gratitude, and am inundated with His love and offer myself to Him and with Him in sacrifice. Sometimes I have wished you were near to tell me how to act and what to do to render Him a becoming homage and to entertain Him as I ought, I mean as the saints have done. Yet poor and miserable as my return is, He makes me feel how it pleases Him, and I think He is glad I have nothing but my poor wretched self to offer so that all is His, for I have nothing; and I forget myself and look only to Him and His wonderful condescension and familiarity, for no one could imagine that the Almighty God could so empty Himself and make so free with *nothing*, and I could never have believed such things. Oh He is truly a God of love, the Essence and overflow of love, oh my Love, Love uncreated, Love inexhaustible, Love incomprehensible, Love of Jesus my Love, how could I see anything but Thy love and other infinite perfections?

"I have just come from church and will try and finish what I had to leave. Rev. E. Powell did write and I tried in some way to

---

[1] Letter 254.

answer, but I don't know whether he could make out anything from what I said. You know as well as him how stupid I am about spiritual things through my great wickedness, but you I felt understood everything, and I never felt uneasy because I was so certain that it was our dear blessed Lord who had said all these things and wrought such wonders, and I never for an instant doubted the author of this unspeakable favour. I was and am so certain that it is my Spouse and my only Treasure, my own dear Jesus. So all He said were words of truth and I never thought how they might sound to others. If it were not so true, it would to me look like blasphemy it is such an inconceivable condescension, and you and rev. E. Powell must know that better than anyone but myself, for you know so well what I always have been. And so I feel you do really praise and thank Him for me and all that He has done for me, for I always ask Him, in the way I know he loves best, to give you both especially every good gift and make you partakers in the favour He in His love has bestowed on your poor child His unworthy Spouse.

"I do wish to glorify Him and do something to praise and thank Him this year for all He has done for me and *I will try and begin*, and if you would write me out some things, I would really try and persevere in doing them better and better. You see I am the same as ever, wishing much and doing little. With very many thanks for your care and goodness to me and begging your prayers and blessing.

"I remain dear rev. Father
"Your obedient and devoted child
"in the s. Head and loving Heart
"TERESA HIGGINSON
"Enfant de Marie."[2]

In this letter she refers to a correspondence she had had with Father Powell, who had taken exception to a phrase in her account of the Mystical Marriage, in which she compared her union with our Lord to that of His divine and human natures in

---

[2] Letter 263.

one Person. He had consulted Mons. Weld and Father Wilberforce on the matter, and had then asked her for a further explanation of her words, which she gave as follows: —

"In grateful love and to the glory of the thrice holy Trinity and Jesus my dearly beloved Spouse, I write in obedience about the union which He accomplished (in His infinite love and of which I am most unworthy) between Himself the all holy One and me His own poor little one. When our dear Lord said to me that our union was as the union of the two Natures in the one Person of Himself and as the soul and body are one person, I understand that as the divine Nature did not mix or commingle with the human Nature (only making it divine or belonging to the Person of God the Son), yet at the same time it raised the slightest act of Jesus Christ to infinite value, each act being a divine act and each atonement an infinite atonement, so henceforth each act of mine will be of more value before God and each little sacrifice made in union with Him is most efficacious, not through any merit of mine, but on account of the union He has established between us. And perhaps you will understand me better if I use the words of St. Paul which express something of what I experience: 'Now Christ liveth in me.' And as the soul is the life of the body so, far more truly, is Jesus the life of my soul and body and I am one with Him more closely than words can convey. For instance, I realise that when I speak to the sick and poor and dear sinners, that He speaks through my poor words and comforts and consoles and softens and enlightens them, and I rejoice that they hear His sweet voice speaking to their hearts and souls.

"Oh that I could give some faint idea of what the soul experiences in this, the closest union possible between God and any human soul, and I say all the united sorrows of every human being united into one, if it went on from the beginning to the end of time, would be nothing when compared to one moment of such union.

"If I am not sufficiently explicit, write and I will say more, yet in my idea the more we say the less we explain."[3]

She also wrote to Father Snow:

"The union our dear b. Lord established between Himself, the Uncreated Light and Life, and my poor soul is so substantial and real that it seems to me we cannot (see) where it begins or ends, just like a little drop of rain mingling with the mighty ocean no one could discern again which was the drop of rain. And I realise how truly He is the Light and Life and support and nourishment of my poor soul and body — not that He is in every part of the soul the same — no. He appears to rest in the inner chamber of the soul and there hold His court, as it were, regulating, governing and holding all things in a wondrous peace, and the powers of the soul do not seem to me to act as it were. For instance the soul sees in a mystic light, not with her understanding certainly, for she does not understand what she sees, and she knows things in God which she cannot remember by her memory because all is fixed so clearly without any image intellectual or imaginary or substantial, yet it is the most perfect vision that my divine Spouse has ever revealed to me. Blessed be His holy Name for ever and ever.

"I am so very ignorant on all spiritual things through my own wickedness that I may be talking rubbish to those who are wise upon these subjects, yet this is what I feel is the case in me and find a separation of the soul and spirit if this can really be — I mean if the spirit can be divided from the soul, for to me it appears very evident. I have wondered whether this abiding presence of our Lord, my Light and my Life, my God and my All will always be so perfectly felt. If so, I cannot ever suffer again as I have hitherto, neither have I any wish either to suffer or to rest, only what He wishes I will. Yet I remember how our dear Lord Himself and our holy Mother suffered, and I know too, if He should again separate or hide Himself, what I would endure. May His holy Will be done in all things."[4]

---

[3] Letter 261.

Father Snow, who had made so close a study of mystical theology since he had undertaken the guidance of Teresa's soul, had from the first been perfectly satisfied as to her meaning and wrote to Father Powell:

"ST. MARY'S AUGHTON ORMSKIRK.

"29 12 87

"MY DEAR FR. POWELL,

"Both St. Teresa and St. John of the Cross use language similar to that of Miss Higginson in speaking of the Mystical Marriage. St. Teresa says: 'More cannot be said than that the soul *becomes one with God*. It is like water descending from heaven into a river or spring where one is so mixed with the other that it cannot be discerned which is the river and which is the rain water.'

"St. John of the Cross says: 'The soul becomes *divine* and by participation God.' 'As by natural marriage these are two in one flesh, so also in the spiritual marriage between God and the soul there are two natures in one spirit and love, as we learn from St. Paul who made use of the same metaphor saying, 'He who is joined to the Lord is *one Spirit*', 1 Cor. 6.17.

"St. Teresa quotes on the same subject the words of our Lord in His prayer for His apostles (St. John 17): 'Holy Father, keep them in Thy Name whom Thou hast given me, that they may be one as we *also are*. And not for them only do I pray, but for them also who through their word shall believe in Me, that they may all be one as Thou Father in Me and I in Thee. That they also may be *one in Us*. And the glory which Thou hast given Me I have given to them that they may be one as We *also are One*.'

"These words surely imply a comparison to the Hypostatic Union or else to a still closer union — the union of the divine Persons of the Father and the Son in one Substance. There is of course much more to the same purpose in the writings of both saints.

"I wish you had spoken to me about it before asking Miss Higginson to explain her words. Believe me yours affecly.

---

[4]   Letter 264.

"ALFRED SNOW.

"P.S. — Eusebius Amort thinks that if revelations are very theological, they ought to be suspected. — Faber."

These explanations appear to have fully satisfied the critics, and Father Wilberforce wrote to Father Powell: "Many thanks for your beautiful words on the union of the soul with our Lord. It is a high and most wonderful mystery, and when the saints are favoured with the union of the Mystic Nuptials, it is the completion in the highest way of that mystical union between Him and every soul in grace. May His Name be ever praised for all His graces and for all He has done in the soul of His Spouse. She must be very faithful after such a grace."

The Mystical Marriage produced another effect m the soul of Teresa (one also remarked on by her great namesake) about which she consulted Father Snow.

"Do you know that since the feast of St. Raphael that agonising pain I used to have so *dreadfully* has gone and I don't seem to have any great desires as I used to have, neither have I that extreme thirst for suffering and great desire for death — and I seem to have no power to wish for anything only just whatever it pleases the adorable Trinity (Who seem to dwell in the inner chamber of the soul) to give me.

"I think (which may be a great imperfection) I am becoming very much attached to the poor body and look to those things far more than ever I did which give it ease and comfort, for I feel a power from within (at least so it seems to me), which makes or inclines me to do any thing and everything which would prolong my existence here, I think that so I may give Him greater service and a little more glory. This may be a temptation or a delusion, but so it is. Pray, dear rev. Father, do pray for your poor child that I may be as faithful as I ought to be, and that I may never through my own wickedness (drive) the All holy God from His sanctuary."[5]

---

[5] Letter 265.

This feeling that she must take more care of the body caused her considerable anxiety and she wrote again:

"In speaking of the feeling I spoke about, I do not refer to that sweet peace and sublime quiet which fills the soul, and in which the brightness of eternal life teaches the soul the hidden secrets of the King her divine Spouse and makes her understand the truth that God the Father, Son, and Holy Ghost are substantially united to her and dwell in unity of essence in the inner chamber of her soul, filling her with a most perfect knowledge of the power of God, of herself, and the nothingness of all created things. It seems to me that at times the thrice holy Trinity treat the soul as though she were Their guest, condescending to lavish caresses upon her in what would seem extravagant to relate. Oh what a firm confidence rises up in the soul and how she fears without alarm to do anything to lose this sensible presence. But this is not what I wrote of, for though I feel forgetful of myself and look only to His adorable Will, yet there arises in me at times a feeling that I must take care of the body as well as the soul, I mean that I feel I must take more care of it, and little mortifications I used to practise, I feel they are better left undone. For example, I always made it a rule if the body wanted anything to give it the opposite — when I felt very worn and needed more rest, I would take less, or none at all: If one part of the body called for more sympathy through pain etc. I always tried to make it bear the weight of the rest of the body. If my eyes ached and I wished to close them, I would do all I could to keep them open. These are all little trifles, but such like things were all this poor little worm had to offer. But now I feel I should take more rest that so I may be better able to work with greater profit and be better fitted to do the things He intends me for. This feeling comes on me very forcibly at times; it seems to me that I pay little attention to mortifications etc. though I have not as yet broken through anything I have been accustomed to do thinking I was safe (even though a kind of reproof was given to me for not doing) I made up my mind not to change anything unless you told me to, fearing that the Devil might be trying to make me lose in one way what the dear good God, my divine Spouse Jesus, gave me in another."[6]

Father Snow soon reassured her on this matter. With regard to the question of food, in a letter written after her death he says: "She was nourished by the blessed Sacrament and took no food whatever. She sat at table with others and appeared to take simple food, but she was very carefully watched, and nothing was seen to pass down her throat. But after the Mystical Marriage, the highest state of union on earth, there is a change, and souls feel that the body requires nourishment to enable them to do what God requires of them and they have a doubt as to whether this feeling is a temptation to sensuality. Teresa had this doubt and consulted me. The whole question is treated by St. John of the Cross. I told Teresa she might safely take what she thought necessary. Thenceforth she took food — a little tea and bread and butter, and about midday a plate of mashed potatoes."[7]

In the first rapture of her Mystical Marriage it had seemed to her that suffering could never again come near her, but she soon learnt that the more closely she was united to her divine Spouse, the more intense was her agony when He saw well to hide His presence from her. In January, 1888, she wrote: "I have found out that the soul can suffer most terribly, even though the thrice holy Trinity are actually united to her, for we are having a mission at St. Patrick's and I felt urged to offer myself to suffer for them, that God would give grace and blessing to the work, and on Wednesday and Thursday nights the blessed Trinity seemed to withdraw (though I know they did not), yet They hid Themselves and inundated my poor trembling soul with fearful agony. Oh what a void is felt when They retire — though the soul is at peace, yet how terribly she suffers and she sees how her strength is increased and how much more she can endure for love of Him whose holy Will she adores. Yet I felt as though I

6 Letter 267.
7 Letter from Father Snow to Father O'Sullivan.

must cry out for mercy and, with my agonising Jesus, felt that I too must ask for the bitterness of that fearful chalice to pass away. Oh my God, my God, Thy holy Will be done in all things; I am all Thine do with me as Thou pleasest."[8]

Our Lord accepted the offering and the Mission at St. Patrick's surpassed all expectations.

As Lent drew near she was again overwhelmed with dread of what lay before her. Her words re–echo those of St. Paul when he thrice besought the Lord that the sting of the flesh might depart from him. "And He said to me: My grace is sufficient for thee: for power is made perfect in infirmity. Gladly therefore will I glory in my infirmities, that the power of Christ may dwell in me."

"Today", she writes, "I am full of fear and dread and trembling in expectation of what has to come. I had hoped to be more courageous, but I am really as bad if not worse than ever and have been on several occasions, but if it is His holy Will that I shall always be so cowardly, then I say He knows what is best. He knows I feel it very keenly, not being as valiant as I would wish to be, and I am sure you will be astonished to see I am no different in spite of all that my dear divine Spouse has done for me. Oh Jesus, my dear Jesus, be a Jesus to me and save me. Remember by how many rites and titles I am Thine. I am the work of Thine hand made after Thy true image, and who can dispute that Thou art my Father. I am the temple Thou hast chosen out of thousands and sparkling everywhere with the ruby drops of Thy most precious Blood. I am the Spouse of Thy choice and therefore one with Thee, and Thou hast given me the keys of the inner chamber and shown me Thy hidden secrets. Thou hast placed my lips on Thy Breasts and I have drawn forth sweet nectar; Thou hast fondled and caressed me, and wilt Thou allow me to be another's — to be a castaway? Ah my Lord, behold the bond of our union, the pledge that I am all Thine own and Thou (God almighty though Thou be) art all mine for ever,

---

[8]   Letter 268.

for Thou hast said it and Thy word is truth. Oh my dear Mother Mary, sustain and strengthen me with thy aid, for you understand so perfectly what I suffer. The brightness is taken from the sun and the beauty from the flowers, for He has withdrawn His sweet countenance and all is gloom and weariness, and emptiness is seen in everything that the eye can rest upon. Every sound seems to tell most that He is gone and is not here. Oh what a sepulchre is the soul without Him, her only Love, her Light, Support and only Treasure. My God, my God! why hast Thou forsaken me? Oh I know Thou hast undergone this cruel separation too. Thou hast suffered this unspeakable agony felt more terribly by Thee than this is felt by me, but I am but dust and ashes and Thou art the Almighty God, and may Thy holy Will be perfectly accomplished in me, for behold me all Thine own my God, do what Thou wilt with me. I am but a poor weak trembling little bird in Thy Almighty Hand, and in virtue of Thy greatness Thou canst but pity and compassionate and help me to accomplish all Thou shalt appoint. I did not mean to write these things in this letter, but as I have done so, I leave them and send them, they will make you understand better what a vile coward I am, yet He knows I do not mistrust Him or for one moment doubt His fidelity to me. Ah no! it is as He knows, He has made me to know Him and love Him so intimately that I fear through my own weakness and cowardice I may do anything that would cause Him to leave me altogether and I fear that I may prove unfaithful.

"Oh my dear Father do pray constantly and fervently for me, for I feel you know and understand what I am and you know I never forget you. Many times in the day I beg of Him by all the love He bears me, and in virtue of our union I ask Him in my own right as His Spouse to give you and dear rev. E. Powell all that I wish, or He would wish you to have. You may think it strange for me, a poor miserable worm, to speak thus to our dear Lord, but He likes it and suggests it and He has granted me so many things I have asked in this way. Oh praise Him and thank Him each day more and more for me."[9]

(Note by Father Snow: "With regard to a passage in this letter, see St. John of the Cross, 'A spiritual Canticle', stanza 27, vol. 2, p. 146, and read the introduction.")

Her dread of Lent was fully justified and at Easter she wrote:

"It pleased our dear b. Lord that I should have a very hard and dry Passion this Lent, but oh how abundantly He makes up for any little pang. He is indeed a loving Spouse."[10]

Soon after Easter, 1888, Father Powell wrote offering Teresa a post in his school at Lydiate, but she refused it, saying:

"I presume you will have seen rev. A. Snow and he will have explained more fully than I did about me going to Lydiate; it was indeed good and kind of you to offer me it. But I should have been gaining in every way and would have had nothing to offer our dear b. Lord my divine Spouse and only Treasure, and I have such a strong feeling that He wishes me to remain in Scotland for the present, though not at the convent. I think He will very shortly find me a school. I have no doubt you may think it ungrateful of me, but you know I must do as far as I can His divine Will, and you can little think how hard it was for me to say *No*, for all my natural inclinations went with it, for, besides having everything spiritual and temporal, I should be so near Rev. A. Snow, but I wish only His adorable Will — though I often feel exiled as it were, and for the present I feel He does not wish me to have any settled place. May His holy Name be blessed for ever and ever."[11]

---

[9] Letter 272.
[10] Letter 276.
[11] Letter 280.

16

St. Catherine's Convent, Edinburgh

FATHER SNOW'S wish that Teresa should be left as far as possible unnoticed was loyally obeyed, but many memories of her still linger in the convent. As to her outward conduct and appearance, the testimony of the community coincides with that of all her friends. Despite her sufferings she was always gay and bright. One of the sisters describes her as the "merriest little soul" she ever knew. She had a special affection for the lay sisters who worked so hard and uncomplainingly, and said she was sure they were very pleasing to our Lord. She was delighted when Rev. Mother allowed her to go into recreation with them, and would tell them stories and do all she could to amuse them. One of her favourite entertainments was to dance to the tune of "Paddy on the Green"! She always dressed in black, and usually wore a white scarf round her throat. As will be readily believed, she cared nothing for looks, and one sister declares that she was for ever running after her "putting her straight". She never tired of doing little acts of kindness, and if, as sometimes happened, her anxiety to help merely resulted in her being snubbed for her pains, she was in no way put out, but, on the contrary, seemed rather pleased. The sisters used often to call upon her in any little difficulty, such as the loss of keys or if a drawer could not be opened. She would tell them to try first all natural means, but if these failed anything could be done by the sign of the Cross.

On one occasion Rev. Mother wished to provide lunch for some visitors who had called unexpectedly. It was Friday and she sent out for some salmon, which was long in coming and had been on the fire only a few minutes when the meal was called for, as the guests had to catch a train. The fish was quite uncooked, and the sister in despair turned to Teresa. She quietly made the sign of the cross over the pot and told sister to serve up the fish. The guests, when asked, declared it to be excellent.

She was very kind to the novices and younger sisters, some of whom nicknamed her "Johnnie Love" on account of her fondness for a small boy who came a great deal to the convent, and whom she always addressed in this way. She would save up cakes and dainties for him and one day when she was pressing these things on him, he was overheard to say pathetically: "Eh, Miss, I canna eat ony mair!"

She used to foretell the war and would look with pity on the boys in school, many of whom she said would die in battle, and she described how the fighting would take place in the air and under the sea. The listeners would laugh at her, for aeroplanes and submarines had not then been invented. She seemed often to know of the deaths of people at a distance, and used sometimes to tell how she had been present with them though without leaving the convent. She did not always know who they were, but could often say if they were priests. She told a friend that she had been with Dr. Roskell, the Bishop who was so devoted to her as a child, when he died at Whitwell in 1883, and she once wrote to Father Snow:

"Rev. Fr. Pitter SJ has gone to reap the reward of his labours for souls. He was a real man of God and did much for souls R.I.P.…. He died at about a quarter to six on Wednesday morning. I knew when he died though I was not certain it was him. I told dear Sister Catherine when she came into my cell at five minutes past six, and we both said a prayer for him. Two other holy persons died that same morning, but I don't know who they were."[1]

---

[1]   Letter 321.

Several cases of bilocation on Teresa's part are attested by the sisters while she was at the convent. One day two of them went to visit a poor woman who lived quite alone and they found her very ill. They asked how she had managed during the night with no one to help her. "Oh", she said, "that kind Miss Higginson was here and she boiled the kettle and made me comfortable." It was afterwards found that Teresa had never left her room.

The Devil, apparently, still came at times to torment her, but he seems to have had little power with her and no outward disturbance took place in the convent.

At Whitsuntide, 1888, she wrote to Father Snow:

"Oh what delights the Holy Ghost breathes into the soul at these times, and do you know that when I feel the actual presence of the adorable Trinity within me, it seems as though all Their riches, love etc. were mine, as though I could hold out my hands and claim all the merits and perfections of our divine Lord and love Him with a love equal to His own, for I seem to possess His love etc. and offer it back again to Him, and oh what a bliss this is. Now if this is presumption or in any way not the thing, I am sure you will tell me, for I know how cunning is the Devil, yet he seems to me not to have much power here, I think rather he is filled with a great fear."[2]

On the anniversary of her Mystical Marriage she was again transported with joy:

"The feast of St. Raphael was a real feast for me, and all the week before the very thought of what took place on that day seemed to fill me with an indescribable joy. At times the flames in the centre of the soul seem to rush upwards, and the divine wisdom absorbs and enlightens, though so sweetly and calmly (not with pain as it used to do), and teaches her (the soul) or at least she sees that her very desires are deeds, I mean are made substantial in Him whom she loves and desires with so great a desire — I really don't know how to express better what I mean, and to you who are so well versed in knowledge on this subject

---

[2]   Letter 282.

it may seem foolish. I think I have said before that I had no desire, I willed only what He wished but I have a real yearning for eternal union mingled with the fear of losing Him by my misery and sins, for there is always danger whilst there is life. I think it is the light and knowledge He gives me that makes me see this truth so clearly (though without anxiety or uneasiness). I feel that you will know what I mean. And although I know at all times that I am really and substantially united with the thrice adorable Trinity, yet I do not at all times feel absorbed into that inner chamber of the Divinity. Perhaps this is on account of my many sins and that I may be able to serve Him in His creatures — yet how constantly the flame burns and how sweetly, oh life–giving fire, dost thou kindle — thou art as oil penetrating my whole being. The blessed Trinity now teaches me by showing me everything in Themselves, not as sometimes I used to see God in all things — now I see all things in God, and the love and wisdom which works all things for His greater glory and the salvation of souls."

She closes with a little good advice to her two devoted friends:

"I hope rev. E. Powell and yourself are in better spirits. I think you are both too desponding. Try and have more confidence, looking more to Him and less at your own misery. It is your very helplessness that should give you such trust."[3]

A little later she wrote again:

"I don't think that if the whole world calumniated me now that it would trouble me in the least. I think I have been well taught that either praise or ill–will of the world is but an empty bubble and not worth thinking of. I am glad that I felt it at first, but I do trust it was but a stepping–stone and not a stumbling–block, and as you say our dear Lord in the least of His favours gave me more than all the reputation I have lost or may lose. So long as I am His, what doth it profit me? Nay, I could thank Him for that if I had nothing else, for I feel it makes me more like unto

---

[3]   Letter 303.

Himself, and I don't expect it to die out and for my own sake I have no care in the matter.

"I would be most grateful dear rev. Father if you would tell me the dangers common to the present state of my soul so that I may not be surprised by the wicked One or my own vile self."[4]

To this Father Snow replied:

"MY DEAR CHILD,

"You are now in a state more free from dangers than any you have passed through. The Devil is afraid to approach you and our dear Lord will protect you against your own weakness.

"I think I told you before that though our Lord is united to your soul in a special way, He is not united to the faculties of your soul or mind, and therefore you should often ask Him (as no doubt you do) to guide you in all your words and actions, that you may only speak and act as He would have you to do. I don't know that you have any particular need of this advice, but I know you like me to say anything that *might* be of service to you."

In February, 1889, there was a profession of one of the nuns at St. Catherine's Convent and Teresa wrote to Father Powell:

"I am sorry I was not able to fulfil my promise of writing last Sunday. I was too ill and have been very unwell all week. I am hardly able to write now but will do my best.

"I wrote to rev. A. Snow on Friday telling him all the news so he will be able to tell you.

"The profession came off on Saturday, and oh what a joy saturated me through and through. I felt over again all that I experienced on the 24th Oct. 1887. I renewed all my poor little promises and vows, and our dear Lord made me experience all His love, beauty, wisdom, fortitude, made me feel so thoroughly one with Him — my own wretchedness changed as it were by His sweet touch into His very Divinity. This may seem wrong to say, but it expresses what I really feel. Of course I do not mean that the substance of my being is changed into the substance of God — no that could *not* be — but that, by virtue of our close

---

4   Letter 304.

union, all His merits are mine, so that I love Him with the love of the Holy Spirit and praise and thank Him with a thanksgiving worthy of His infinite Majesty. He has set a lamp in my soul which enlightens and consumes it, and He is the light and the fire. He arises and breathes upon my poor soul, and light and new life are given unto me. He shows me the wedding–garment with which He has clothed me, and the rich diamonds and precious gifts with which He has decorated me, and the rubies are the red drops of His most precious Blood, and the brightness and beauty are His, and I sing in my inmost soul, 'What shall I render to the Lord for all He has done for me?' and I find a recompense and an offering worthy of Himself in Himself. Oh my Love, my Dove, my Beautiful One, my Spouse and my only Treasure, my God and my All.

"I think that the words of St. Paul are the most expressive when he said, 'I live now not I but Christ liveth in me.' and I think when he spoke of seeing 'in my flesh I shall see God', he referred to this state of the soul (as well as to the glorious resurrection).

"I think rev. A. Snow said to me some time since that I was not wrong in thus expressing myself, but you might show him this note and correct anything that is not right."[5]

Teresa destroyed nearly all her correspondence, so very few of Father Snow's letters to her have been preserved, but there is one written about this time when the dread of the coming Lent was again overwhelming her.

"FEB. 14 1889.

"MY DEAR CHILD,

"May our dear Lord be praised for ever for all that He has done for you and the great love He has shown you.

"I sympathise with you very much on the suffering which is before you, but at the same time I rejoice with you. He has detached your heart from every created thing and drawn you to Himself and made you feel and know that all your happiness is

---

[5]   Letter 308.

in Him, and therefore you can have only one real suffering which is for Him to hide Himself from you for a time. Truly no words can express how great this suffering is. But then the greater the suffering the more it is to His glory and the good of souls He suffered so much to redeem, and He will reward you by giving you a still greater knowledge and love of Himself, for being infinite He can always communicate Himself more and more to His creatures. You know these things better than I can tell you, for He Himself has taught them to you. Have courage then my dear child, for He will support you and cannot forsake you.

"I did not think of your being ill or I would not have worried you about writing. If your sickness comes from the cold weather, you must really get yourself proper warm clothing. Rev. Mother would look after you in this respect, if she did not think she was interfering with what I look on as my department."

Teresa did not write again till after Easter, when she sent the following letter, surely unsurpassed as a proof of her heroic charity and love of souls:

> "AMDG ET IN HON BVM ET ST. J
> "ST. CATHERINE'S CONVENT
> "LAURISTON GARDENS. 1889.

"DEAR REV. FATHER,

"I am sure you will praise and thank our dear Lord for all He has done for me in allowing such a vile wretch to participate so much in the fearful sufferings of His dread Passion. All that I had experienced in other years put together seemed to me as nothing compared to what I endured this year and the time too was prolonged. I never was really well since last Lent, but in October I began to experience fearful agonies in soul and mind, far worse than I had been able to endure before, and they increased in severity each week. At times an awful despair would seize upon me and a crushing power seemed to press me down on every side I felt the arm of God's Justice heavy upon me and the breath of His indignation and wrath consuming me as a fire. Oh what a terror too was upon me? for who can withstand an angry God? I was weighed down and hemmed in with sins of every description, and I felt an allseeing Eye gazing and searching me through and through and I cannot tell you how terrible was my plight. I felt abandoned by God for He completely hid Himself. Then my bodily sufferings seemed to me at times to be unbearable. The week of the holy Winding Sheet I felt as though all my bones were crushed in and a fearful retching and vomiting of blood followed and lasted for some weeks, and though I felt giving way on every side, still I begged for more if it would only cause one soul to make a single act of love more.

"There was a poor woman, Jessie King, in prison for the murder of nine children and she was most impenitent, and I begged of our dear Lord, for the glory of His Name and for the sake of the agony His holy Soul had endured for her, to give her contrition and repentance and I would willingly suffer more if possible and would take the punishment of her sins if He would only grant my prayer, and I told Him I would not leave Him till He heard me and granted her mercy — which He did. May He be blessed for ever and ever.

"Then a gentleman in Ireland I heard of who was giving great scandal and I offered myself in a special manner for him, and our dear Lord more than granted what I asked, as you saw from the letter I gave you to read. Then there were missions and very many souls needed help whom our dear Lord mercifully granted me to aid. L.D.S.

"During the whole of paschal tide I have been very unwell, but oh how sweet to be able to suffer a little for Him who has done so much for us, and all the sufferings we could endure for a lifetime are as nothing compared to one instant of that joy with which He saturates us through and through. He has several times lately allowed me to partake of the most precious Blood, I mean to draw It from his sacred Side, and this has given me untold delight and new strength. Oh wondrous love of the Sacred Heart, who can form words to tell of its depths, experience alone can teach. Then our dear Lord has allowed me to hear the prayers of condolence and consolation to His holy Soul ascend to Him from the earth, and I have seen rich graces and blessings untold descend upon those who practise the Devotion, and He is well pleased with them. Oh if we could make all minds see and know Him as He is, then would all hearts love Him and all tongues praise Him. Pray hard, dear rev. Father for your obedient and devoted child

"in the sacred Head and loving Heart,
"TERESA HIGGINSON
"Enfant de Marie."[6]

The spread of the Devotion was ever the thought nearest to her heart and she recurs to it again and again in her letters.

"JUNE 1889

"We have had exposition from 7.30 a.m. till 6.30 this evening. I have been with Him nearly all day, so I have had plenty of time to make many petitions. I do thirst for a due celebration of the feast of the s. Head (and reparation to the holy Soul) by a special feast for this end. Oh how I wish for all minds to see and know Him as He is and all hearts to love Him as He deserves, then would all nations serve Him as they ought and bless and thank Him with a praise worthy of His great majesty. But I suppose we must wait a little while longer."[7]

Much as our Lord urged her to further effort, He never seemed to make clear to her, either her own share in the matter, nor when the Devotion would be established, as she wrote to Father Powell:

"Our dear Lord has not revealed to me the time when the devotion will be acknowledged by the church, nor when dear England will be brought back to the light of the true faith and the love of its saving doctrines. Yet each day and every moment of each day I offer my poor worthless self a living sacrifice in the hands of each priest that offers holy Mass, for the conversion of sinners, the holy souls, the welfare of the church and in thanks-

---

6   Letter 309.
7   Letter 318.

giving and atonement, and I long for His kingdom to come, His holy Will to be done on earth as it is in heaven. Oh there is nothing like suffering for teaching us the wisdom, the love, and the infinite power and beauty of our dear good God, and in proportion as we love so the more we burn with love and zeal for the souls made to His Image and likeness and redeemed by the precious Blood of His coeternal Son. And I ask Mary to remember her Dower."[8]

For her own part Teresa tried to inflame all those with whom she came in contact with devotion to the sacred Head. Father Humphrey S.J., who was then in Edinburgh, took it up most enthusiastically and preached and even wrote about it. So did Father Parker and many other priests. A special shrine was erected in the convent chapel, for which she collected from her friends. The little book of prayers which had been printed with the approval of the Bishop of Liverpool was translated into several languages and spread far and wide. An attempt was even made to bring it to the notice of Pope Leo XIII, but whether this was actually done is not recorded. Happy and grateful as Teresa was for this, the public manifestation for which she looked was still delayed, and so she prayed and waited on, content to do her humble share and trust to our Lord Himself for the fulfilment of His Will in His own time and His own way.

In August, 1890, she again wrote to Father Snow of the condition of her soul:

"DEAR REV. FATHER,

"It is now some time since I wrote to you about my soul or the way in which the dear good God teaches me or deals with me, and really these ways appear to me so subtle that I cannot in any way express them. All words are but so many meaningless sounds and do not in any way express the things of God. How then must I speak when I would speak of God Himself?

"It appears to me that God, having taken up His abode in the soul, reigns in her, rules and enlightens her, even as the sun

---

[8] Letter 340.

shining in great brightness and splendour shows forth clearly those things that were hidden before and draws up moisture from the earth and is reflected in clear water; so as naturally, without any strain to the soul, God penetrates its depths with His rays, teaching her greater depths of His infinite perfections and drawing forth acts of thanksgiving, praise and admiration, adoration and glory to Him who alone is worthy of her love and esteem and gratitude. I cannot say that our dear Lord has taught me anything fresh, for all truths seem to me to be forever old and yet forever new, and the soul has not to go out of herself as it were to reach God or to learn the things He would make known to her. There does not even seem to be any surprise at the great wonders that she beholds in God. All is quietness and peace and calmness even in beholding the judgments of the allpure and Allpowerful God, and the predominant passion of the soul is that of praise saying 'Thank God' in sorrow, sickness or joy. It seems really to matter very little to her now whether she is in sickness or health, prosperity or adversity; His Will is the ruling star and the anchor that keeps all things still and steady. If she can work a little for His glory or if it pleases Him to let her feel that she cannot do anything, it is all one, for she knows His love, His knowledge and His care, and she wants for nothing and her confidence is so great that the smallest little thing she asks for, and every thing she wants she just tells Him that she would like it or is without it and then thanks Him for it, for she is quite certain of obtaining it.

"Our dear Lord often reveals to the soul that certain persons are dying and need help, or glory that is given to Him by the devotion to His sacred Head and holy Soul, and makes her feel how agreeable this is in His sight and how fast it is spreading and how firmly it is taking root.

"I will be better able to make you understand when I have the pleasure of seeing you."[9]

---

[9]   Letter 346.

The next few years passed uneventfully. In October of both 1891 and 1892 Teresa spent some weeks with her sisters at Neston, when she had the great consolation of seeing Father Snow and many other friends, and also of revisiting the humble room at Clitheroe where heaven had come on earth to her. She stayed too at St. Patrick's, Manchester, of which Canon Musseley was now rector, and where she spent many happy hours with her dear Margaret, his housekeeper. Margaret's fellow–servant, Mary Jane, well recalls the radiant atmosphere that seemed to fill the house whenever Teresa came, and she tells how Teresa loved to take her share in all the work, usually singing some hymn to her guardian Angel — she had a very sweet voice — as she came and went, helping with the cooking or the washing up. Sometimes the good Canon would himself open the door and look in upon them and then slip away without a word. He seldom spoke of Teresa, but he had a deep veneration for her, and he told the sisters of the Presentation convent that one day, when passing her room, he saw her, raised in ecstasy, receive the sacred Host.

When staying at St. Patrick's, Teresa usually occupied an upstairs room, from the window of which she could look out upon the church, and so keep her night watches with our Lord. There was a little girl in the house, Kitty Deady, now a nun, whom Canon Musseley had brought over from Ireland and who had been adopted by Margaret. She remembers well the wonderful impression made upon her by Teresa when she first saw her as a little child, how she longed to be like her, feeling it must be lovely to be so good! Margaret told her afterwards that she had been with a saint and that she must never speak of anything she saw or heard. The child faithfully obeyed, but she loved to sit with Teresa, who would tell her sometimes about heavenly things and sometimes about the little children she used to teach. Teresa never looked sad or worried but seemed always happy and content, and yet, in spite of her gentle kindness, Kitty felt that her dark, penetrating eyes could pierce her through, and she was conscious of a feeling of deep awe in her presence and a sense of her own unworthiness. When staying at the rectory Teresa used to rise at 5.30 in the winter and at 5 in the summer. She was in church by six and remained there till 9. Then Margaret would give her a small cup of tea and the thinnest wafer of bread and butter. Often she took nothing else all day. When Kitty came in from school at 12.30, Teresa was generally busy helping Margaret to cook the dinner, and the little girl would be sure to find some special dish waiting for herself. They often went to benediction at the church of the Holy Name and Teresa always joined in the singing, her sweet voice thrilling the child through and through and making her feel God was very near. Kitty also tells how Teresa once bilocated to help her friend. There was a large clergy luncheon at St. Patrick's and Margaret was cooking a huge joint when she fell and burnt herself severely. For several weeks she lay in bed in great pain. One evening she said to Kitty, who came into her room: "I hope you are making Teresa comfortable." Kitty, knowing that Teresa was at Neston, thought Margaret must be wandering, but Margaret, seeing this, said, "No, my dear, I am quite clear in my head. Teresa has been with me. She put her hand on my head and blessed me" (as she always loved Teresa to do). Some time later, when Teresa did actually come over from Neston to see her, Margaret asked if it were not true that she had been there on such a day. Teresa merely answered with a smile.

Margaret outlived her friend by many years, and a priest, once finding her sitting by the fire all alone, asked how she got through the long days now that she was no longer able to work. The old face lit up and, pointing to Teresa's photograph upon the mantelpiece, she said, "I speak to her and she speaks to me." Two days later she died, a most beautiful and holy death, and who can doubt that Teresa was there to help her at the last?

In June, 1893, Father Snow lost his mother and Teresa wrote to condole with him:

"May the adorable Will of God be done in us and by us in all things and at all times.

"I cannot tell you how deeply I feel for you in your sorrow, nor how sincerely I condole with you on the death of your dear good Mother R.I.P. and yet I cannot but rejoice and thank God that another soul is saved and another voice added to praise Him for eternity. For she has fought the good fight and has gone before Him with her hands filled with good works and clothed with His gifts and graces, her lips anointed and her soul saturated with His adorable Blood, and although I will ever pray for her, yet I always will say after the prayers for the dead the divine praises, for blessed in the sight of God is such a death. And what a joyous meeting it would be of your Papa and brother, how they would welcome and greet her and sing new songs of praise to the thrice holy Trinity for all They have done for her, and I am sure we will have a powerful advocate in heaven in her. I would have written before, but I knew you would sooner I wrote to priests to get the holy Sacrifice offered for her repose, so I left you till tonight."[10]

When Dr. O'Reilly, the Bishop of Liverpool, who had dealt so severely with her, fell ill, she prayed much for him, and on hearing of the death of "our dear good Bishop", she wrote to Father Powell:

"What a saintly man he has been and what a glorious work he has done in the Liverpool diocese since he came to it, and I am sure he will pray that someone may take his place who will be suited to fill it. I am saying the hymns of the Holy Ghost, the third glorious mystery of the rosary, and little prayers to s. Head, and St Joseph, foster Father of Jesus Christ, Spouse of the blessed Virgin and Patron of the universal Church, pray for us."[11]

At Whitsuntide Mary Jane came to Edinburgh on a visit. She was speaking of the Bishop's death and wondering as to his possible successor, and Teresa looked up and said simply: "It will be Dr. Whiteside", and a few months later he was in fact elected. She wrote to Father Snow:

---

[10] Letter 409.
[11] Letter 427.

"I have been making a tridium of thanksgiving for the new Bishop and I am sure he will have the protection of our holy and Immaculate Mother Mary on whose Assumption he was consecrated. I feel sure he will be a jewel to the Church and a star in the diocese, a real father to his priests, although so young, and a friend and shepherd to his people. We are all in retreat. It commenced on the 15th instead of the 16th. Pray for each and all that we may be truly generous and ask that we may now at last begin to do something for our divine Spouse. I really cannot bear the thought of appearing before Him empty–handed. His excessive goodness to me makes me quite ashamed of myself."[12]

Truly her humility seemed to increase day by day. With all her deep knowledge and experience in spiritual affairs, we find her consulting her confessor quite simply on the matter of religious vows.

JAN. 1ST 1895.

In the holy Name of Jesus and Mary I write to enquire about the difference of vows, those of *religious* and those taken by myself *private*. If I understand properly, I believe that those taken by nuns etc. give far greater glory to our dear good God than private can ever do. Is that a fact? Last midsummer rev. W. Humphrey S.J. spoke at some length concerning them and I could not see him to ask any questions. Then Fr. Benson S. J. at this tridium said that the religious state, or those who took religious vows, were in the most perfect state that could be attained in this life, and though many people had taken private vows there was *no* comparison between them, one was so much more perfect and rendered so much more glory to God, yet it was not God's holy Will for every one to embrace the religious state. Then I wondered if it was the adorable Will of God for me, for you know God's greater glory is the one desire of my whole being — and to do His holy Will.

"I am sure you will tell me exactly what you think. I am not in any way disturbed about this, I mean it does not ruffle that deep

<hr>

[12] Letter 432.

and beautiful peace with which God fills my soul to overflow, yet what would give to Him one degree of accidental glory more I feel I should strive after if such were His holy Will in my regard. I have thought for the last seven years and over that our union was so complete — I was so closely united to Him and He absorbed me so entirely, that it was the most perfect union that could exist in this world, a union so wonderful that one would marvel how it could be without the destruction of one party or the other (of course I know the eternal God could never be destroyed). I mean it seems as though the personality of each *alone* remained distinct, at least so it appears to me, and if I do not explain myself properly, you I feel will understand what I mean."[13]

Father Snow replied as follows:

MY DEAR CHILD,

"You must distinguish in your mind between a *perfect state of life and a state of perfection*. The religious is the most perfect state of life but anyone can with God's grace reach a state of perfection in any state of life. And we have also to distinguish between what is best and more perfect in itself and what is best and more perfect with regard to each individual. Now no one can possibly be in a more perfect state than to fulfil in everything the Will of God and have one's will made one with the Will of God. And he gives most glory to God who most perfectly fulfils His Will. So if one person in obedience to God's Will takes no vows and if another in obedience to God's Will takes private vows and another in obedience to God's Will takes vows in religion, all three cannot do anything more perfect or give more glory to God in that particular matter. The father of St. Lewis Bertrand after the death of his first wife had an ardent desire to become a Carthusian in order to devote the remainder of his life to prayer and penance. On his way to the Carthusian monastery to ask for the habit, St. Bruno and St. Vincent Ferrar appeared to him and assured him that it was not God's Will that he should become a

---

[13] Letter 439.

monk but that he was to marry a second time and serve God in the world. Whereupon he married again and became the father of a great saint. And he could not have done anything more perfect or given more glory to God. And though it is true to say that the state of life of a Carthusian is a more perfect state than that of a married man in the world, yet there is no reason why a man like the father of St. Lewis might not reach a much higher state of perfection and union with God than many a Carthusian.

"The application of all this to yourself is simple enough, and I hardly need make it. The grace of God urged you to take private vows even before you properly knew the meaning of them, and the same grace urged you to renew them at your first Communion and many times afterwards, and as far as I know you have never had any indication whatever that it is God's Will that you should take vows in religion.

"You may therefore conclude that you are perfectly doing His Will in *not* taking vows in religion — and giving Him more glory thereby. He has been pleased to make use of you for His glory first in one place and then in another, and it may be His Will to do so again in the future And therefore you would be doing wrong to tie yourself to any particular place unless you had strong indications that it was God's Will you should do so.

"I hope this makes clear what you wanted to know. If not I will write again if you will let me know exactly what you want.

"With love to my sisters and kind remembrances to all,

"Yours affectionately in Christ,

"ALFRED SNOW."

This explanation fully satisfied Teresa, who wrote:

"Very many thanks for your beautiful letter and for the clear manner in which you explained about the vows. I am quite satisfied that you know exactly what I meant and I thoroughly understand your explanation and am most grateful to you for all your care and trouble for my soul's welfare.

"Sometime since I wrote you that I had on several occasions taken something to drink (milk water and tea) and, as you never made any reference to it, I begin to think that perhaps you did not get the letter. I do not do so regularly but sometimes I get such a burning thirst that I feel quite exhausted and I felt that I had a real inclination for it so I took it, humbling myself before the adorable Trinity and tried to make a very devout spiritual Communion before I took it. I am not telling you this as if I thought there was any wrong or imperfection in doing so — only that I think you should know, and I wondered why you did not mention it as I asked you would it not be better to tell dear rev. Mother at *once* for fear she should tell anyone that I did not and had not taken anything for years. And besides I think too it would be acting a lie not to tell her, though perhaps you have already done so...

"I heard that some of the African chiefs had brought their whole tribe to the priests for instruction and baptism, and I fancied that perhaps they may be some of those whom it has pleased our dear good God that I should instruct, and perhaps the missionaries may find that they have a pretty fair knowledge of Christian doctrine though mixed up with their pagan practices."[14]

In October 1895 Teresa went for a short time to Selkirk, to Father Forbes Leith S.J. who was in difficulty owing to his inability to find a certificated teacher for his school, and in January she was again at Neston. A remark in one of her letters shows her readiness to enter into the little events of daily life and the pleasures of her friends. Her sister took her to some entertainment "to see Constantinople and have a sail" and she advises Father Snow, if he goes to Liverpool, to see it as it is very pretty and she is sure he would enjoy it!

[14] Letter 440.

17

A Life of Hidden Service

LIKE so many of the saints Teresa had a very deep appreciation of the feasts and seasons of the Church. On Trinity Sunday she wrote: "Blessed be the most holy Trinity and undivided Unity now and for evermore, Amen. I love this feast so much, and all this time with its beautiful feasts are days of celestial peace and holy joy days of love so exquisite that words cannot express them. Oh how grateful it makes us feel that we are children of His Church; how thankful that we are nourished with its divine truths and fed and regenerated by His holy Sacraments.

"Corpus Christi. I wish you dear Rev. Father a really happy feast in holiness. You will see that I commenced this letter on Sunday but did not finish it. I have been nearly all day with our dear divine Lord drinking in the nectar of His sweetness, hovering round this chalice that inebriates, that makes music within us, feeding on its memory, feasting on its anticipation, gazing deep down in the ocean of His love, asking much for each and all, praising, adoring and thanking Him, trying to make reparation for myself and others. And He has given us His divine benediction; may we give Him all the glory we are capable of."[1]

Year by year she followed Our Lord closely through all the stages of His earthly life.

The beautiful feast of Christmas was always a time of especial joy and consolation to her. In 1896 she wrote to Father Snow:

---

[1] Letter 429.

"You say rightly our dear Lord does indeed give me happy feasts and fills me with joy and peace so sublime and sweet that it would be useless for me to attempt to explain: "Eye hath not seen nor ear heard" etc. etc. I often feel as if our Lord were really giving me my Heaven upon earth, and I do so little in return, yet I know that the smallest act I now perform is of far greater value and gives a far greater degree of accidental glory to the adorable Trinity than the greatest I did some years ago. May His holy Name be praised and blessed daily more and more.

"I seem to understand so well how little I can do and how short time is in which we can do anything for Him, that I am afraid of doing anything that might prevent me, I mean that I take more care of myself, remaining in bed when I feel very tired even for three or four hours and sometimes all night, only rising for a short time and returning to bed again; but as far as I can remember, you told me some years ago that this feeling was not from the devil, but that since our divine Lord, my Spouse and only Treasure, had united Himself so closely to me, there was not the same necessity for these things that there was before. So I have not the slightest scruple about it, only thought it better to mention it again as it has several times come into my mind to do so. And in the little room where I now am, I can as it were look straight into His tabernacle. It used to be a part of the choir and was boarded off and I know walls cannot separate us. Besides the home He has made for Himself in the very centre of my poor soul, I have Him so near in the Blessed Sacrament of His Love."[2]

As Lent drew on, she once again accompanied Our Lord on His way to Calvary.

"I am sure in your compassion you will pray very fervently for me during the remainder of this Holy Week. Although I do not often write, yet I always feel that you pray for me and beg our dear Blessed Lord to ever have me in His holy keeping.

"Though from time to time, our dear Lord has graciously allowed me to participate in His sorrow and sufferings, yet I

---

[2] Letter 470.

254

have been able to teach nearly the whole of the year, and this week I am attending most of the meditations and considerations of the retreat, but I am very weak and cowardly and I fear that I may give way in some way or other. You know me of old, how much I tell our dear Lord I wish to do for Him and souls, and when I have the chance I behave like a base coward that I am, oh God help me. Looking into the soul of our Lord our divine Spouse as He has shown me, what a garden of pleasure the human soul should be for the thrice adorable Trinity, and what glory it is capable of giving to its Creator and Lord, and how, on the other hand, it is such a terrible horror to spoil the image and likeness of God therein, my fear increases more and more; and in this dreadful darkness that now encompasses me I see nothing but desolation and misery within and without. I say over and over again, Jesus my true and only good, I wish for naught but Thee, behold me all Thine own, my God *do what Thou wilt with me.* And it echoes back like a mockery, for I do not feel one bit of it, and I dreadfully fear that I may have more when I feel I cannot continue with what I have. I know He will not desert those who trust in His tender fatherly love, yet I am so mean and weak and worthless. Pray for me and ask good Father Powell, Mary, to pray also."[3]

She had followed closely in the Way of the Cross and, when Easter came, our Lord allowed her to share too in the triumph of His glorious Resurrection.

The following beautiful letters were written at Easter, 1897.

APRIL 1897.

"May the peace of our dear Lord and His celestial joy be yours at this holy Easter time, and may our souls be ever glorious palaces and worthy habitations for the King of Kings to rest in. Truly He has led captivity captive. He has slain our enemies and broken the fetters that in any way tethered us, and made the citadel a strong fortress by His presence within. He has enriched it with His spoils and decorated it with the rich treasures pur-

---

3   Letter 472.

chased with His precious Blood. The golden walls are studded with celestial jewels. The throbbing of the poor human heart are as little wavelets beating against the crystal sea wherein the divinity rests in the very centre of the soul, the secret chamber where our risen Lord at times allows His poor little spouse to enter and forget herself in His loving embrace. He is proud of His dwelling and what He has made it. You will, I am sure, think me foolish but it seems to me a false humility to be silent when the God of love and wisdom has lavished upon us. The work is His and the glory thereof, and if He is magnified when we extol His gifts in nature, how much more when we sing His praises for the supernatural gifts He so magnificently bestows upon the soul, for deigning to dwell in so wondrous a manner within us. I have sung with my whole heart with our dear Blessed Lady, our Mother, 'My soul doth magnify the Lord, and my spirit has rejoiced in God my Saviour, because He has regarded the humility of His handmaid.' Because I was empty He has filled me to overflow. May His holy Name be blessed for ever and ever."[4]

Again our Lord impressed her with His great desire to be honoured in His sacred Head.

APRIL 23 1897

"Our dear divine Lord has not told me positively when the Devotion will be authentically established, but He frequently shows me the glory that will be given to the thrice Holy and Adorable Trinity through the devotion to the Sacred Head and Holy Soul. He has shown me lately more and more how great a glory can be given to God and what a worthy temple He can make the human soul for the adorable Trinity to dwell in. And when a soul such as mine for instance, can give such glory to Him and be so pleasing in His sight, how much more the Adorable and Divine Soul of Jesus Christ. How proud the Holy Trinity must be of Their work in His Soul when our dear Divine Lord showed me how proud He was of His work in mine.

---

[4]   Letter 473.

"When I have felt the time so long and felt that I was perhaps the real cause of its delay, Our dear Lord has shown me how pleasing my longing was in His sight, and very clearly He has made me understand that all things are present to Him. And when I have said, 'How long dear Lord, how long shall I not see Your wish accomplished', then I understand that it will very shortly be fulfilled — but all time is but as a second to His Eternity, that I do not know when. Then again I have seen little silver streams of light as it were threading their way through different places of the earth, and our dear Lord gave me to understand that in these places the Devotion was practised and they are ever increasing...

"I am most grateful to our dear Lord, for this year I did not miss holy Mass one day during Lent. I even got down on Maundy Thursday for holy Communion, though at times I was very ill. Each year I can bear so much more and show it less, I mean I can bear up under it better, not being obliged to go to bed. I did not go to bed after holy Mass on Wednesday and Thursday, and stayed in all Good Friday."[5]

In the summer she again visited Neston and, before returning to Edinburgh, she went by urgent request to stay for a few weeks with some friends at Clacton-on-Sea. While there, she went over to the Convent of the Canonesses of the Holy Sepulchre where, to her great joy, she found that the nuns had long been practising the Devotion to the Sacred Head. "How kind of our dear Blessed Lord to give me so many little pleasures", she writes.

In the same letter she tells how she went to confession and was afraid the priest was not going to give her absolution; "He said that 'disobedience' was not sufficient matter. However, after a little, he asked if the priest I usually went to gave me absolution and who did I go to — then he asked me how long

---

5   Letter 474.

was it since I committed the sin[6], and how old I was now; he gave it to me in the end, but I think he hardly liked doing it."[7]

At Christmas she was back in Edinburgh.

"AMDG AVE JESU AVE MARIA.

"ST. CATHERINE'S CONVENT.

"EDINBURGH,

"27. 12. 1898.

"DEAR REV. FATHER,

"Peace and joy in Our Lord. I don't think it is possible for us to find words to express what these words really mean. To those only whom God in His tender compassion and Fatherly tenderness has allowed to taste, they only can understand what they mean. As the year is drawing to a close, naturally we look back to see what we have done for Him who has done so much for us; what we have rendered to the Lord in return for all His mercy and goodness to us. And as usual I find my hands empty. Every year He seems to find new ways and means of proving His Infinite Love and all I can do is to give myself unreservedly to Him that He may do with me what He pleases. May His holy and adorable Will be done in us and by us and all creatures in time and eternity.

"I love to consider even as Mary was a Ciborium, the first Ciborium, so our souls are too. And as I think of the joy that filled the heart of Mary as she carried her God and Son about with her, I feel He is always with me too. He allows me to call Him my own, and I feel quite inundated with joy and a sweet peace that no words can express. He so often too brings before me what He has done for me, and I repeat again and again the Magnificat, and each time I say it, it seems better to express what I would say to Him.

---

[6] The sin she refers to, is doubtless the act of disobedience in her childhood which Father Snow later declared to have been, in his opinion, the only true matter she can have had for absolution.

[7] Letter 478.

"During our Quarant Ore when I was entreating our dear Divine Lord to enlighten the minds of men by the Wisdom of His Sacred Head, and show Himself as He really is that all hearts might love Him, all tongues praise Him and all minds bend in adoration and in obedience to His teaching — I reminded Him as I often do of His expressed wish to have His Sacred Head honoured as the seat of Divine Wisdom. He brought before me very clearly how He had wished at the same time to have the mystery of the Incarnation preached and the Rosary said, as a means of teaching the people better the mysteries of the Incarnation, and that that was being done and so the Church was preparing the world for the practice of the Devotion to the Sacred Head and Holy Soul. He showed me how His Word was an act, that what He says must be, and I have felt a great delight and secret joy when I think of it or say or hear of others saying the Holy Rosary.

"I am sure this is a very funny letter, but if you understand what I mean that is enough.

"Begging God and our dear Lady to remember what you have done for me and to repay you according to the greatness of their majesty. Thanking you and begging your prayers and blessing, I remain dear Rev. Father,

"Your obedient and loving child,
    "In the Sacred Head and loving Heart,
        "TERESA HIGGINSON.
            "Enfant de Marie, Tert. of St. Francis."[8]

About this time Archbishop Vaughan made a most earnest appeal for the Foreign Missions, a work in which Teresa had always taken a keen interest — in fact, it was the one to which she would most gladly have devoted her life, in the hope of final martyrdom. Many years ago she had told Father Powell how ardently she had desired this grace and how our Lord Himself had come and given her the martyr's palm:

---

[8]   Letter 502

"Oh my Father, I have such a longing to do something for souls and to shed the last drop of my poor miserable life's blood for Him who is my only Treasure; and as I craved this favour from Him, He Himself appeared well pleased with my desire and presented me with that palm which I have so long desired, not only bearing leaves but most fragrant and sweet scented blossoms. May it not be His holy Will that I should go out to Africa, for there is little chance here, at least so far as I can see, to win the martyr's palm."

Then, feeling that in such a death there could be naught but joy, she begged that she might at least be allowed to shed her blood for those who were her enemies: "I have said, Lord, there could not be any pain or sacrifice in dying actually for Thee, that bliss is too great for me, but may I not like Thee, oh Lord, die for those who would injure me if any such there be — at least that one may I spare, who wishes me most wrong. But Thy holy Will is my only desire. May it be done in all things on earth as it is in Heaven."[9]

And now again, on hearing of the archbishop's appeal, she wrote to Father Snow asking whether she ought not to offer herself for service in the mission field.

12 Jan. 1899. "May the pure love of God and a desire to fulfil His adorable Will in all things reign in our hearts for ever. I received your letter of the 9th, and am most grateful to you and thank you for it; and although I cannot say that our dear divine Lord and Master wishes me to go on the foreign missions, yet for a long time, as I think I have several times told you, He urges me to offer myself to do something for Him and I say, 'Behold me all Thine own my God, do what Thou wilt with me'; or 'Behold Thy handmaid' etc. etc. or 'Lord what wilt Thou have me to do? Teach me to do Thy holy Will for Thou art God.'

"Then my health is much improved and I look well and stronger than I used to be (as you know). And I think I told you that I took more rest and I am taking more food, and you told me

---

[9] Letter 87.

not to take corporal punishment, yet I do not think I have any desire for it or mortifications as I used to have. And as I do not know really whether some of this comes from self–love, yet on the other hand I have a strong inclination to give these things (not the mortifications) to the body in order to make it able to undertake and do better whatever our divine Lord wishes me to do, at least so it seems to me. And as I was told the Archbishop (Vaughan) made a touching appeal for people to go out to foreign missions, I thought that perhaps that was what He wanted me to do. Yet I have not that enthusiasm about it as I used to have. My only desire is to do His holy Will as perfectly as I can…

"Of course I go to Holy Communion every morning at Mass, but our dear divine Lord has not given me holy Communion at other times during the day or night as He so often did a few years back, neither do I desire it as I now have the thrice adorable Trinity and the Sacred Humanity present within me in a most sublime manner. Yet this does not express correctly what I would say, for I understand each day more perfectly that we and all things are in God as the fish is in the water, and at times He saturates us in such a manner as we become like bread steeped in wine or water. There is something so subtle in this presence of God in His mansion in the soul, or the soul in Him, that I cannot explain — yet I know you understand. There is such a close union that I have only one desire and that is to do His Holy Will perfectly. He is a true and loving Spouse, one who seems to forget His Infinite Majesty in His loving caresses for the soul who wishes to please Him. When I sometimes ask Him to let me do something for Him before I die, that I may not appear before Him at death empty–handed, He makes me understand that one act of love since our union (on the 24th Oct. at Clitheroe) gives Him greater glory than anything I did before. Then I feel such firm confidence, holy joy, and I may say celestial peace that I think I have no desires and no wish to do anything in particular, and no fear only to offend Him. I often wonder how He can trust me as He does. Though this worm is so mean and cowardly and but dust and ashes, worse than nothing, yet she knows how rich she is, what virtues He has given her, and she (I mean the soul) feels as if she could sing His praises if she could for all the world to hear.

"It is a long time since I wrote about my soul and, though I may have told you all these things before, yet I feel that it relieves me to do it again. I think I sing the Magnificat oftener now than ever. I used once to think when my beloved Spouse took me to Thabor that He did so to prepare me for Gethsemane and Calvary, but now I do not think anything about whether on Thabor or under the Cross, I feel now I can say from my inmost being, 'My Lord, it is good for me to be here.'

"I am sure you will smile when you read this as you know how basely cowardly I am when crosses and desolation come upon me. Pray for me my Father as I always do for you and good Father Powell, for I know what I owe both to the one and the other, and I am grateful and ask our dear Lord to bless and reward you according to His kingly greatness and make us all saints that together we may sing His praises and love for all eternity."[10]

To this Father Snow replied as follows: —

> "ST. MARY'S,
> "AUGHTON,
> "ORMSKIRK.
> "13th Feb. 1899.

"MY DEAR CHILD,

"The letter you sent me just a month ago about the present state of your soul interested me very much, and I thank our Blessed Lord again and again for all the wonderful graces He has given to you. All that you say quite agrees with the teaching of St. John of the Cross who was enabled by our Blessed Lord to write most beautifully and clearly (as far as such things can be made clear) about the state of the highest union of the soul with God that can be attained in this life. Our Blessed Lord has made

---

[10] Letter 504.

you understand that one act of love since your union gives Him greater glory than anything you did before. So also St. John teaches that one prayer for the Church is more efficacious than any amount of active work. This is why I urged you at the time to give as much time as possible to prayer, though when you told me that outward occupations did not prevent you praying while you were doing them, I was satisfied to let you do such good charitable works as came in your way. In one sense we are all empty–handed, in another sense no soul in the state of grace is empty–handed. It is *His own works* that our Lord rewards in us. He has done great works in you by raising you to this degree of union and thereby enables you to do great things for Him in a single act of love or the most momentary petition for the needs of the Church."

In July, 1899, Teresa received an urgent letter from her sisters begging her to go home and help them. Fanny, always an invalid, was very ill, and Louisa felt unable both to nurse her and to carry on her duties in the school. Teresa wrote at once to Father Snow:

"You know dear Rev. Father that I shall be quite glad to do whatever you think best, but where home is concerned I would never trust myself to decide, for naturally I have an intense love for my family and a deep sympathy for whatever concerns them."[11]

This is one of the rare occasions on which Teresa lifts the veil with which she so carefully shrouded the deep affections of her heart.

Father Snow of course consented to her going and she left the convent, little thinking it was a last farewell. She took her leave of the nuns who had been so kind to her, fully expecting shortly to return, but in point of fact she never again went back to Scotland. She stayed at Neston until her sisters had recovered and no longer required her help, and then began to consider the

---

[11] Letter 508.

idea of once more taking up her teaching. She wrote as usual to consult Father Snow.

"What I said about taking a school, of course I meant if you thought it would be for His greater honour and glory for me to do so. You know I have all that I could wish for at dear St. Catherine's, and far more than I deserve, and it would be very ungrateful of me not to acknowledge all the kindnesses and goodness I have received from the dear nuns, and I should be very sorry to leave as I look upon the convent as home while I am here. My room is next to the Church, and I can get holy Mass every morning without going out, make a visit when I please, and am continually under the one roof with Him which I regard as it is a real privilege and honour. But I think you understand me and know that so far as I am concerned, I have no wish either one way or the other, but willing and waiting to do whatever you think is the best."[12]

For the moment no post was forthcoming, and she went to stay with her friends, the Garnetts. Miss Maggie Garnett had been for many years mistress of Father Snow's school at Aughton, and her sister Annie lived with a brother in Liverpool where she kept a little shop. They were in great difficulty at the time, owing to the serious illness of another sister, and Father Snow suggested that Teresa should go and help them. She was only too glad to be of use, and Miss Garnett declares that in spite of their troubles, the time of her stay with them was the happiest of their lives. They called her Little Mother and she did all she could to help and cheer them. When not required at home she would slip away to church, revelling in the rich religious life of the great city.

"How can I thank our dear divine Lord for all His loving kindness to me. I get three holy sacrifices every morning and sometimes four, besides Benediction nearly every evening, and visits to the churches where the Quarant Ore is going on. You know as well as I how little I deserve these favours, and I wish

---

12 Letter 512.

you to join with me in thanking Him for them and also for allowing me to drink of the drops that flow from His chalice of suffering and desolation. Though I mention suffering last, yet I know its precious worth and look upon it as a great grace and as a caress from our thorn–crowned and crucified Spouse. You know how cowardly I am, so I know you do and will continue to pray that I may not offend Him or give way in anything. I am all His and He must do with me just as He pleases. Though during the last few days and nights I have suffered much, Deo gratias, I am able to go about and do all the little kindnesses I came to do for dear Annie."[13]

At one time Miss Maggie came home very ill, and Teresa helped to nurse her. During her convalescence she did all she could to cheer the invalid and would sing and dance round the room to amuse her. Sometimes she would pat her on the shoulder and say: "Now, my dear, if you are very good I will dance for you in my shorts!" She would then slip off her skirt and proceed to dance a *pas seul* in her flannel petticoat!

One day seeing Annie was worn out with her nursing, Teresa put her into a chair saying: "My dear, you are not to run up and down stairs any more. Sit there and I will tell you a story."

She then told the following curious little tale.

She once found some children teasing and making fun of an idiot boy who was known as Silly Billy. She sent them off and took the child to his home. Some time afterwards she heard that Silly Billy was dying and she went to the house, where she found him lying quite unconscious on his bed. The mother begged her to pray for him. She at once knelt down and began to do so. All of a sudden the child, who had never spoken in his life, sat up with wide–open eyes and cried aloud: "What does Silly Billy see? Three in One, and One in Three", and fell back on his pillow dead.

As usual Teresa was very retiring and, though she was always eager to help in any way she could, she kept as far as possible in

---

13 Letter 528.

the background so that no casual visitor to the house even suspected there was anything in the least remarkable about her.

At Easter she wrote to Father Snow:

23. 4. 00.

"Resurrexit sicut dixit, Alleluia! Alleluia! Alleluia! I wish you the fullness of Easter joys and that peace which our dear Lord gave to His apostles. How beautifully the church expresses the feelings of the soul at this holy season, and how thoroughly the soul echoes and re–echoes the praises of her Lord and her God in His glorious resurrection. Oh how good is God! How abundantly He rewards the poor little nothings that we do for Him and the love of Him. Oh that I had the hearts of all the creatures to love Him with! the tongues of all to praise Him and the senses of all to serve. My will is His and His adorable Will is all I desire. I am my Lord's and He is mine.

"Today is the feast of St. George and I have assisted at three Masses, and received Holy Communion for the conversion of our much–loved land. What thousands of prayers are being said every day for the return of England to the faith of our forefathers, and yet how far away so many are from the barque of Peter and the Sacred Heart of our dear Lord, and yet Mary is still our Mother and England her Dower.

"I commenced this last week but had to leave it to do something that was wanted. This is my little Nazareth and I have great joy in doing the little needfuls. Do you know, when I thought I was not going back to the convent, I told our dear Lord that He knew what was best for me, yet I fear I had a feeling that I was losing something — and how ashamed of myself I have been when I found that He had really prepared more for me than I could possibly get at the convent. Three and sometimes four Masses, a nice visit and Benediction nearly every night besides being able to visit the different churches where the Quarant Ore was going on. I am ashamed and really sorry for my want of confidence. I know I do not deserve these favours from His Hands and yet how tenderly He caresses and how lovingly He chides. Let us at least learn to know Him as He is so that we may love and serve Him as He deserves."[14]

She was always most careful to keep the feast of the Sacred Head on the octave of that of the Sacred Heart, the day specially appointed by our Lord for its celebration. In this year (1900) she wrote to Father Powell.

"May you have a really happy and holy feast day! Oh how admirably is the devotion to the Sacred Head and holy Soul adapted to the wants of the present day, perhaps more than in any of the past ages. For now, more than ever there seems to be a division between the intellect and the heart. There is a want of discipline as the powers in the same personality are ever warring against the other, and there is no union between the intellect and heart, and the practising of this devotion teaches us to see things in their proper light and makes us love the things of God and despise the deceitful glare and empty bubbles of vanity and sin — brings as it were these two parts together, and unites them even as the devotion to the Sacred Head and loving Heart are united and are one. For the devotion to the Sacred Heart is completed in the devotion to the Sacred Head and Holy Soul.

"Oh Wisdom of the Sacred Head, guide us in all our ways!

"Oh love of the Sacred Heart consume us with Thy fire! Make our hearts love and our wills bend to all that we see and know is for God's greater glory, no matter what it may cost us."[15]

In September a great and joyful undertaking broke into the outwardly uneventful course of her life. It was the year of the Jubilee, and one of her Edinburgh friends, Mrs. Fleck, took her on a long–desired visit to Rome. Unfortunately there is no record in her own writings of this pilgrimage. Either she did not write or her letters have been destroyed, but Mrs. Fleck has been able to supply some details of their journey. They met in London and crossed over to Dieppe, sleeping a night in Paris. Next day they visited the most famous churches and proceeded by the night

14   Letter 529.
15   Letter 532.

train to Genoa. Here they had to wait some hours and found Benediction at a church close to the station. They arrived in Rome at nine in the morning and went straight to the Scots College, whose rector, Mons. Fraser, was a friend of Mrs. Fleck's. Unfortunately he and all the students were away at their summer house at Marino. However they managed to find rooms at the Hotel Minerva, where they came across an old gentleman, Mr. Smith, who was very kind to them. He knew Rome very well and showed them round and got tickets for them for the Papal audience. There was an English pilgrimage in Rome at the time which they joined. Mrs. Fleck says that in spite of the crowds and their inexperience, they never found the slightest difficulty in getting about, and even managed to see several places of interest which the other pilgrims did not see. In fact, Teresa seemed to have a special guidance in all her actions. On the day of the audience, when everyone was struggling in the crowd to find a place, she and Mrs. Fleck went quietly up the stair past the papal guard and walked leisurely round, to find themselves close beside His Holiness. They were duly presented to Him with the other pilgrims, but, true to the rest of Teresa's hidden life, no outward sign marked this meeting between the chosen Spouse of Christ and His aged Vicar.

The travellers visited the Basilicas and all the chief places of interest in Rome, mounted the Scala Santa, and heard Mass in the Catacombs. On leaving Rome they spent a few days in Florence and then went on to Venice where they saw the Patriarch, afterwards Pope Pius X, in his cathedral of San Marco. Thence they proceeded to Padua and Assisi, which must have given great joy to Teresa, who was one of the Tertiaries of St. Francis. They knelt by his body in his beautiful church and then prayed at the tomb of St. Clare. They visited the little old convent of San Damiano, unchanged since the day when St. Clare herself inhabited it. They brought away some flowers from her little garden where St. Francis sang his hymn to Brother Sun, and they saw the miraculous crucifix which spoke to him. Afterwards they wandered among the olive trees on the hillside looking over the beautiful plain. They stayed the weekend at Milan to pay their respects to the famous shrines of St. Ambrose and St. Charles, and returned home via the St. Gothard and Lucerne, arriving in London in time to celebrate the feast of All Saints at the Brompton Oratory. In London they again met Mr. Smith, who begged to be allowed to take their photographs in memory of their pilgrimage. To this happy thought we are indebted for the only real portrait existing of Teresa. Mrs. Fleck says that Teresa spoke very little on their travels, though she was full of admiration and gratitude for everything and her sweet smile was more eloquent than words. Daily Communion was an absolute necessity to her, the Blessed Sacrament was her only sustenance. She sometimes drank a cup of tea, but never partook of any food, and this used to be remarked at the hotels so that Mrs. Fleck had to make excuses for her, saying that she was rather an invalid.

When they reached Liverpool, Teresa wrote to Father Snow:

"May the adorable Name of Jesus be praised and blessed by us and His holy Will be perfectly accomplished in us at all times and places. Really I do not know what to say to you, my poor heart feels too full to speak when I think of all His tender care and kindness to this poor little worm."[16]

Father Powell was taken seriously ill at this time, and Teresa went for a little to help to nurse him and then returned to her friends the Garnetts. In February of the following year she set out on another journey, this time to escort their invalid sister to Bruges. She seems thoroughly to have enjoyed the journey.

"You will see from the above address that I am in Belgium. I had a very nice journey the whole way, leaving Liverpool from Central Station and arriving at Bruges between three and four. I had to stay in the waiting room here at the station till five o'clock. I managed to hear holy Mass and receive holy Communion at six, and assisted at two other Masses later on. There is a beautiful custom here of having exposition during seven o'clock Mass

---

[16] Letter 535.

every Thursday and First Friday, then, as Saturday was the Purification, we had it during the last Mass, so I had a real little feast. Three Masses every morning, one of them a singing one with exposition and benediction, then we have benediction every evening as well. On Friday we visited the church and venerated the relic of the Precious Blood and assisted at a solemn requiem for the late governor, whose month's mind it was. How grand and solemn it was! They always are venerating relics here of one saint or another, and have grand processions. There is to be one tonight or this afternoon. I believe the principal persons and acts in the life of the saint are gone through and represented."[17]

The following letter, also written from Bruges, is interesting as showing how she managed to turn every little event to the glory of God and the good of her neighbour.

"12 QUAI DES TEINTURIERS.

"BRUGES.

"12. 2. 01.

"DEAR REV. FATHER,

"May the adorable names of Jesus and Mary be for ever blessed! Oh how wonderful are the ways of the dear good God. Here in this little old town of Bruges how many chosen there are, souls that truly love Him for His own sake and who delight to suffer for Him in both body and mind. I cannot tell you how edified I am with all I see, and how humbled I am before these noble and generous souls. There is one dear old lady, the wife of the late governor, R.I.P. who has suffered desolation for the last twelve years without one little gleam of consolation and who for the last seven years has had gangrene in her feet, one of which has fallen off and the other causes her such fearful pain that she writhes in agony. Yet she is so sweet and patient. This morning she received Holy Communion and I followed the procession which left the church as a guard of honour to our chosen Lord and King. (She is to undergo an operation at ten o'clock to cut the

---

[17] Letter 544.

nerve in the remaining foot, and it is to be done during the Mass that is being offered for her at the church of St. Walburga.) She opened her heart as it were to me when I first saw her, and this seems to be a great consolation to her, for she says she is so reserved that she can speak to so few. I cannot tell you what a wretched little mite I feel beside her, but as I know humiliation is good for the soul I am grateful to Him for it. Then there is another loving and devoted child of His Sacred Heart whom I go very often to see — who is much like her friend that I have just spoken of, but she is not suffering such extreme agony of pain, but she has been obliged to sit in the one position for over twelve months, and not able to get out, but she has suffered fearfully in other ways for over twenty years. She loves Him so tenderly that His Holy and adorable Name is her consolation and delight. We really love each other and seem to know and understand each other without speaking many words. She has asked and told me many things of which she was in doubt and suffering about, and our dear divine Lord has made use of his poor little handmaid to give her comfort and consolation... When I have finished writing, I am going to sit with a poor old woman who is dying of decline, and she has a little orphan grandson, a cripple, for whom I have made a very pretty scrapbook which I hope will please the dear child.

"I cannot tell you how grateful I am to you for all your fatherly care and tender kindness to me, the very last of His little ones, and I feel ashamed of my expressing any desire to take a school or do anything else, for I see your wisdom in leaving me without a settled occupation, for if I had a school I should not have been able to do these little acts of charity. I always have the greatest confidence in my obedience to your wishes and each thing confirms it, for I know His greater glory is your only consideration."[18]

After her return to Liverpool she wrote again to Father Snow:

---

[18] Letter 545.

"How wonderful are the ways of God. You see I went to do a little kindness and our dear divine Lord made use of me to help and comfort many. I am sure you will pray for all who have asked my poor prayers. I thank Him for all and each, and also for the chances He has given me to practise humility. I know and you know that He who has taken up His abode within me is He who comforts and enlightens those whom He wishes me to help and strengthens those who are weak or in doubt. Oh my Father, what a great and noble Lord we serve, what a mighty and all powerful God He is under whose standard we fight. May He strengthen all our weakness and give us the grace that will make us saints, and great saints, that we may know, love and serve Him each day better here, that we may give Him all the glory we are capable of, for all eternity. I think it will be so hard if He is disappointed in us at the end."[19]

Father Powell, her faithful friend and advisor, died on 26th December, 1901. She wrote to sympathise with Father Snow:

"I trust I shall be able to prove my gratitude to our dear holy Father, E.P. R.I.P. by all the indulgences and holy sacrifices I can procure for him now. His death will in many ways be a sorrow to you, yet I know you will gain a great merit through it and give glory to our dear kind and loving Spouse who has taken him only a little while before us. He can do now a great deal more than he has ever done for the devotion and we shall soon have another dear advocate in Heaven to help and intercede for us now, and welcome us at the end of our journey home."[20]

It was with Teresa, as with other saints, the more she advanced in the love of God the more she also loved her neighbour. Her growing sanctity in no way cut her off from her friends, in fact, she seemed to care for them more tenderly. After the death of Miss Maggie Garnett, which occurred a little later, she wrote:

---

[19] Letter 547.

[20] Letter 552.

"I often think what a joy it will be in Heaven, to see and be with those whom we love and to feel that nothing can ever separate us. There will be no more parting."[21]

When in June, 1902, Father Snow was made a Canon of the Diocese, she wrote to congratulate him.

"I made a tridium of Masses for you praying that the Holy Ghost would enlighten your mind and inflame your heart and make you wise as a Solomon, and strong in goodwill as Samson was in natural strength, and humble as a real servant of God should be. For a canon without humility would be of little use. But I know how well you love humility and hate pride."[22]

Seldom as Teresa refers in her later letters to her interior life, it is clear that she was all this time following closely in the footsteps of her Crucified Spouse. But now, as she so often said, it was different from of old. She no longer had that insatiable desire for suffering which had formerly consumed her — whether in Gethsemane or on Thabor, it was all one to her. It was not that the pain was less; on the contrary, she found that, since her Mystical Marriage, the periods of darkness were far more terrible than before and she dreaded them accordingly. But they did not disturb her peace — she knew that in God's own time they would pass and she realised with St. Paul that the sufferings of this time are not worthy to be compared to the glory that is to come.

"May Jesus Christ be praised for ever for all His goodness and tender kindness to us", she wrote to Father Snow. "Well may you say that we could never thank Him enough in time, so He has given us an eternity to do it in. Though one is so full of dread and fear and suffers so terribly in the utter darkness and desolation that encompasses the soul in the hours of agonising anguish which seems as if it would annihilate her — when it is passed and she again sees Him enshrined in all His beauty and glory in the centre of the soul, when she basks in the sunshine of His

---

[21] Letter 562.
[22] Letter 553.

divine presence, she forgets the death–struggle that has taken place and feels mean in speaking of that which seems then so little to have purchased such an increase of knowledge, peace, and glory and joy. She feels to understand so well what the holy Apostle St. Paul says about the sufferings etc. of this life."[23]

She never ceased asking for prayers, for the greater the heights she trod, the deeper did her roots strike in humility, and she feared lest, left to her own weakness, she might even yet turn traitor. In the June of 1903, she wrote:

"I must beg most earnestly of you to pray hard and frequently for me. You know how weak and cowardly I am, and though I know full well that my divine Spouse is near and will not leave me in my hour of need, yet I have a fearful dread and awful fear. May He be loved and praised by all. I trust Him yet I know and feel my own weakness terribly. I do not wish this suffering to be taken away, but pray that His holy, adorable, and amiable loving Will may be done in me and by me now and always. This day, the commemoration of the Precious Blood, should give me confidence. May He be praised for ever for all He has done and given to us through it."[24]

In November of the same year she wrote:

"Thank God I am much the same on the whole, but I have had two short spells of the most agonising desolation and trials I have ever passed through. May His adorable Name be blessed for ever Who is mindful of His poor little worm. And instead of being full of joy in suffering something for the glory of His Name and the good of the Church, I am full of fear and dread of the same thing returning. I know I am always a coward but I am worse than ever I was. May His Holy and adorable Will be fully accomplished in me and by me. I know you will pray earnestly for me that I may never turn traitor."[25]

---

[23] Letter 548.
[24] Letter 560.
[25] Letter 567.

18

Recalled to Teach

AFTER Miss Garnett's death, Teresa returned to Neston and began once more to look out for a school. It was sixteen years since she had last had a definite post, and in the interval her life had been composed of trivial duties and little acts of kindness, but she had long learnt that human measures are of no account in the things of God and that the tiniest action will weigh down the scale, if undertaken in accordance with His holy Will. During these years of seeming uselessness our Lord had taken her up into a high mountain apart and shown her things which eye hath not seen nor ear heard, and now, as a last token of His favour, He was bidding her come down again into the plains — to an obscure cottage school, there once more to take up her high calling of "teaching little children how to love Him".

On November 23rd, 1903, she wrote to Father Snow:

"Today I received a letter from Sister M St Philip. I went to see her and she told she had sent a letter to you the copy of which she enclosed. It was from the chaplain at Chudleigh. What shall I do? I told Sister I was grateful to her but that I should prefer a convent, but she said the nuns she had written to did not answer, so she thinks they may perhaps have got someone. She also says there is no hurry and if in the meantime she is applied to by the nuns, she will at once let me know. She talked for a long time and thinks that any teacher who can manage it at all ought to look upon it as a sacred duty, for protestant teachers have in several cases been installed in Catholic Schools."[1]

The enclosure she refers to is as follows:

"DEC. 6 1903

"The rev. H. J. Dowsett has applied to rev. Mother of Mount Pleasant Training–College Liverpool respecting a mistress for the school of the Rt. Hon. Lord Clifford and has been advised to write to Miss Higginson.

"The school is a small one, at present only 24 children on the books, but the number after Christmas should be close on 30, though it could not for a long time at least exceed that number. The children are clean, bright and exceedingly well–behaved. They are all children of the people employed on Lord Clifford's estate. A mistress is required fully certificated to take up the school after Christmas. The school has not yet been definitely accepted by the County Council, but there is no doubt that it will be. The buildings and other parts of the school are in good repair, but Lord Clifford is awaiting the report of the County Council when he will erect new schools as they may wish. At present the mistress, Article 50, is receiving £40 per an. with three furnished rooms (one sitting–room and two bedrooms) and firing. The caretaker is required to make up the mistress's fire and do up the rooms each morning and the sum of £5 extra is given the mistress to engage the caretaker or anyone she chooses to do her cooking or other work required. A fully certificated mistress would of course receive such a salary as her position demanded.

"The school is not very far from the church and in future would probably be nearer. The country is very beautiful and the climate soft and healthy.

"If Miss Higginson would care to know more about the school, Fr Dowsett will supply information. He would like to know Miss Higginson's qualifications, past schools, and salary required *with or without* the arrangement made between the present mistress and caretaker. These are not necessary adjuncts

---

[1]   Letter 568.

of the position." He then gives a list of the services in the church, and continues: "The school–house adjoins the school. The fact of having three rooms allows the mistress the pleasure of having one of her friends to stay with her.

"On receipt of the County Council's requirements, the probability is that a new school and house will be begun as soon as possible. The rooms were furnished throughout in 1902. Fr Dowsett would like an early reply to put before Lord Clifford."

Teresa seemed irresistibly drawn to this lonely spot in far–off Devon, so far removed from friends and advisors. She felt that her divine Spouse was asking something special of her and never for a moment doubted that the call would lead her still further along the road of suffering. Accordingly, with the consent of Canon Snow, she accepted the position. When she went to say goodbye to him he writes, "She asked if I would come to her when she was dying. I said I would if I knew. She said she wanted to take an oath when receiving viaticum that all her writings were true."[2]

She set off on her long journey in January, 1904, and having missed her connection at Exeter, she spent the night there, and took the opportunity of visiting the cathedral.

"I did go into the old cathedral at Exeter and prayed, and asked all in heaven to intercede, for the restoration of the Church, all who prayed and received the Sacraments there who had learnt the truths of our holy faith and enjoyed the peace and blessedness that can only be found in the Church of Peter."[3]

She arrived at Chudleigh in pouring rain and there is a note of desolation in her first letter to Father Snow:

[569] "Thank God I have been very sick all the week but feel rather better tonight. We begin school on Monday, so I am sure you will make a special offering of me and my work to our dear divine Lord… I do not know how I am to get stamps here as there is no post office nearer than Chudleigh and no letter box in

---

[2]   Letter to Father O'Sullivan.
[3]   Letter 570.

the wall nearer than 2½ miles off. The house is between two hills and no other house near that I can see. I shall be most grateful for a few penny and half penny stamps. I shall write again after tomorrow... I am writing under difficulties — have no lamp and only a very thin candle."[4]

Nearly all her life had been spent amidst the busy stir of great cities, and now to find herself buried in the very heart of the country in the depths of winter must have seemed strange indeed. But the greatest blow was her distance from the church. For so many years she had lived almost within touch of the tabernacle, and here she found herself far away, for the little church was attached to Lord Clifford's house over a mile distant. The road was very hilly, though there was a shorter way across the fields, and this she used except when, in wet weather, it became so swampy as to be impassable. Her very soul seemed to bleed in the anguish of her desolation, but she knew she had come here to share the Cross, "and what could really be a cross, only something that could keep me from Him?"

The schoolhouse stood at the head of a little valley, or coombe as it is called locally, and was reached by a steep path leading down from the road. The building consisted of two houses under one roof with a wide stone passage in between. The door on the left opened into the house of the caretaker (a Protestant woman with a large family). The other door led into the teacher's sitting–room, a pleasant, low–ceilinged room with two windows looking out over the meadows. The two bedrooms were upstairs and the school premises round to the back. There was a nice garden and a porch which in summer was covered with climbing roses, but when Teresa arrived in the middle of winter and in pouring rain the place must have looked sadly desolate. The house was terribly damp and the buildings were in bad repair and infested with rats and it was a long time before anything was done to put them right.

---

[4]   Letter 569.

As usual in country places there was considerable curiosity about the new teacher, and one of the Catholics remembers her first sight of Teresa and the feeling, half of consternation and half of amusement caused by her appearance. It was a Sunday morning and on her way to Mass she overtook a little shrunken woman looking far older than her years, creeping along the road in a tall old–fashioned hat, wearing galoshes and huddled up in no fewer than three shawls! The woman could not help wondering how one so frail and simple–looking would be able to deal with her own big, unruly children.

On the Monday after her arrival Teresa attended a Christmas party given by Lady Clifford to the Catholic children on the estate. There was a grand tea and one of the monks from Buckfast showed a magic lantern.

"Between the tea and lantern Lady Clifford played for the children to dance. It was a real farce for they had not the slightest notion of dancing. I think they can never have seen anyone dance. However they seemed to enjoy it and that was everything.

"Lady Clifford said she hoped I would be very comfortable and that I would stay with them for many years, to which I made no reply. I am afraid I shall not be able to manage the walk to and from the church. It is a great distance for me and up and down hill all the way, and no made road up to the highway, nothing but ruts and puddle mud over the shoe tops. It has rained every day since I came and rev. H. Dowsett says that this part of Devon is called the watering can of England.

"There are rats in the house and as soon as I put out the candle I can hear them at it and they eat it all or take it away. Today Fr. Dowsett has sent up a lamp and a coal scuttle. There are only six geographical readers and Burns and Oates' Catholic History of England to read from and these all torn. A register recording three whole years attendances and room for another. I have been busy adding the years attendances as none had been added. There is *no* summary and an old admission book with record of baptisms in it. No timetable, conscience clause and hardly anything for the children to work with. I gave Fr. Dowsett a list of books etc. required but have not heard anything about them. He came into school for a short time on Monday morning and said he would bring some charts of Lord Clifford's estates which they must learn for geography — he said that grammar, geography, and history was all bosh for that class of children and too much reading was not good for them either. He said that he wished me to work up the prayers, catechism and religious knowledge of the children as they had utterly failed at the religious examination. He said also he could not believe children could be so ignorant of the simplest truths. He blames the parents and teacher. I do not find them so bad as he makes them. They are very good children and above the average for intelligence in country children. Not having tools to work with, I have found it rather hard work to keep all the children well employed. When I get books it will be much easier.

"Do pray very earnestly for me. Rev. H. Dowsett kindly gives me holy Communion before Mass and I leave the church at the post communion and am only back in time to open school and I get a cup of tea at the play time. As soon as Lord and Lady Clifford go away, holy Mass will be at a quarter to eight so that I shall be better off. Last Sunday when I was going for holy Communion, I fell in all the slutch and had to go back and change my dress, etc. and wash myself, so of course I was late, but Fr. Dowsett came to me as he came down from the altar and said he would come out again in about a quarter of an hour. He really is very kind in that way.

"I think I have now told you everything about the school, children, and other things. Mrs — and Mrs — are in a great stew about me. They say I will soon go to the next world if I stay here. But I must be about our Father's business — whatever He has for me to do here. His holy Will is all I desire."[5]

At the end of the month Teresa wrote again to Canon Snow:

---

[5]   Letter 570.

"It is a month tomorrow since I came south and no one has been to see me since I came. The pane of glass has not been put in nor the window frames mended, so each morning I have to wash up large pools of water both upstairs and down. Last week was the worst — on Monday it was freezing and bitterly cold, on Monday night there was a thaw and regular storm of rain and wind which has continued with more or less violence all the week, and what is worse I have not been able to get to holy Mass except Monday and Saturday. The latter and today I really had to wade through the water ankle deep in some places. Fr Dowsett said I was not to attempt to go down for Benediction as I have a very bad cold, stiff neck and swollen face and black and inflamed eye. I am telling you these little things that you may thank our dear Lord with me. For our dear divine Spouse will not be outdone in generosity and for the little I can give to Him He lavishes in abundance. I feel so keenly not being able to get to holy Mass and holy Communion that I told Him that my very soul bled with anguish. And I knelt to assist in spirit at your holy Sacrifice and others, and He filled me so with His adorable presence that I feel certain it is His Will that I remain here in spite of everything. And right glad I am that I have so much to remind me of Bethlehem. Deo gratias. I can teach these little ones to know and love Him, for they are good children and anxious to learn."[6]

Although she did not know for what purpose she had come, she was quite sure our Lord had called her here and she wrote again to Father Snow:

"Although it is not my turn to write, I thought I would do so tonight if I possibly could, for I wish you to pray for me more earnestly than ever. I am quite convinced that this is the place I had to come to and that I saw some years ago. The school is what I thought was a little white church on a hill side — for as I came along the low road and looked up at it and saw the four windows and a door at each end on a line with the windows and

---

6 Letter 571.

looked at the roof etc., I felt quite convinced that this was the place in which God wished me to do something for His glory and the good of souls. If it were not for this certainty, I do not think that I should venture to stay here as Lent is approaching, and be so far from the church and such a difficult road to go to it. Besides before I came I felt and knew quite well that I was going to have a share of the Cross. And what could really be a cross, only something that could keep me from Him? And several times I have not been able to get to holy Mass and holy Communion — I must try and welcome these disappointments and try to thank and bless Him for them. I know I am not worthy of any or all of His great gifts, but I have been so spoiled and He has lavished so many favours upon me that I look for them as a matter of course, though I hope that I do not look for anything that is not His adorable Will."Lent was drawing near and she was alone in a strange land far from friends, far from her director, and, above all, far from our Lord Himself in the blessed Sacrament of His love. She had said some time before that each year she found herself able to bear more and to show it less, and we have no record of this her last Lent on earth. She wrote to Father Snow:

"And now dear rev. Father I must beg of you to renew your earnestness and please do all you can for your poor child during these next few weeks. I think I need prayers more than ever I did and as you know what a fearful coward I am, I trust very much to your intercession for me...

"If we have all Easter week as a holiday, I propose going to Lancashire on the Monday and returning on Friday, at least if you think I should. Of course it is a long time to look forward to and we do not know whether we shall be here or not at that time or what might happen between this and then. But if it is for the best, I think I should like to go."[7]

She did go home and on her return fell ill with an attack of bronchitis:

---

[7]   Letter 572.

"I have had a rather bad bronchial cold ever since I returned and had linseed and mustard poultices on day and night, and, as the congestion did not give way, I gave a holiday and tried turpentine. I am a little better today but very weak. I have not been out all the week. I wrote and told Fr. Dowsett but I have neither seen nor heard anything from him. No one ever comes near school or house. The place is so damp that a pair of slippers that I left in a cupboard near the fire had long blue and green hairs about half an inch long grown from them when I returned on Saturday. I do hope that you may have fine and warm weather all your holidays and that the change and rest may really do you both permanent good.

"I am really grateful to our dear b. Lord for whatever He sends or permits. May His holy Name be praised for ever and ever."[8]

A week later she wrote:

"Thank you for your kind and sympathetic letter. ... I am a great deal better today. I have been to holy Mass etc. and Benediction was immediately after Mass. It is the first time since last Sunday that I have been. I did not get to Benediction on Sunday for I could hardly get home from Church in the morning I was so faint and my heart was so bad. I sent for rev. H. Dowsett and he came up yesterday, Friday morning. He says he will see that the house is made airtight. The rat holes are made up and tarred and a shed is built up over the passage to the school. I succeeded in getting him into the house and I showed him the doors etc. and he says I shall have curtains also and some other things.

"Lord and Lady Clifford will be home for the first week in May, Sunday or Monday, Fr Dowsett says, and I will then see Lady Clifford and know what is going to be done. I do not know that I have done what ever it is that our dear Lord wishes me to do here. If I did, I should leave at once, but under the circumstances, as I am somewhat better and the weather is more settled, with your prayers and blessing I shall wait a little longer."[9]

---

[8] Letter 576.

She recovered very slowly. On May 8th she wrote:

"I hope that I am among your offerings to our dear and Immaculate Mother this month and that you are uniting my intentions with yours in your May devotions. We had a singing votive Mass of the blessed Virgin this morning. Somehow I always feel great joy when a feast of the glorious St. Michael falls on one of our dear blessed Lady's like today.

"I am still on the sick list, but I have been able under great difficulties to get to holy Mass these last three days, though I shall not be able to get back again to Benediction, the distance is too great for me at present. I keep so very weak and my heart is bad and cough also. Thank and praise the adorable Trinity with me and for me. I wish only what They appoint and I say very often with St. Peter, 'Lord it is good for me to be here', but I do not finish the quotation, for I really wish to go home where there will not be any danger of offending Him Whom I love above all things."[10]

"We are having very nice weather just now and I am feeling a good deal better and have been able to get to holy Mass each morning, and I trust that with the next week's rest and the good weather I shall get all right and strong again. I have really been very ill, Deo gratias, but am picking up nicely again. I am grateful that you had such nice weather at Ventnor and hope you may long feel the benefit of it. Even when I was so bad and could not get out, yet I had a great joy in knowing that I was doing His adorable Will during the darkest days. This may seem very contradictory but I always have a kind of peaceful joy whether I am in joy, light or darkness. I mean a real joy and desolation together."[11]

She loved the beautiful flowers which grew with such profusion in that soft climate and often packed off boxes of roses to Canon Snow for his church, sending, as she used to say, a little

[9] Letter 577.

[10] Letter 579.

[11] Letter 580.

message in each petal of every flower. She does not say what arrangements she came to with Lord and Lady Clifford, but she must have agreed to remain on, for after the Summer holidays which she spent at Neston, she returned to Chudleigh. Various alterations appear to have been made, and she says the school was much improved and the valley had also been drained and was much better.

She had completely won her way with the children, whom she constantly refers to in her letters as her "dear chicks". She had her own way of managing them. There were several big boys in the school at the time, and no doubt at first they expected to have things all their own way with their gentle little teacher, but they soon found she was not to be trifled with. She could be severe enough when necessary, and her own evident distress when they were naughty worked upon their better feelings. She once caught one of the older boys playing the fool during prayers in order to make the others laugh. She at once punished him, but the rest of the children were so astonished to see that teacher herself was crying that they ran home to tell their mothers that the boy had done something terrible indeed. Teresa, fearing the mother would be seriously alarmed sent for her to talk the matter over.

The girls were devoted to her and she would often keep them after school hours to give them lessons in cooking, allowing them to take home the results of their efforts. In wet weather she was always careful to have something dry for each child to put on, and would give them hot cocoa and provide meals for the poorer ones, and when she came back from her holidays she brought each of them a nice present. For the rest she kept very much to herself and never went into the neighbours' houses, unless they were ill or needed help, when she would be the first to go to them. She was always busy, and did a great deal of needlework, making vestments for the Canon or clothes for the children. Her sewing was most beautiful. She once made a baby's dress which was sent up for some competition of Queen

Alexandra's and won the first prize. She hardly ever went anywhere except to church, and the impression grew that she wanted to avoid attention. Accordingly little heed was paid to her and
she got the name of being somewhat eccentric. Her chief companion was a little dog called Rough which Fr Dowsett had sent
her to keep away the rats.

In September, 1904, she wrote to Canon Snow:

"Adore, thank and praise Him for me, and offer Him my
whole being, my heart with all its love and affections, every
beating and desire, my soul with all its powers, my body and
mind with all its senses, that every action of mine may be one
perfect act of resignation love and glory to Him who is my Lord
and God, my Spouse and only Treasure, here and in heaven. Oh
how I loved the minutes I spent before Him the last few years,
and how I treasure them now that I cannot be actually present
with you during the Quarant Ore, but I shall be with you in
spirit...

"We are to have Confirmation here on the 9th Oct. so I am
sure you will pray for my little chicks. Thank you for the prayers
you have already said for them and their unworthy teacher. The
religious examination is to take place on the 10th and the Bishop
and Lord Clifford will be present, so I hope the children won't be
too shy to answer."[12]

After the Bishop's visit she wrote again:

"The Bishop administered Confirmation to seven of the
school children and one boy made his first Communion last
Sunday. The Bishop and Lord Clifford visited the school on
Tuesday afternoon and seemed well pleased with the children.
The religious examination is postponed till Oct. 26th, Wednesday week, in the morning. I am sure you will remember us all on
that day."[13]

Her letters grow very homely and simple and are full of
inquiries for her far-off friends. Her thoughts often dwelt on her

---

[12] Letter 588.
[13] Letter 589.

early days, and the feast of the Presentation carried her back to the wonderful occasion when almighty God had first made Himself known to her as a tiny child.

"I wish you the very happiest of feasts, and I am sure you thank the adorable Trinity for me in an especial manner on this feast of the Presentation, for I always feel that I owe so much to God and our dear Blessed Mother for the great grace that was given to me on this feast day, and my whole soul and heart feels bursting with loving gratitude to our dear good God for all He has done for His poor little worm. I think I did write to you the last, but it appears such a long time since I heard from you that I must write." She then sends love and messages to many friends and closes: "Asking a continuance of your good prayers for all my poor people here and also for myself, and thanking you again and again for all your kindness in the past, begging your prayers and blessing, I remain dear rev. Father your obedient and devoted child

"in the sacred Head and loving Heart
"TERESA HIGGINSON,
"Enfant de Marie, Tertiary of St. Francis.
"L D S."[14]

And now at last the long awaited time was at hand and she was to learn the purpose for which her divine Spouse had led her to this distant, lonely spot.

---

[14] Letter 590.

19

Per Crucem ad Lucem

THE school at Chudleigh broke up early and Teresa had arranged to spend the Christmas holidays at Neston, leaving on the morning of December 14th. She was all ready for the journey; her box was packed; she had given Rough his breakfast and was waiting for the cab to take her to the station, when she was seized with a sudden stroke. When the cab came, she was found lying on the floor, the little dog trying pathetically to rouse her with a bone. The neighbours carried her up to bed. She was fully conscious but quite helpless. Her speech was somewhat affected and her mouth drawn a little to one side, but this soon passed off. Father Dowsett at once wired both to Father Snow and to her sisters. He told them that there was no real danger and that he was arranging for careful attention, and so, as the school at Neston was not yet closed, her sisters decided not to go at once but to wait until she was able to travel and they could bring her home. The doctor hoped she might be well enough to undertake the journey in a few weeks' time. Meanwhile Father Dowsett suggested that the Canon should come and stay with him in order to see her, but it was a busy season and the Canon could not get away.

For a week she was left to the care of the neighbouring women, who were well meaning enough, but quite unskilled in nursing. Then, seeing that further attention was necessary, a nurse was sent for. Father Dowsett himself went into Newton Abbot in search of one and engaged Miss Casey, who was a Catholic. She has described her feelings when first offered the case. It was close on Christmas and great festivities were being planned in the hospital. She was looking forward eagerly to these entertainments and had sent to London for a new blouse for the occasion. It was, not unnaturally, rather a blow to her to be asked to go instead to a lonely cottage in the heart of the country to nurse an unknown patient, one, moreover, whom she had already heard spoken of as an "eccentric old Frump"! She would gladly have refused the case, but her mother persuaded her that it was her duty to accept it, and to her lasting joy she did so. Still, all the way to Chudleigh she nursed her disappointment, until, on reaching the cottage, her better feelings got the upper hand, and she went in with a bright smile determined to think only of her patient. She at once had her reward, for the moment she entered the room a great feeling of awe and reverence came over her, almost as though she had come into the presence of God. All her regrets vanished — rather they were changed into thanksgiving for the wonderful favour which had been bestowed upon her in being allowed to tend one whom she felt to be so near to God. Later, on Christmas Day, Teresa asked her if she regretted the festivities she had missed, and on being assured that she would not resign her post for all the pleasures of the world, Teresa smilingly told her she had known of her struggle and had begged our Lord to make it up to her. Then she added that, although leaving herself entirely in the hands of God to arrange for her as He knew best, she had asked Him to send her a Catholic nurse and one who knew and loved Him, and as soon as Miss Casey came into the room she felt her prayer had been answered.

The nurse found her patient in a sadly neglected condition. She had not been washed or her bed made, nor had her room been dusted since she was taken ill a week before. She had been carried down to the sitting–room and an old towel horse put by her bed to keep off the draughts. Teresa said no word of complaint and insisted that nothing should be done for her until nurse had first had some tea. Then only would she allow herself to be made comfortable. Nurse soon set things right and made the room cosy, borrowing a screen from Lord Clifford's house and covering the table with a dainty little cloth made by Teresa herself.

Father Dowsett was very attentive and brought the Communion when he could, but he was lame and not able to manage the distance very often. Her longing for Communion was intense and during the night nurse would hear her say repeatedly: "Oh when will He come, when will He be here?" After receiving the blessed Sacrament she would be completely unconscious of her surroundings, sometimes for hours. At first nurse, not understanding, would gently rouse her and she obeyed as simply as a child. She had no wishes of her own. Her one thought was the will of her divine Spouse, and when Canon Snow wrote to her that it was her duty to do all in her power to get well in order to do more for God, she readily obeyed to the smallest detail. The doctor ordered her nourishing food, and tempting delicacies were sent her from Lord Clifford's house. She took whatever nurse gave her without a word, but the unaccustomed food merely produced the most violent indigestion, and both nurse and doctor were much puzzled until she at last explained. The doctor said he had never seen anyone so childlike, and Mrs. Statt, the nurse's sister, who came over to visit her, said she could not help feeling all the time that she was in the presence of a beautiful innocent little child. Mrs. Statt loved to sit and talk with her. One day she was speaking of her house in Newton Abbot and Teresa told her that she had once been passing that very house and been impelled to stop and pray for its inmates, feeling sure she would some day be brought into touch with them. She had stood outside while she said a decade of the rosary. Mrs. Statt, like Teresa, was a tertiary of St. Francis, and when Teresa happened to say that in case of her death she had no habit in which to be buried, having already given away three in succession,

Mrs. Statt gladly promised to give her hers should she require it first.

Another visitor was Father Dawson, the priest from Teignmouth, who had made her acquaintance when she took the children there for an outing. He was at once impressed with her saintliness and when she was taken ill went to see her. For a long time he sat beside her and they talked of holy things, and he said afterwards that he had learnt many lessons from her and was loath to leave. Among other things she told him was that at one time she used to pray for suffering, feeling she could not live without it, "But now", she added, "I do not feel like that. I just take whatever our Lord sends."

At first the patient seemed to make rapid progress. Father Dowsett wrote to her sister: "There is a still further improvement in your sister's condition. She has, of course, to be kept very quiet, but she is bright and cheery. It is best not to let her know how ill she is at present."

On December 26th nurse wrote to Canon Snow: "Deo gratias she is getting much better and the doctor is very pleased at the rapid progress she is making. She wishes me to tell you that our Lord has sent her every comfort, screens, curtains, etc. everything to make her cosy and keep out the draughts. She is so touched with the loving sympathy of the little children and their parents. Everyone has been so kind and considerate."

During the following night she took a turn for the worse, and nurse sent a hurried line to Canon Snow:

"7 a.m. There is a decided change in her since I wrote your letter. The use of her limbs is quite gone again for the present. She has had a very bad night. I don't wish to alarm you but she certainly appears worse than I have seen her yet. I am just sending a note to Fr Dowsett asking him to come at once. If there is another change for the worse, I will wire immediately."

Father Dowsett came up and gave her the last Sacraments, some of the older girls being brought in to assist at the ceremony. On January 6th nurse wrote again:

"It will comfort you to know that Miss Higginson is much better. There was a marvellous change in her since she received Extreme Unction and holy Viaticum, which Fr Dowsett administered early on the Wednesday morning that I wrote to you. Our Lord has again restored the use of her limbs. She was able to use her hands almost immediately after the reception of the holy Sacraments. Deo gratias."

Canon Snow replied:

"Your welcome letter with the good news came on Saturday night and I am very grateful to you for writing. I trust Miss Higginson will now speedily get better and be able to travel. You will be sorry to part from her but you must comfort yourself with having made so good a friend and thank our Lord for what He has done for you through her. She will not forget you. Tell her I both sympathise with her and congratulate her: sympathise with her because the going home day is deferred, and congratulate with her because she will have further time to do more for her Spouse and merit more for herself."

She continued to improve slowly and her sisters were very anxious to get her home, but the doctor was afraid to risk the long journey and it was proposed that nurse should first take her for a little change to Teignmouth.

But again she seemed to fail and Miss Casey wrote on January 16th:

"Miss Higginson is not nearly so well again. She has been suffering very acute pains in the head since last Thursday 12th, and it affects her eyes so that I am obliged to keep the room almost in perpetual darkness. She cannot even bear the fire in at night, for the glare, although shaded by a screen, seems to make her as she says seasick. The doctor says the heart is much weaker and is the cause of these severe pains in the head. It prevents her from sleeping. She can neither sleep night nor day."

These fearful sufferings in the head were no doubt allowed to be her final offering for the promotion of the great Devotion whose Apostle she was sent to be.

This state of things continued until the 31st when nurse again wrote:

"She is still very up and down. One day the tiniest bit stronger and the next down at the lowest. She has had one or two very bad turns since I wrote before asking permission to move to Teignmouth, and at present her heart is in such a weak state and her nerves are so unstrung that I doubt that we shall have to postpone our going to Teignmouth at least for a few days more... She cannot do anything for herself, but she is not helpless. She has recovered from the seizure but it has left her nervous system in a frightfully weak state. She cannot bear now the least sound and light is a torture to her. She suffers acute pain in the head and flatulence is another great trouble to her."

Her physical sufferings were visible to all. Of her spiritual trials none can tell. She could not write and she never spoke of them, but it is evident that they continued to the end. A great sadness would at times come over her and she seemed quite changed, so that nurse was sure she must be sharing the sufferings of our Lord in His agony, or taking on herself the punishment of other souls. She would implore for prayers saying again and again: "Oh why do you not continue to pray for me. Do pray for me", and one day Father Dowsett came out of her room after hearing her confession in deep distress saying: "The poor soul is suffering terribly. Go in and try to comfort her", but human consolation was of small avail. She was the "Spouse of the Crucified". Our Lord had brought her to this far off lonely spot to accompany Him on His way of the Cross, and where else could it lead her save to the summit of Calvary?

All her life she had begged our Lord most earnestly to remove all external signs of the great favours He had bestowed upon her and her prayer was granted, for no outward marvels marked the course of her last illness. Even the marks of the sacred Stigmata were withdrawn and nurse knew nothing of them. The only thing she noticed was the reserved way in which Teresa shook hands. She never allowed more than the tips of her fingers to be taken, and this struck both Miss Casey and her sister as very strange in one who was so warm–hearted. She was often rapt in prayer and a wonderful atmosphere of sanctity seemed to radiate from her, but that was all. Even the Devil appeared to have little power, though he still came at times to torment her. Nurse relates how one night he kept throwing water over Teresa's bed. Time after time she woke up to find her patient's coverings all wet. She was completely mystified until Teresa explained to her that it was only the Devil trying to annoy her. Nurse, with not unnatural impatience, exclaimed: "Well I wish he would go to sleep and let us get a little sleep too!" "My dear, he never sleeps", said Teresa with a smile.

Meanwhile rooms had been engaged at Teignmouth, but both Father Dowsett and the doctor doubted the wisdom of moving her. The former wrote to Father Snow:

"Feb. 4th. I do not think Miss Higginson is quite well enough for a day or two to take the journey to Teignmouth. Is there a possibility of your being able to come down here and see her within the next few days? I should be very pleased to put you up. I will let you know how things progress. Her heart is so very uncertain and I am consulting the doctor as to the possibility of Miss Higginson being removed without any danger of catching a chill, as the weather is not very propitious here. Please do not think I want to interfere with any arrangements made for Miss Higginson. The truth is that Lord Clifford and I are under a great obligation to Miss Higginson for all she has done, and I could not risk her being removed unless the doctor not only gave the permission but really advised the removal. I am sending for the doctor to ask him to call and see me, then I will telegraph you the result. I think Miss Higginson would far prefer your opinion than even that of her sister. This is my reason for writing to you. I could not in a letter tell you all the circumstances of the case. I do not think there is any danger of death, but such a valuable life deserves all the care and consideration that those who know Miss Higginson can possibly give.

"Yours truly H. J. DOWSETT."

Canon Snow was unable to accept Father Dowsett's invitation as he had just lost his own brother and could not get away. The nurse knew how Teresa would have rejoiced to see him and sympathised with her on her disappointment, but Teresa seemed almost surprised at the idea of being disappointed at anything that happened to her. "My dear", she said, "how can I be disappointed at anything our dear Lord sends to me? He is Wisdom and Love and I can only press His hands a little closer in mine and say, 'Dear Lord Thou knowest best'."

Love of God's holy Will was in truth the keynote of her sanctity. It was no mere question of submitting to His Will: since her Mystical Marriage she knew no other will but His. This was the great lesson she taught her nurse during those last weeks of her earthly life. "My dear", she said again and again, "Love the Will of God and you will enjoy heaven on earth." In everything she saw the hand of God. Nothing was too small or trivial to speak of Him. She who had been allowed to hear the things that it is not given to man to utter: who had seen our Lord revealed in glory, could equally discover Him in the most commonplace details of everyday life. If a little child came to the door, she saw the Infant Jesus; when the lamp was lighted, it spoke to her of the light of His countenance; even when the kettle boiled over, she thought of the overflowing of His love. In the same way everything had to be done for His sake; and nurse found that no matter how good and apparently important a work she might be doing, it must be promptly set aside for the smallest duty, until under Teresa's gentle guidance she came to understand that it was not the work itself but the fulfilling of God's holy Will which was the one thing necessary. And so, after nearly sixty years of heroic sanctity, Teresa had reached the pinnacle of perfection — that spoken of by our Lord Himself, for she, the teacher of little children, had herself become as a little child and was at last ready to enter into the Kingdom of Heaven.

On February 9th she said goodnight to her nurse with special tenderness, thanking her for all her devoted care. "Do not fear, dear child", she said, "but put your hand with loving confidence into your Father's Hand and He will guide you safely through every path, and where the road is rough and stony He will carry you in His arms."

They were her last words. About midnight nurse noticed that her breathing had become very quick and laboured, and asked if she were feeling ill. Receiving no reply, she got up and went to her. Teresa was unconscious and completely paralysed. The nurse called up the caretaker and sent for the doctor, but when he came he said there was nothing more that could be done. In the morning Father Dowsett wired to Canon Snow:

"10.21. Feb. 10. Patient unconscious. Sudden relapse. Can you come?"

The Canon could not get away, but her sister Louisa started at once and on her arrival wrote to him:

"Teresa is still unconscious in an uncertain heavy drowsy sleep and then apparently not breathing at all. God has been so good to her that I trust she may be spared to travel home. Unless the good God intervenes in some miraculous way, she cannot last very long. The doctor shook his head this morning and said he was not looking for this new development... Teresa does not take any nourishment. Of course she cannot. I hope consciousness may return to her before I have to return. Her teeth are clenched together and she looks so livid... The nurse is a little body and so devoted. Fr. Dowsett honoured me as her sister by sending a groom to meet me for which I was very thankful although there was a bus at the station."

On the 18th she wrote: "Tess is still unconscious although at times she seems to have lucid intervals and will press your hand although she has not known me yet."

Nurse also thought she had glimmerings of consciousness. It had been her habit every night to anoint her five senses with holy water saying at the same time the prayers for the last anointing:

"By this holy anointing and by the Cross and Passion of our Lord Jesus Christ and the prayers of the Church, pardon me all the sins I have committed by my eyes, ears, etc." After she became unconscious nurse continued to do this for her, and when it came to the anointing of the palms, the hands would open and a sweet smile came over her face as though she understood and were grateful, but when spoken to she showed no signs of consciousness.

Miss Louisa wrote to Canon Snow telling him not to come, as he could do nothing for the patient in her present condition, and promising to wire to him if she showed any sign of coming to herself. On the 14th she sent a card: "No change; there was a slight improvement but not maintained today. Sleeps and breathes loudly and fitfully."

On the 15th it became obvious that the end was near, and Father Dowsett wired in the afternoon: "Patient dying. Cannot last long."

About five o'clock the last struggle began. Her face took on an expression of the most intense agony and there were continual convulsive movements of her mouth as though she were undergoing terrible sufferings in her soul. Her face every now and then became livid and distorted and her breathing was loud and laboured. Her sister and the nurse knelt beside her saying the rosary, litanies and prayers for the dying, and sprinkling her frequently with holy water, but she made no sign when they spoke to her. For six long hours she lingered thus until, at ten minutes past eleven, her beloved Lord came at last to clasp his faithful Spouse in His own everlasting embrace.

"The end came unexpectedly", wrote Louisa, "although we were looking for it all day. Sister never regained consciousness, and it was God's almighty Providence that she was in that state, for she suffered terribly."

The nurse also said that never before or since had she seen so heartrending a death agony, or one that lasted so long.

The secret of those last hours is her own. All that we may guess of them is that the "Spouse of the Crucified", who had clung so closely to our Lord through life, was allowed to follow Him unto death — even the death of the Cross.

Nurse had promised Teresa that in the event of her death no other hands should touch her and so now, unaided, she performed the last offices and laid her out in the brown habit of St. Francis, given as arranged by Mrs. Statt. It seemed as though even after death Teresa would claim nothing for her own. Her body was carried into the school where the children and their parents came to pray beside her. Many of them still remember the beauty of her face, for the look of suffering she wore at first gradually gave way to one of peace and happiness. A delicate tinge of colour came into her cheeks and she looked so lifelike that they hesitated to close the coffin, doubting if she were really dead. Louisa wrote: "Sister is looking more like herself. She had such a suffering look but now she is changing." And on the following day she said: "The undertaker has brought the shell and Sister looks happy. I would like her to be left in the church over night and buried on Tuesday morning. As she is in a shell, it will not matter. There is no smell of death about her and no discolouration."

It was arranged that she should be taken back to Neston in Cheshire and buried in her mother's grave.

When all was over, Nurse Casey[1] sent a long account to Canon Snow, to which he replied as follows:

"ORMSKIRK.
"8. 3. 05.

"MY DEAR MISS CASEY,

"I cannot thank you enough for the very full account you have sent me, and this too when you were ill in bed. I expected this was the cause of the delay. I trust you are now well enough for

---

[1]   Miss Casey is now a Poor Clare at Lynton in Devonshire.

work again. Alternate work and suffering and prayer is excellent discipline for the soul.

"Miss Higginson desired that her death might as far as possible resemble Our Lord's. Hence the desolation she suffered. That she might endure this desolation, He hid from her that she was going to die. Had she known that He was about to take her to Himself, so great would have been her joy that the most intense bodily pain and any other suffering would have been as nothing. All during her life He permitted her to participate in His Passion and it was fitting for her own greater reward and for the good of the Church and of souls that her death should be in suffering and not in consolation. You say in one place she clung to the hope she was going to get better and teach again. This was simply impossible. She had reached the highest degree of union it is possible for a soul to reach on earth and a soul in such a state cannot cling to anything but the Will of God. The Will of God and the will of the soul are one. But as I have said, our Lord concealed from her that she was going to die, and when someone about her said she would get better, then no doubt she would consider it her duty to get better as soon as possible, and, if Teignmouth was to do her good, to get there without delay. This was not undue eagerness.

"I am not in any sorrow about her death. Immediately I got the telegram I went into the church and, standing in the sanctuary, I said the Te Deum with great fervour and consolation thanking our Lord for all the marvellous graces He bestowed upon her and for her glory and happiness. I have not said one single prayer for her, being sure she is in heaven. Knowing all I do about her, I should feel I was not doing right by our Lord to imagine she was in Purgatory. Some here have told me that, when they tried to pray for her, they have found themselves praying to her. Nor do I feel any sense of loss, for I feel her nearer to me now than when she was at Biddlecombe."

And so at last the work for which our Lord had called her to Chudleigh was done, and in the darkness of a winter's morning, when the ground was white with snow, her earthly remains were taken home.

"The ground was white with snow at Biddlecombe", wrote Miss Louisa, "when we left at seven o'clock to drive the seven miles to Newton Abbott. We just had a hearse and one coach and a wagonette to take the seven carriers back, as we could not find men on the estate. Lady Clifford is abroad, but she ordered a beautiful cross of arum lilies and bunches of violets and her card attached. His Lordship came home late on Sunday evening, but he allowed us to travel through the park as it shortened the distance considerably. She was shown every mark of respect, and kind large–hearted Fr Dowsett would have liked her to have lain amongst them. Mass was said for her every day and this week also. I must tell you things more fully if ever I have the pleasure of seeing you. Sister and I at Newton Abbott were placed in a separate coach and we never left it till we reached Neston. We were several times hitched off and left for a short time. I had all her luggage placed in the carriage with me... We had only a float and a cab at Neston as the distance is so short, and she was taken straight to the church. Fr Thompson was very kind. Mass was at eight–thirty, and after Father Thompson had breakfasted, she was interred."

Thus was this great servant of God laid to her rest, simply and unnoticed even as she would have wished, her sisters and the faithful Margaret alone with her at the last. And surely her humility has been satisfied to the full, as she lies hidden in her mother's grave awaiting the good pleasure of her divine Spouse who in time of trial had said to her:

"Take courage my loved One for the Seat of divine Wisdom shall be praised, known and adored as I wish, and I will glorify My Name in thee."

20

Canon Snow's Testimony

CANON SNOW was Teresa's old and trusted friend. For over twenty years he had been her spiritual father and director and she had laid bare to him all the secrets of her heart and soul. Who could speak of her with deeper knowledge or with greater truth? His testimony can scarcely be ignored and this is what he says:

"At the very forefront of these observations I think it right to say that I have the firm conviction that Teresa was not only a saint but also one of the greatest saints almighty God has ever raised up in His Church. The grounds of this conviction will appear in the course of the observations I feel it my duty to make.

"I became her director in September 1883, hearing her confession for the first time on the 14th day of that month, and remaining her director until her death on the 15th of February 1906. She went to confession to other priests according to convenience but was under vow of obedience to me and to best of my knowledge and belief never sought any direction in any one particular concerning her soul and temporal affairs from any other priest. At this time she was in that degree of union known as the Mystical Espousals. This took place, as she describes in letter 39, on the feast of the Sacred Heart 1874. In this degree the soul is being prepared for the Mystical Marriage and this took place on the 24th Oct. 1887. St. Teresa fully describes the sufferings the soul has to undergo in this period, and mystical theology teaches that the higher is the union with God in the Mystical Marriage, so much the longer has the preparation to be and the more intense must be the purifications and sufferings. We have here the long period of over thirteen years in which this highly favoured soul was being prepared by prayer and constant suffering of all kinds for the highest degree of union a soul can attain on earth. Our b. Lord allowed her frequently to participate in His Passion and especially in every Lent for very many years before her death. This participation in His sufferings our Lord made known to her was not only in expiation for sin and for the ends for which He Himself suffered, but was also purification for further union with Him. How great then must have been her holiness when she received the wonderful favour of her Mystical Marriage.

"Then again, although the Mystical Marriage is the highest state of union a soul can attain in this life, still God is able to communicate Himself more and more to the soul, and the soul can more and more advance in holiness and merit. Now Teresa lived seventeen years and nearly four months after the Mystical Marriage. During this long period of closest union with her Divine Spouse she lived the same life of constant prayer, suffering, participation in the Passion and work for God. Who shall put a limit to her perfection and holiness?

"Once more, in a letter written to her confessor on the 27th Apr. 1880 describing a manifestation our Lord had made to her concerning the devotion to the sacred Head, she wrote: 'Our beloved Spouse' (He then quotes letter 36, p. 107 relating to the soul she so often saw in vision and continues): I have copied this passage in full because I take it to be a divine revelation of her perfection at the time it was written (April 1880) and I add what must have been her perfection at the time of the Mystical Marriage which took place more than seven years afterwards, and what at the time of her death which took place nearly twenty–five years after."[1]

---

[1] "Observations on the life of the Servant of God, Teresa Higginson", by Canon Snow.

Such a statement cannot be lightly set aside. But Canon Snow points out that Teresa was essentially a contemplative and not an active saint. She never did any great outward work. She was always weak and feeble and suffered without ceasing — truly meriting her title of "Spouse of the Crucified". Both he and Father Powell fully expected that great miracles would take place in proof of the Devotion and of her own sanctity, but they learnt that the ways of God are not as those of men, and he goes on to say: "In any place in which she stayed many interesting and edifying incidents took place such as what I may call little miracles and miraculous answers to prayer, and these would be known only to a few and they kept the knowledge to themselves. Such things would make interesting and devout reading but would as it were be out of proportion to the greatness of her sanctity and the work she did for God, the Church and souls as a mystic and as revealed in her writings. I do not know that anything happened anywhere that attracted public attention. This seems to me to be according to the design of God in her regard acting in great part through her profound, and I may say *abject* humility. Remember that our Lord was spoken of as the 'most abject of men'. She looked upon herself as the vilest wretch on earth and was willing to be treated as such."[2]

As the years went on, this hidden aspect of her life grew more and more pronounced. Even the little miracles which happened so often at Wigan and at Bootle became less frequent. It was the same with her ecstasies. At one time she might almost have been said to live in a continual state of ecstasy, but from the great day of her Mystical Marriage all the outward marvels became more and more rare, until towards the end of her life they seem practically to have ceased. It was as though, having attained such perfect union with our Lord Himself, even the choicest of His favours faded into insignificance.

---

[2] "Observations on the life of the Servant of God, Teresa Higginson", by Canon Snow.

But although Almighty God willed that while on earth she should remain hidden from the eyes of men, He has so provided that in His own good time this priceless work of His hands may be made known. Few of the saints have left so full a revelation of their souls as is contained in the series of letters written under obedience to her directors. They are mines of wealth and would supply many volumes on the spiritual life, whether from the mystical, ascetical or psychological aspect. Canon Snow treasured them most carefully, for he was convinced that it would be principally by their means that the great object of her life, the establishment of the Devotion to the Sacred Head, would be brought about. He never tried to bring her forward: even after her death he made no effort to vindicate her name or to make her sanctity known, but was content to leave things in the hands of God. That Almighty God is never in a hurry was, he said, a lesson he had learnt long ago, and he perceived no clear indication that the time had come when, according to His promise, our Lord would glorify the name of His chosen Spouse. But that this would happen he never for a moment doubted, and towards the end of his life the old man loved to linger on her memory and could scarcely speak of her without tears.

Teresa's letters are no great models of human culture — her style is often faulty, she pays small heed to punctuation, and her words even are not infrequently misspelt, yet these writings have been submitted to many priests and others learned in mystical theology, and all are agreed that the knowledge and understanding they display are beyond that of the most wise, and could come from God alone. She seldom made use of books. At one time she thought that by reading the works of some of the greater saints she might be able to explain herself more easily to her confessor, but our Lord showed her that this was not His holy Will. She wrote to Father Powell:

"JUNE 1880.

"I think the reason our dear b. Lord makes it impossible for me to read is that I may not be disheartened in reading of what the saints have done for His greater honour and glory and the salvation of souls. Besides you will perhaps remember me asking you for some book, if there was any, about the great favours that our dear Lord bestows on me that I might be better able to put in words what I want to express, and my Lord and my God greatly rebuked me for doing so saying: 'In what have I been wanting to you?' Oh my Jesus, Thou hast given me all things good in abundance, for Thou givest Thyself and in Thee is all perfection and infinite treasures of wealth and I have drunk freely of the waters of life and eaten of the good fruit of knowledge. And our dear b. Lord, knowing my excessive wretchedness and misery, has compassion on my weakness and teaches me Himself those things He wishes me to know, and even when others read out, I seldom know anything of what they read... I never did make spiritual reading a part of my daily exercise. The Crucifix is the Book of books and to me the Tree of Life and contains never ending volumes: and it is from this book He has taught me what I know, and from the holy tabernacle He has spoken and filled me when hungry with good things beyond description. I don't think I have ever heard of Sister Emma Rick without you mean Emma's Cross and that I have never read but know the name well, but I am so stupid that, if I could read, it would avail me little. (He had probably asked her if she had read the revelations of Anne Catherine Emmerich!) And I have always felt that our dear b. Lord did not wish me to read or He would have enabled me to so. And when on several occasions Fr Wells gave me hymns to say as a penance that I did not know, if our dear b. Lord had not said them for me, I could not have fulfilled the requirements of the Sacrament, and I told Fr Wells I could not say my penance. He told me to ask our Lord to help me and He did so but I never told Fr Wells how: I don't know whether he knew or not, he certainly knew many things which I never told him."[3]

---

[3] Letter 54.

It is impossible in the space of one short book to do more than sketch in the bold outlines of this wonderful life, but a few words may be added to throw some slight lights and shades on the portrait. Much could, and no doubt will, be written about her striking personality and virtues, but no mere description can compare with the living and convincing picture so unconsciously unveiled in the sublime simplicity of her own writings.

It is clear that the great aim of her life, the end for which it would appear that almighty God had sent her into this world, was the promotion of the Devotion to the Sacred Head of our Lord, the Seat of the divine Wisdom. All her prayers, all her sufferings, tended towards this one object, and our Lord gave her to understand that this would become a great devotion in the Church and be a sure means of bringing England back to the ancient faith. It was in England, in the dark days of persecution, that the sacred Heart was first preached by the Ven. Claude de la Colombiere, and it must be a matter of great thankfulness and hope to us that it should be in England, and through English lips, that our Lord has chosen to make this fresh revelation of His Wisdom and His love. May it be perhaps that the untiring fight the Catholics in England have waged for the preservation of their schools has won for them this singular favour from almighty God, and that it is in reward for the heroism of the teachers, who for so long bore the heat and burden of the day, that He has chosen His special messenger from among their ranks? And if, with the blessing of God, Teresa's fervent prayers and hopes bear fruit, it is to the poor and humble streets of one of our great industrial centres that we must go to find the spot selected by our Lord for this manifestation of His divine Will.

Meanwhile the mustard seed to which He likened the Devotion still remains hidden in the earth, but signs are not wanting that it has taken root and, watered by the approval of the Church, we may hope that it will soon develop into a mighty tree. Teresa herself laboured hard to sow the seed and she often marvelled how our Lord could delay so long the fulfilment of

His great desire, but as her life drew on she learnt that time is swallowed up in His eternity, and she too was content to wait. After her Mystical Marriage she wrote:

"I ask Him most earnestly for the spread of the Devotion, for this seems to be His adorable Will (yet without that eagerness and burning desire which I used to experience), in a calm and trusting manner, knowing His time and manner is best, without any anxiety concerning it, feeling confident of its spread and success, that it is God's work and God's holy Will and it must be done. Feeling as though it were already accomplished, yet offering myself as a willing sacrifice in what way soever He shall desire."[4]

Her last mention of the Devotion in her letters is on the day appointed for the celebration of the feast four years before her death. From that time, in this as in all else, she withdraws from the eyes of men, hidden in her perfect union with her divine Spouse.

There is no need to enlarge on Teresa's devotion to the Blessed Sacrament. It was the life of both soul and body, and the miraculous way in which our Lord fulfilled her longings has already been described. A priest who knew nothing of her was once giving Communion at Lydiate, when he found the Host had left his fingers. He was very startled, fearing he had dropped It, when he saw It entering the mouth of a little woman dressed in black. He was so upset that he spoke of the occurrence to another priest, who exclaimed: "Oh, that must have been Miss Higginson!"

In one of her letters she describes how the very thought of our Lord's presence threw her into ecstasy as she was changing the curtains on the tabernacle:

"When I went to change the tabernacle curtains — you know far better than I can tell the adoring awe that naturally creeps over one when they stand face to face with the veiled Creator of the world, when we enter the circle where cherubim and sera-

---

[4]   Letter 281.

phim lie prostrate in wonder and silent admiration. With them I
bent in profound adoration, but love and desire seemed to fill my
whole being and I forgot my own nothingness and misery as I
gazed upon His s. Head beaming with the ethereal light of God's
eternal day and His sacred Heart glowing as a burning fire with
its consuming flame. I know not what I saw, for I was lost in the
excess of His infinite Wisdom and boundless Love, and I remained for some time with the curtains in my hand quite unconscious of all save Him who drew me as it were entirely into
Himself. (This had not happened for more than a fortnight before) and since I have felt inflamed with a desire to die or waste
away my poor life in furthering this desire of His sacred Heart.
Oh that I had the tongue of men and angels that I might proclaim
every day and at all times this burning desire of the God of all
power wisdom and knowledge."[5]

Someone once asked her if she had ever seen our Lord and she
answered Yes, that in former years she used to see Him with her
corporeal eyes, but that such visions were lower in kind and far
more subject to illusion than the intellectual ones she was granted later.

Frequent as were her ecstasies, Canon Musseley is the only
one among her friends who claimed to have seen her actually
raised in the air, but that this did happen is clear from her own
letters, where she describes her sensations on such occasions:

"SEPT. 20 79

"I have written twice this week a private letter but have each
time destroyed it for I know not how to express what I heard or
saw. The only thing I can say is it is beyond the power of human
intellect to comprehend, for all the powers of the soul and senses
of the body are lost in God. I spoke to you about this before and
I have been afraid of it, though this time I did not try to resist as
I had done before, and this I think was pleasing to our Lord (as
you told me to give myself entirely into His Hands to do with me
what He pleased), for He filled me with unspeakable delight,

---

[5]   Letter 82.

and yet I think I was much wanting in confidence, for I was much terrified at finding myself raised up as I told you before. I mean that at first I knew I was being raised up and I was greatly humbled when I felt His infinite power, and He seemed to kindle a fresh flame of love within me which seemed to consume everything that was not for Him. Then He seemed to draw me entirely into Himself as a drop of rain is lost in the waters of the mighty ocean, so does it seem here with the soul etc., but we cannot say for we do not know what God then allows us to enjoy, but the good effects are very great, for we become much more disengaged from all things here. Our Lord also takes away all the strength of the body and I remained very weak and hardly myself for two whole days."[6]

"I told you I think that I could not write on Thursday evening, for I was about to write as you desired me when our Lord surprised me as it were by drawing me up into Himself as a little bit of paper is carried up by a mighty wind. So at times He carries me up, drawing my poor soul into His very essence or as one drop of water mingles with and is lost in great waters of the ocean, and the body too is raised and I know at the time that it is being raised; and I used to dread this immensely, but I see now so clearly it is folly to try to resist, and the sweetness that fills even the poor body if we give ourselves entirely into His hands that I have learnt to say, 'Lord I am Thine, do with me what Thou wilt'. It seemed to me at these times that the soul really left the body, she was in such agony (though filled with delight and sweetness) and remained cold and stiff and unable to move for so long afterwards, but you know better and I submit to what you say. I know not what I saw or heard. I think the whole being is lost in God at these times, and afterwards our dear b. Lord shows us by degrees what He then teaches the soul. And she is so filled with the majesty and greatness, the wisdom and beauty of God that those great desires and impetuosities that fill the soul make this life a continual death. Oh my Father, do you think He

---

[6]   Letter 15.

will leave me here very long? I wish only His holy Will but He only knows how I sigh and long for His eternal possession, and yet I cannot really wish to die, for in death I know I could not suffer for Him nor merit for those souls for which He died."[7]

Again she says:

"Oh great and almighty One, who can withstand Thy majesty and resist Thy power, for we are as a kite in the air or matchwood in the torrent. What Thou willest must be, yet I beg of Thee to remember that I am but dust and ashes and to take pity and compassion on my misery and nothingness. Today it has pleased our dear b. Lord to confer one of those great favours on me that I have before spoken of and He has shown me in some manner the glory that He would receive through the Devotion to the seat of Divine Wisdom, and He filled me with such a love and desire of Himself that my body was raised: I could perceive it though I tried not to resist, yet I always have such an unspeakable fear at these times."[8]

She never mentioned these supernatural favours except under obedience, but her friends, who often loved to tease her a little, would sometimes try to trap her into speaking of them unawares. Some of them once spoke of being raised in ecstasy and casually asked Teresa a question about it. She quite innocently replied: "Yes it is a most strange sensation", and then suddenly drew herself up, realising how she had given herself away.

Teresa's love of our blessed Lady shines forth in all her letters. Among them is a long account of the Seven Dolours which would furnish grounds for many meditations. The following needs no comment:

> "AMDG et in hon BVM et ST J
> "Bootle, Aug. 20 81
> "Feast of St. Bernard

"DEAR REV. FATHER,

---

[7] Letter 36

[8] Letter 58.

"In the holy Name of Jesus and Mary and in obedience I write of that glory etc. which our dear b. Lord has shown me respecting His ever Immaculate virgin Mother.

"Oh my Father, how can I tell of that which cherubim and seraphim cannot comprehend, and it seems to me that it is only the rays (from the sun as it were) of her glory that they feel and yet they are overwhelmed with awe, wonder, admiration and love, at the excessive power and majesty and beauty with which the adorable Trinity have clothed their Queen — As the heavens are above the earth, so is the glory and majesty of Mary above the highest of God's creatures, and their beauty fades almost to nothingness beside her. For in the very instant of her Immaculate Conception, she far exceeded the cherubim and seraphim in knowledge, love and every perfection, and each breath she drew, every motion and action of her whole life and being was one of next to infinite homage, adoration, and profoundest knowledge and love; each beating of her heart was an immeasurable height and depth of perfection, and all the love and perfection of all the angels and saints united in one would not reach to her perfection at her birth.

"At different times I have seen her under different titles — as Queen of Angels — Queen of Martyrs — Queen of Virgins — Queen of All Saints — as Virginal Mother of the King of kings — as our most powerful Advocate and Comforter of the afflicted, and each title has a world of glory peculiar to itself and far beyond any description I can give; but if it seems that no tongue of angel or man can express, or mind conceive, the glory which God has prepared for us poor miserable creatures who try to love Him, what is to be said of that of her who is crowned and adorned by the Eternal Father as His Daughter, by the Coeternal Son as His Mother, and the Holy Spirit as His Spouse. Oh Tabernacle of the adorable Trinity, Thou art so closely united to God so as we cannot go down into the deep depths of Thy Dolours — for whose sorrow is like unto thine, for it was lost in the eternity of God, for it was as an ocean without limit, for God was its centre its cause and its end — so now that your sorrow is turned into joy, who can tell the glory, power and beauty which are thine, for you are clad in the majesty and splendour of the triune God, and, great and rich and almighty as God is, there is not anything He could give thee more than what He has. Thou art above all others and next to the King in a vesture of gold and sparkling crystals; thou dost shine in the brightness of eternal light and the brilliancy of His countenance is upon thee, Thou art far above the angelic choirs, for you are their Queen and Queen of All Saints, thou art Mistress of the Apostles and Queen of Prophets, for whose knowledge of God approaches to thine? Thou art Queen of Virgins, oh Virgin Mother of our Redeemer, and thou art our Mother, and God has laid up His treasures in thee and He will give whatsoever thou desirest. Ah well may the Psalmist cry in admiring wonder: 'Who is she that cometh up from the wilderness laden with (delights) and leaning on her beloved?' For you are the vine laden and bending under the weight of its rich grapes. You are the Lily in which He delights and the mystic Rose whose perfume He exults in. You are the Apple of His eye — the first fruits of His redemption, the Cedar from which He built His living Temple. Is she not the high rock in whose cave He has made his nest and the Garden in which He loves to repose? Is she not the land overflowing with milk and honey, and the Ark of God's Covenant with man even in the Garden of Paradise. You are the good Tree whose fruit is Jesus. Surely thou art the honeycomb of Samson, Thou art a tower of strength against the face of the enemy, for thy foundations are in the mountain heights, thy walls of adamantine and thy gates of diamond, gold and pearl, Thou art truly the City of God in which He holds His court. Thou art the dispenser of His gifts. His dying Gift upon the Cross.

"Oh adorable Trinity, I return Thee everlasting thanks for all Thou hast done in and for Mary, and Jesus, my beloved Jesus, I thank Thee far more than I can tell for making Your Mother mine. And grant that for all eternity, with the angels and saints, we may praise and bless Thee and may gaze on that beautiful loving face, so full of glory, so full of grace.

"Our dear b. Lady was represented to me in her glorified body, not that I could notice her exact appearance, only I knew or understood that she was there in person. I experienced such a love and admiration and astonishment at the excess of glory and knowledge, wisdom and love which was hers that I could not if I had wished describe or form a picture of her in her corporal form. It was her wisdom and knowledge and therefore her love for God and God's goodness to her that was most impressed upon the soul, and I felt that Jesus was so proud of the work of His hand, and I felt something of that glory that she rendered to the adorable Trinity. How They loved and how she loved."[9]

Teresa had a great devotion to the holy Angels, especially our guardian Angels. It grieved her that they are so little thought of and she loved her own angel and made use of him in many ways. She would send him on messages and communicate through him with her confessor or others at a distance. Sometimes he would replace her at table when she did not wish to eat, as has already been told. Mrs. Fleck relates a little incident that happened on their travels in Italy: "When we were leaving Venice she mislaid her rosary ring and when we got seated in the gondola she seemed rather anxious over the loss, and I was trying to help her to remember where she had it last, but she said: 'Don't be disturbed. I will ask my good angel and, unless the person deliberately keeps it, he will restore it.' A few minutes afterwards she drew my attention to the lap of her dress, and there was the ring right enough. She said, 'I felt it fall and there it is.'"

Another incident is told by one of the nuns at New Hall who had known her as a child.

"When Miss Higginson came here on July 22 1897, I was still in the noviceship, so knew nothing about her coming till late on in the day and I only received leave to see her about 5 o'clock.

---

[9]   Letter 109.

When I entered the room, she was standing facing a large picture of our Lady with her back to the window. She did not move when I entered (the door was on the side of the picture), so I said, 'I don't suppose you know me?' She answered, 'Of course I do, you are —. I knew you were coming in.' I said, 'How did you know?' (because only the portress knew besides the Mistress of novices and she had not told her). She replied, 'I have always honoured some people's guardian angels and you are one of them. He told me you were coming in.'"

The sister gives an interesting description of Teresa's appearance on this occasion:

"She had black silk gloves on, though it was a *very hot* day, and she held my hands in hers very tightly all the time. Her hat was very much over her forehead, and her face was quite *smooth* and *pale*, just like a corpse."

It was the custom at Bootle to toll the church bell when anyone died so that all might join in the de profundis for the departed soul. On one such occasion there was no one about, and Teresa went into the church wondering whether she could ring the bell herself. As she stood there, a little boy came in and, running up the belfry steps, began to ring the bell. Just then Father Powell arrived and asked who it was who was ringing. Teresa answered, "That little boy: it is the little boy who helps me to carry the big candlesticks when I am not able. I often see him kneeling in front of the altar praying."

The bell stopped, but no little boy came down. Father Powell said: "No little boy could carry those candlesticks. It must be an angel or the Child Jesus."

Teresa had a large correspondence, for many people, religious, superiors of convents, etc., wrote to her for advice and help. She treated these letters as absolutely confidential and was always careful to destroy them. When, during her last illness, she could no longer answer them herself, she told her nurse to do so. The nurse asked what she was to say, and Teresa said she was to go upstairs and ask her guardian angel and he would direct her.

And so it happened, for she found herself writing almost without knowing what she wrote, and, curiously enough, she could never afterwards recall any detail of the correspondence, though she always found that these letters brought light and comfort to those for whom they were intended. She noticed too that, though this writing often kept her up till two or three in the morning, it never seemed to cause her the least extra fatigue.

Like all the great saints of God Teresa was consumed with the love of souls, and, as we have seen, she constantly prayed to be allowed to take upon herself the punishment due to the sins of others. There is a letter dated January, 1880, written in the trembling hand which denotes that she was hovering on the verge of ecstasy, in which she says:

"I really do not know how to contain myself, I feel so urged to take upon me the punishment of the sins of those who are not attending the holy mission, that so God may have mercy on them. But Fr Wells told me I must never again do so without permission, and now I ask you to allow me for the love of those souls for which our dear Lord suffered and died. Ah my Jesus, remember the smart of those many wounds and the precious Blood which flowed from them, and all Thou didst endure in soul and mind for them; and Mary, by thy love and zeal and by the pain and sorrow thou didst suffer beneath the Cross, join your sighs and tears with His voice and precious Blood and cry aloud: 'Father forgive them for they know not what they do.' Oh dear Father, I know you will not refuse me when you see I have an opportunity of doing something for Him who has done so much for me. I ask it in the name of Jesus and Mary and that allsaving Blood which He shed for their and our immortal souls. I hardly know whether or not I made an offering of myself for this purpose (but He knows I did not mean to be disobedient if I did), but He has certainly increased the pains I usually suffer — but suffer is not the right word I know, it is so sweet yet so excessive. You I think know what I mean.

"I should have stayed in the church to see you but I felt myself becoming so very weak I thought I had better come out for awhile. If I do not get in again, I know you will say a few words to our dear b. Lord and our holy Mother for me and say good-night to them for me."[10]

Again in 1882 she wrote:

"He let me feel a little of what He who is infinite Purity felt at taking sins of impurity upon Himself, and He who is infinite Truth at clothing Himself with lies and deceits etc. etc. Oh my God, my God, Thou hast shown to me that Thou art the almighty God, the holy and strong God, the God of justice and at the same time the God of wisdom mercy and love, the God of compassion, our Emmanuel. He has shown me too the value of a soul and I feel that to save one I could endure these sufferings for ever, for I know how He loves a soul and I feel that I could go the round of the world proclaiming His wisdom and love and showing the emptiness of worldly joys, the smoke and bubbles after which men run in search of pleasure, and tell that God alone can satisfy the soul or heart of man, for He has made us for Himself and we cannot rest till we rest in Him.

"I feel that there is such a desire for souls eating me up that, if it would profit one anything, I would willingly give up daily holy Communion, and in doing so I feel I should give all I have."[11]

She often took upon herself the physical sufferings of others also. As Rev. Mother at St. Catherine's wrote to Father Snow, she was always offering herself for someone or something.

Margaret's adopted daughter, Kitty, was very ill. She lay for six months at death's door, and Margaret wrote to Teresa begging prayers. Teresa replied: "Kitty will not die yet. It is our blessed Lord's Will that she should still suffer and that she should get better when it shall please our Lord that I should take her sufferings. I will ask Him in due time that I may take her sufferings and sickness."

---

10 Letter 22.
11 Letter 121.

On the 15th of February the invalid was worse than ever. Suddenly she felt all her pain leave her and, though very weak, she was able to get up and put on her clothes. A few hours later a telegram brought the news of Teresa's death.

Teresa had devoted her life to teaching little children. She always laid far more stress on the training of their characters than on the mere imparting of knowledge, and her influence with them was wonderful. She seemed able to read their very hearts and to tell at once if a child were speaking the truth. She could never do enough for them, for she saw in them the infant Jesus. She liked them to have the very best of everything in the way of food and clothes, and often sheltered little waifs from the wet and cold, clothing them with the finest material at her own expense. When remonstrated with on this seemingly unnecessary extravagance, she replied with her sweet smile: "How could I give anything but the very best to the Holy Child?"

She was also devoted to the sick and poor and spent much of her time in visiting them. She would nurse and tend and comfort them in all their troubles, and one of her greatest delights was to cook nice things for them.

As for her own comfort or appearance, as will be readily believed, she cared less than nothing. Very early in life she took a vow of poverty and would henceforth claim nothing for her own. Even the very clothes she wore she looked on as a loan and was always ready to give them to anyone whose need she thought was greater than her own. Her mother used to say: "I don't know what Teresa does with her clothes. Each time she comes home I get her things and when she returns to me she has hardly anything to wear." During her visits to Neston her sisters would try to renovate her wardrobe. Miss Catterall tells how Teresa returned from one such shopping expedition with a new bonnet trimmed with a large ostrich feather. By some strange chance the feather soon got burnt in the gas jet, after which mishap Teresa seemed to take much more kindly to her bonnet!

After her death her sister Louisa wrote: "Nearly all Sister's clothes were missing. I suppose she must have given them away. If she had recovered, I don't know what she would have done."

Once at Bootle she took off her flannel petticoat to give to a woman who begged of her. The woman went round to the priest's house and showed it to the housekeeper, who at once took it to Father Powell. He told the housekeeper to give her something else and, sending for Teresa, told her to go home and put on her petticoat at once.

Towards the end of her life Teresa was asked which virtue she had practised most and her answer was: "My dear, I don't ever remember missing an opportunity of being kind, for nothing makes us resemble our dear Lord so much as kindness." She then went on to explain how people may be self–denying, merciful, even charitable, and yet not kind. True kindness she said must be a conscious imitation of our Lord, and by this beautiful apostolate many souls may be won for Him, for kindness brings happiness, softening hearts and preparing them for His grace. How perfectly she herself carried out this teaching is amply confirmed by all who knew her.

By this means she brought many souls to God. A poor prisoner was awaiting execution. He was utterly hardened and unrepentant, and rejected all the efforts of those who tried to soften him. Teresa had a method of her own. She bought a bunch of grapes and went to the prison. The wretched man was sitting on his bed in sullen despair, but she gently put her arms round his neck saying: Look dear father, what a beautiful bunch of grapes I have brought you!" Even the hardened sinner was not proof against such an appeal.

Another virtue she never tired of teaching was that of confidence. She used to say that what grieves our Lord most is our want of confidence in Him. No generous person can bear to be distrusted and our Lord is most generous and feels it more than all.

Teresa had many accomplishments. She was a most beautiful needlewoman, though her friends never doubted that it was her guardian angel who often did her work for her. They would come home and find her lost in prayer, and yet any work she had in hand was always ready at the appointed time. She was also an excellent cook. Sometimes during her visits to Liverpool she spent a day or two with Canon Snow, and, if any of his friends came to see him, she delighted in preparing the dinner for them. She never tasted the dishes herself, but would call upon the housekeeper to try them. The Canon had some little wards who sometimes came to tea and Teresa was sure always to have some special dainties ready for them. She sat at table with them, telling stories and asking riddles and entering into all the fun. She appeared to eat, but those who watched her closely saw that she never took more than a little piece of bread and butter, and they noticed too how her lips moved in prayer when the rest were too busy to heed her. She loved nothing better than to have good things to set before her friends, and took special note of their likes and dislikes. She was most hospitable to anyone who came to the house and it used to strike people as somewhat surprising where the necessary supplies came from at some unexpected call. And only the best would serve her to set before her friends. One day during her last illness two men called at the cottage. They had known her in Liverpool and were tramping through the country in search of work. She told the nurse to lay the best cloth and to provide the best meal possible for them, adding with her sweet smile: "We must do all we can in honour of this visit of St. Peter and St. Paul." Her guests were quite overcome, and went away full of awe and reverence for their hostess.

She was at times allowed to foresee the future, and our Lord revealed to her the terrible judgments of war and famine that were coming on the world. In 1880 she wrote to Father Powell:

"If it were not in obedience, I should never attempt to describe the dreadful things which have been shown to me, but, trusting in that wisdom and power, I hope He will give you a right understanding and knowledge of all that you wish me in His Name to relate. Oh Jesus, my beloved Jesus, be Thou a Jesus to us and save us whom Thou hast redeemed by Thy most precious Blood. I know not how or where I was taken, but it seemed to me that I was in a high place and looked down upon the earth. First I saw a cloud of darkness encompass the earth, a real thick material darkness which I understood too was a figure of the darkness of the intellect into which man had precipitated himself, then I heard the sound of mighty thunder and saw the lightning flash, and it seemed to me as if balls of fire fell upon the earth and struck it to its centre splintering the rocks to fragments. And I heard the rush of waters and a fearful wail of mourning arose from the earth, and humbly prostrating myself I craved for mercy through the Blood and bitter Passion of Jesus Christ, for through this darkness could be seen distinctly shining stars on the bosom of the earth (the holy tabernacles of His love), and I begged God not to look upon us but on the face of His Christ. And I heard a mighty voice say, 'I will not save this people for they are flesh. Ask me not in His Blood for His Blood is upon them.' (I understood to condemn them). But still I continued uniting my poor prayer with that of our dear crucified Jesus, saying over and over again, 'Father forgive them for they know not what they do. Jesus, Mercy! Mary, help!'

"I cannot say how long this lasted, for I was as much afraid as I was humbled, but then I heard a voice I knew full well to be that of our dear Lord and Saviour Jesus Christ saying: 'Say that not one of these that are given to me shall be lost.' Then the earthquakes stopped and the lightnings ceased and I beheld starved and maniac looking forms rise trembling to their feet, and I saw the sign upon their foreheads, and with them and the whole court of heaven I praised and blessed that God of infinite wisdom who in His mercy has redeemed us in His Blood.

"On another occasion I saw the stars shining brightly in the firmament and I saw a smoke arise, then I saw numbers of them fall and our b. Lord made me understand that through levity, want of mortification, and intellectual pride, many of His priests will presently fall away. At other times I have seen dried up herbage, dead cattle and fainting forms of human beings which I think indicates famine but I have not been distinctly told so. I do not know either the exact time these things will come to pass, but I understand that they are now hanging over our heads. The sign which marks the foreheads of the saved is the Wisdom the seat of which He expresses shall be duly and publicly worshipped."[12]

After these terrors she understood that a great peace would follow: "When these things shall have passed, there will be very few left who have not His seal upon their foreheads, yet these will be brought to love and adore the Wisdom of the Father in person of Jesus Christ, and the Holy Spirit dwelling in the hearts and minds of His people, the Church will enjoy a great peace and calm, and God will be adored, loved known and served verily and indeed."[13]

Many volumes might be written of the virtues of this great servant of God, but perhaps no words can more fully or more simply express her marvellous sanctity than those of her own favourite versicle. They were ever on her lips, her refuge in desolation, her delight in times of joy:

> *"Jesus, my own, my only Good,*
> *I wish for naught but Thee:*
> *Behold me all Thine own, my God,*
> *Do what Thou wilt with me."*

---

[12] Letter 57.
[13] Letter 58.

21

Letters

THE following are among the most striking of Teresa's letters, and need no comment. They are taken from the series written in obedience to Father Powell during the years 1879 to 1883, and give a deep insight into her spiritual history.

On July 16th, 1879, shortly after her first revelation with regard to the devotion to the Sacred Head, she wrote:

"In obedience to your wish I write to let you know that that excessive darkness has again passed away.

"Yesterday at noon, when I was trying to say the Angelus, my poor soul was more afflicted I think than ever I had been before, when suddenly I felt myself drawn into God as it were even as the fish is in the water, and since I have been as it were over-whelmed with the presence of God — not by way of feeling the actual presence of our b. Lord in His glorified Humanity of which I have before spoken, but as all things are in God — so I feel myself engulfed in the most holy Trinity. Blessed be the most holy Trinity and undivided Unity now and forever more amen.

"I see how worthless is all of earth and how mean are the painted shadows which the world calls honours. I feel that I could endure the greatest torments and long to lay down my life in proof of my love for Him who alone is worthy of being loved.

"There is such a burning desire of the possession of God within me that it seems inwardly to consume me, and that pain is so great yet so sweet that I feel my poor heart is breaking, and my poor soul seems really as if it were striving to be released from the body, on which I feel I could inflict all kinds of tortures. Oh what a sink of misery and iniquity I am and how little I am able to do for our good God. I have noticed particularly of late, during dryness as well as at other times, when I see how little I am able to serve God and the souls for which He died, such trouble comes upon me that this anguish seems to tear my soul to pieces."[1]

When she first went to Bootle, though she entered with so much zeal and interest on her new duties, her soul was suffering the most terrible desolation:

OCT. 1879

"I am sure you will join with me in thanking our dear good God for His goodness to me and in asking Him to give me grace to cheerfully embrace all the desolation etc. which it shall please Him to send me. I know how unworthy and miserable a wretch I am and yet this does not move me. Neither His great love nor His awful bitter Passion make any impression. I seem to have no compassion or love for Him. It seems as if faith, hope, and charity were all dead — as if God had entirely abandoned me for my base ingratitude to Him, and all His favours are forgotten. I know how empty is all of earth and yet I am perfectly indifferent and insensible to Him who is my only Treasure. I am grateful to Him for giving me an opportunity of suffering something for Him and I wish to praise and bless Him if it should continue for ever. I know His grace is sufficient for me, and He will not try me above the strength He gives. But on the other hand you know as well as I do my infidelity and misery, and if He should leave me as I deserve, what would become of me? Everything I do seems done through habit and as it were an empty nut without any good in it. I remember Fr. Wells telling me to be very calm at these times, but it is this very calmness and indifference that is now as it were a sword to punish me. Oh that I could only love Him, then every other trial would be as naught! May His holy Will be perfectly accomplished in me and His holy Name blessed

---

[1] Letter 9.

for ever. I do not wish that He would lessen this hardest of all crosses. I have often complained to Him that he did not let me suffer for Him, and asked Him to give to others who knew Him not as I did the favours and consolations He gave to me (that so they might taste and love Him if only for that sweetness which surpasses all else) and give me instead a great spirit of self–denial, obedience and a more burning love of Him and His holy Cross. You said something last night about human consolation, but I think when it pleases Him to draw or hide Himself from the soul, nothing can console or comfort her..."[2]

Father Powell having questioned her as to the way in which our Lord instructed her, she replied:

"In the name of the most high God and in obedience to your wish, I will try and put into words that which our dear blessed Lord my Spouse and only Treasure, has made known to me, and as you asked me the other day in Confession how our b. Lord made these things known to me, I asked Him to let me know how these impressions or knowledge were conveyed to the soul. And this is what I understand: that, as I have said before, our b. Lord places in the very centre of the soul those things which He wishes her to know, without any words or image being formed, and this comparison will make clear I think what I mean — that as one looking glass casts those things that are reflected in it to another, so the soul being entirely in God, He impresses, infuses, or reflects in her what He desires she should learn. And some-times He does this without the powers of the soul being sus-pended or the senses of the body being lost, certainly they are riveted so to speak and made to drink in whatever He desires. But oh my Father who shall find words to express the delight and glory the whole being enjoys at being thus instructed by so heavenly a tutor!"[3]

AMDG et in hon BVM et ST. J
"Jan 8 81

---

[2] Letter 20.
[3] Letter 34.

"DEAR REV. FATHER,

"In honour of the Seat of divine Wisdom, and in the holy name of Jesus and Mary, and in obedience to your wish, I write of those things which it has pleased the All–wise to show me. Oh Spirit of wisdom and understanding help me, Jesus, my beloved Jesus, do for me what I am unable to do. Oh my Mother Mary, pray for me and watch over me for I am thy poor sick child.

"After five o'clock Mass on the Epiphany, in fact during the whole Mass, I was extremely recollected and I saw, as I have often done before, the great mysteries unveiled as it were, I mean as the angels and the blessed in heaven see these things in God in Trinity of Persons and unity of Essence. Oh most sublime and stupendous Sacrifice, oh unfathomable mysteries of wisdom, oh height and depth of immeasurable love, oh my God, how can I find words to express the least of what You have shown me? Oh most comforting and consoling mystery, for here we have a worthy return for all that God has given us, here we offer to the adorable Trinity a price which far exceeds all that God (though He is omnipotent) could bestow on any or all of His creatures united, His holy Mother and all the court of heaven included — nay if each favour was multiplied by the favours God ever has or will bestow on any or all His creatures, we still have a price to pay which far exceeds all. For we have the second Person of the blessed Trinity, the co–eternal Son of the Father, Jesus Christ, having the same substance as the Father etc.

"It seems to me that at holy Mass we are as it were almighty (not through any merit of our own — ah no for surely here we sink into utter nothingness, surrounded as we are with the over-whelming power and majesty of God) but on account of the greatness of our offering. Ah my Jesus Thou mightest well say: 'Ask and you shall receive', for all things else are only Thy gifts, but here we have You in person. Oh my Love, my Love, what can I say — all that I can say is that I can say nothing.

"Of this I have written before, so I think at least, but what I meant to write was what happened after. We had all to leave the church very shortly after the holy Sacrifice was over and I felt so sorry, but I went with the rest, and when I came in our dear Lord allowed me to see in the very centre of my heart as it were the divine Infant, I mean Himself in that form as the Light of lights, not in a corporal form but impressed on the heart and in the soul, so that I understood that He wished me to adore Him specially as the little Babe of Bethlehem. And so I tried to do with Mary and Joseph and begged of them to offer me to their Jesus and mine, and I offered to Him their ecstatic love, nay I tell Him that I love Him with the love of His own most sacred Heart (for He often shows me my poor heart lost in His adorable Heart as one tiny rain drop in the mighty ocean). I am afraid I am writing what has nothing to do with this great favour which our dear Lord in His wisdom and love has bestowed upon me and with which you know I have nothing to do.

"You understand the manner that our dear Lord showed Himself to me (I think) in some way the same as He forms those words which He from time to time speaks to the soul. His sacred Head was as it were the fountain of that flood of light in which He appeared to me, and I felt that He was glorifying the blessed Trinity in the resplendent light that was centred in the Seat of divine Wisdom and He was the Light that enlightened the Gentiles, and I thought this feast had a special connection with the Devotion to the sacred Head.

"Oh Seat of divine wisdom and guiding power which governs all the notions and love of the sacred Heart, may all minds know Thee, all hearts love Thee, and all tongues praise Thee now and forever more amen.

"Dear rev. Father, if I was not bound by holy obedience, I think I should really run away somewhere to hide, not that I think that you do not really know me as I am, but I feel at times that charity gilds my many faults and prevents you seeing me as I see myself. For some time past I seem to have forgotten myself, I mean my unfitness to teach others, but this evening for a short time I have looked into this pool of iniquity and see myself as I am. It seems to me that my Lord and my God hides from me *myself* that so I may open the eyes of the soul in Him and behold His awful purity, boundless majesty and infinite wisdom and love. Oh my God, that I had the voice and heart of men and angels to make Thee known to the whole world as Thou art that so we might all love Thee as Thou deservest.

"TERESA HIGGINSON
"Enfant de Marie."[4]
LDS et hon BVM et ST J

AMDG et in hon BVM et ST J
FEB. 1881

"DEAR REV. FATHER,

"In honour of the sacred Head and to the glory of the Sacred Heart, I write in obedience to your wish. Oh that I could find words adequately to express what I would say. You know it has pleased our dear divine Lord to allow me to suffer in part the agonies of the bitter Passion for some length of time (more acutely than usual) and for the past few weeks an inexpressible fear and dread of Lent has at times taken possession of me, yet how willingly I submit myself and how ardently I have longed for, and even anticipated them, He only knows. I sometimes fear too that my weakness may prevent me from bearing what His love would otherwise allow. But on Thursday 17th, during Benediction, I grew very weak and the suffering of soul and body increased, as I think I never experienced them before except in Holy Week. I begged the holy and strong God to help me to go out of church, I went at once to my room, and when I lay prostrate on the ground offered myself with our divine Spouse praying in the garden as a victim of expiation and reparation.

---

4   Letter 77.

Then our dear b. Lord opened the eyes of the soul to see clearly the sins and the punishment thereof I had taken on myself. I saw the awful purity of God which they had outraged and I felt how heavy was the arm of His divine justice, and I saw the excess of my own weakness and nothingness, and my heart sank within me and my will seemed to have no power to act. I may say I was completely overpowered and annihilated. I tried in my heart to say the Glory be to the Father etc. but ended with 'Thy holy Will be done!' I never experienced such a struggle before. I cried again and again: 'My God my God, why hast Thou forsaken me? Oh Mary, my Mother Mary!' But she too seemed deaf to my cry. I tried to say: 'Jesus my true, my only Love, I wish for naught but Thee. Behold me all Thine own my God, do what Thou wilt with me.' But I could not articulate a sound. Hell itself seemed let loose upon me tempting me to cowardice and despair. I tried to open wide my arms to show my ready willingness to accept all, for crushed down as I was beneath the weight of this seeming heavy cross I said: 'Thou too, oh Lord, didst fall beneath the weight of Thy cross, and by Thy falls on the way to Calvary I trust for strength and grace to rise and bear mine side by side with Thee.' Then I saw the holy angels of God coming to strengthen and comfort me, and my divine Spouse impressed these things in the very centre of my soul — that hitherto I had prayed and suffered with Him under the shade of the olive trees, now His love required that I should go forth with Him to be publicly crucified, but I was left at will to choose. Oh Lord, Thou knowest all things, how then canst Thou doubt my love for Thee? Oh how these words pierced my poor heart and soul, yet from them I gained strength and will to act as became the Spouse of a crucified Lord. I must now no longer look at all to myself but seek only His greater glory in all things. I am ready oh Lord, I am ready and waiting Thy holy Will. I may say that for several years I have experienced a crucifixion of body and heart, and I have tried to resign my poor miserable will to that of the great God of heaven and earth, but last Lent I experienced as it were a crucifixion of soul as well also, at least in part. You know words cannot express what I would say, but I know He who is the God of wisdom and understanding will give you to know what I have written in obedience. Pray dear rev. Father for your obedient and devoted child

"In the s. Head and s. Heart
"TERESA HIGGINSON
"Enfant de Marie."[5]

AMDG et in hon BVM et ST. J
FEB. 28 81

"DEAR REV. FATHER,

"In the holy Name of Jesus and Mary and in honour of the Seat of divine Wisdom and to the glory of the sacred Heart I write in obedience to your wish. On the evening of Thursday 24th, as soon as I went to my room I knelt down to say the sorrowful mysteries of the rosary, and our dear b. Lord really represented to the soul these dreadful mysteries in the manner that I described them last year. That is, while I actually gazed upon our dear b. Lord suffering these indescribable torments in soul, heart, mind and body, I also was allowed to partake in them (but in a greater degree than I have done before). Other years I have not been able to comprehend half so clearly the infinite attributes of God, His awful purity, justice love etc. nor the enormity of sin, and therefore I saw things only through a wall as it were; and I was completely overpowered with each individual sorrow of soul and anguish and suffering of mind and body, and I was as it were stupefied as to what was to come and I hardly realised the extent of suffering till it was past. And I see selfishness in those things which I had looked upon as entirely God's. I think I mourned more over my divine Spouse and the sins which caused His sufferings because I actually endured a

---

5   Letter 97.

little of the smart of those many, many wounds — I mean that I think I grieved for sin more on account of the pain I endured for it than because by it the awful majesty and beauty and love of God are outraged. Oh my Jesus, my Lord and my Love, make me all Thine own. You know how I now wish to suffer and love Thee, oh make me ever love Thee more and more.

"When I say that our dear Lord allowed me to see and to suffer in the mysteries of His bitter Passion, I do not mean all — I did not reach the top of Calvary, I saw nothing of the 10th or 11th station. I went with Him from the supper room. I saw Him crushed in anguish and agony in the garden. Oh my God, my God, my dear Jesus, Oh that I could help Thee loved One in Thine agony.

"Oh Eternal Father, behold the breaking Heart, the sorrow of that Holy Soul, the red drops that trickle down from every pore of His most sacred Body. Stay the arm of Thy divine Justice for already the price is more than paid for every erring soul. Oh eternal Father, remember it is Thy coeternal Son, He in whom Thou art well pleased. My God my God! When wilt Thou be appeased? Oh my Jesus, remember that Thou art the Almighty God. Oh Mary, where art thou? Ye angels, come and help Him. Oh love of God! Oh Sin, Sin…

"Dear rev. Father I was obliged to leave off. I could not write and I know not half I have said, but I saw Him fall and brutally kicked and dragged I was with Him all that night of untold horrors — denied by Peter, condemned to death. I saw Him fall beneath the cross, comforted by St. Veronica and the holy women, and I felt something of that sea of sorrow that inundated the souls and hearts of the Mother and the Son as they first met each other on this Way of the Cross. Oh my soul, how can I express these fathomless mysteries, so sublime, so dreadful and so unsupportable to human nature that nothing short of a miracle could enable us to endure in any way the smallest portion of them or the knowledge of them. As a tiny raindrop is to the mighty ocean, so is all I could say (or all the united sorrows and sufferings of every created being multiplied together) to the least of these impenetrable mysteries. Words here seem to lose all meaning, they are as so many ciphers. While almighty God allowed me to endure these sorrows of soul, desolation of spirit, anguish of heart and suffering in body, I saw at the same time the infinite homage that was paid in each to the infinite majesty of God, the graces that were to flow from this plentiful redemption, the souls saved, and the glory won for His elect. I saw the blood of martyrs flow, the tears of repentance glisten in many an eye. In short I have seen what these excruciating sufferings, this most precious Blood, has purchased for us and the infinite glory It renders to the adorable Trinity. I feel something of His thirst for souls, and, if it be to His glory and the good of souls, I would be content to suffer (as He alone knows I do) to the end of time. It seems to me as if each smart or suffering were a flame of fire consuming my whole being and at the same time supporting life, for I verily believe I could not now exist without this living death. Oh my Lord and my only Love, many things Thou hast given me but this I prize above them all. Oh Wisdom, oh Love, which is for ever contriving new ways and means of forcing us to love Thee more. Oh my Spouse and my Treasure, my crucified Jesus, give me suffering if it be Thy holy Will, not in proportion as I love Thee, but Lord as Thou lovest!

"Oh my Father, He has given me a greater portion of His bitter Passion than I am able to express. I used to think the sufferings of body were beyond expression far, but they are as naught in comparison with these other treasures He has entrusted to me. Oh my God, grant that I may not bury these talents but make them fruitful through Thy most precious Blood.

"These sufferings do not in any way stun the soul or stupefy the senses of the body. They open wide the eyes of the soul and quicken the senses, and it seems to me that this knowledge which it brings is the very cause of greater suffering and makes us thirst for more. It appears that when we are thus suffering with our dear b. Lord, we become as it were one with Him so entirely that human nature hardly exists, if I may so speak, for it is facsimile with that which happens in time of consolation, though the effect differs. I do not seem to regain my strength from one week to the other. I have been rather uneasy at missing holy Mass so often lately, for I see so clearly the inestimable value of *one* holy Sacrifice I feel that I should not miss it even if I had to crawl on my hands and knees, and yet I feel I am not able. May He who is the almighty God bless and reward you for all your care and kindness to me His poor miserable child.

"I have been permitted to endure different parts of His dolorous Passion all the week, and my head bleeds more frequently than it ever has before. I have also been taken up, I do not know where, but so that I looked down upon the earth as I have mentioned before, and I have seen the infinite wisdom and love of God in a most extraordinary way. I felt the clouds beneath my feet and saw many holy spirits going backwards and forwards to the earth, some bearing censers and other caskets, and some fire etc. I know not what it means, I was as it were annihilated. Oh my God, my God, have mercy and pity upon us whom Thou hast redeemed with Thy most precious Blood. Begging your blessing etc. I remain dear rev. Father

"your obedient and devoted child

"in the s. Head and s. Heart

"TERESA HIGGINSON

"Enfant de Marie"[6]

LDS et hon BVM et ST J

"169 ST. JOHN'S ROAD

"BOOTLE SEPT. 23RD 1881

"DEAR REV. FATHER,

"In the holy name of Jesus and Mary and in obedience to your wish, I will try and explain as far as I can the state in which it has

---

6   Letter 98.

pleased our dear Lord to bring my poor soul, and I trust in the infinite Wisdom of His sacred Head for light and knowledge to do as you require.

I think I have before written how the soul suffers a pang beyond that which the lost soul feels in being obliged to remain in the awful purity, the dread justice and infinite knowledge of the all powerful God. Here it seems to me that the whole being is crushed as it were into nothingness, and if it were possible for the immortal soul to perish it would do so in an instant. And she feels she would gladly suffer the pains of every mortal suffering for ever (rather) than endure the searching gaze of that allseeing and knowing Eye for an instant, and it seems too that eternity has really commenced with her, her suffering is so great and it seems to have lasted so long, for she forgets everything although she knows fully all that God has done for her. I mean it seems only to be an additional pain to her. She sees herself wrapped closely round with the punishment of mortal sins taken upon herself (and this she feels and knows, as God only shows in this particular light what each individual and all the malice of the united guilt is before Him), and yet pains that in the excessive love and mercy of His compassionate Heart He allows her to suffer, she now feels a burden beyond endurance. She trembles and dreads beyond description the favours He allows and gives to her. I mean when He would embrace her as it were, the thorny crown seems to pierce too deeply her aching brow, and the flame of fire which consumes His sacred Heart to burn too acutely. I mean that sword of fire (typified by the angel of old guarding the entrance to the terrestrial Paradise) seems to cut too deeply her cold and cowardly heart, the nails seem too coarse and she quivers at the very thought of them fastening her to the cross which seems far too heavy for her to carry. I mean in other words that, though she has a burning desire to suffer and die with her Lord and Spouse, she feels she has no energy, no real love, no generosity, she is a base coward. And though she tries to comfort herself by telling our dear Lord that He too fell beneath the cross, and that before He died He raised one loud cry for pity and compassion, yet her very words turn into so many spears to rend her heart and soul. She cannot look to God for consolation, for He alone seems to be the cause of her suffering. She desires to come to Him, but she is held back as it were with the dread of this overwhelming awe of His infinite wisdom, knowledge, purity and justice, and she feels too His very love and mercy must bid her depart from Him whom she knows to be her only Treasure, her only Love. Oh, I know not in what words to express this most terrible and excruciating pain which God can cause the soul to suffer, and she knows that He permits it also, so that He may fit her for the place He has prepared for her from the beginning."[7]

JAN 7. 1882

"The last two or three weeks our dear b. Lord has from time to time inundated my whole being with such a celestial sweetness, a holy joy which is I think a foretaste of that everlasting bliss which He has purchased for us in His Kingdom and is inexpressible in words, and we must feel it to understand it. One second of this delight is more than sufficient to repay a thousandfold the services of a long life. Here all care, sorrow and suffering are entirely forgotten, great desires rise up in the soul, and above all a power to act which could not otherwise be acquired, and things are made easy which before we were hardly able to think of.

"I was very recollected all the evening and those weaknesses kept coming upon me and I felt that I could not wait till morning for holy Communion, I felt almost dying of desire of Him. I may have begged of our dear b. Lady to come and give Him to me, but I really do not know, when all at once I felt crushed into nothingness, as it were — almost annihilated in the awful majes-

[7] Letter 111.

ty of His glory. I do not mean that there is a confusion in the soul — no, that which was calmness before is made more calm — and peace which He alone can give with a wonderful light of knowledge deluged my poor soul. I understood that Jesus the divine Infant had really personally come to visit me and that Mary had brought Him, and I knew I felt that He desired to come to me. I would not dare to hold Him, but stretching out His infant arms I felt the thrill and pressure of His sacred lips, my whole being was lost in His infinite beauty and love. I know not how long He thus remained with me. I think I lose sight of Him that so I may enjoy Him and admire His infinite perfections and praise His excessive love and goodness to me. But I notice that I always lose sight of Him or am lost in Him that I may enjoy Him, and little by little those divine truths He has taught come before the mind. But I am not able to do much for some time, for I find myself every now and then quite absorbed in His greatness, and it is only at intervals that I can consider these things. And if I wish to express His praises, I find myself unable even to utter one word, my poor heart is too full to speak. And as I held Him, the eternal Son of God and Mary's Son, our dear little infant Jesus, that instant I perceived these words infused into the very centre of my soul: 'Take courage my loved One, for the Seat of divine Wisdom will be known, praised and adored as I wish, and I will glorify my Name in thee.'

"I am all Thine, oh my beloved Jesus, do with me what Thou wilt. Remember too, oh Lord, all my misery, that I am but dust and ashes, the very slime of the earth, and pity me. Oh that I could do something to honour and glorify Thee, for Thou art my Lord and my God. The feeling I experienced when I felt His divine touch was the same as when it pleases our divine Lord that the sacred Host should dissolve into His most precious Blood. I think by this you will understand me."[8]

---

[8]   Letter 117.

AMDG et in hon BVM et ST. J

"AP. 1882

"Oh Wisdom of the sacred Head guide us in all our ways.

"Oh Love of the sacred Heart consume us with Thy fire.

"DEAR REV. FATHER,

"In the holy Name of Jesus and Mary and in obedience I will try and write something of that which it pleased our dear b. Lord to show me concerning the excessive sufferings He endured for us in His holy Soul, and yet I feel that I cannot say anything, for I do not know anything when speaking of the bodily agonies of Jesus in His awful bitter Passion — human words long since dwindled into ciphers. How then can I speak of the sufferings of soul which the living God declared was sorrowful unto death, for they are too deep to express and too excessive for us to understand.

"Of course we know that all the atrocities and outrages, all the tortures and agonies He endured in His adorable Body were but a faint shadow of what was being effected in the powers of His holy Soul, and yet these bodily sufferings were so great that it is not given to the mind of man to comprehend.

"It seems to me that when almighty God pleases that a soul should be instructed in these fearful mysteries, He draws that soul in a wonderful manner into Himself, giving it a supernatural life and endurance and that the understanding is not able to comprehend at all. All I know is that I do not know anything. It is as the Apostle says: 'Eye hath not seen nor ear heard, nor hath it entered into the heart of man to conceive.'

"It was in His adorable Soul that Jesus endured a torture equal to the eternal punishment due to each separate mortal sin, and the exact suffering and torment appointed for each peculiar mortal sin. I mean each kind of sin has a special punishment, and He endured each and all collectively.

"We often witness the effect produced by the meeting of bodies of different natures: see the explosion caused by the meeting of two gases of opposite natures; see how a little water flowing into the fire in the earth's centre causes earthquakes etc. But are they as opposite as infinite Holiness and Purity are to mortal sin? Think then how the Soul and Heart of Jesus the Man God were torn asunder, what a rending of His whole being took place when He clothed Himself with the iniquities of the whole world. Oh my God, my God.

"I do not know what to give as a comparison. As flowers have different scents and colours, so have different sins horrible stenches each according to its kind, and I verily believe that if almighty God allowed the stench of one mortal sin of impurity to be felt upon the earth, everything would be poisoned by its foulness. Oh how horrible is the disgust felt even by us poor sinners when we take upon ourselves the sins of others — if we were to wrap ourselves up in a decomposed body, what a terrible loathing we should experience, and yet this is nothing compared to the loathing disgust the soul endures, for the senses of the body cannot convey the smallest idea what the sensitive part of the soul is capable of enduring. So all that any human being could suffer would be but as a grain of sand compared to the whole earth, there is such a difference between our dear b. Lord and ourselves, but as our understanding is so finite we feel obliged to make these comparisons to be understood.

"Think of the terror of the soul that departs this life in mortal sin as it stands before the allpure God to be judged. Oh what a terror filled the Soul of Jesus as He took upon Himself the sins of the whole world and not only stood before, but was actually drawn into, the infinite purity and infinite justice of His eternal Father. His understanding comprehended God in the very essence, knew His infinite purity, dread holiness, and strict justice on one hand, and He saw sin as He only can see it in all its infinite malice on the other, and knew that He must pay to the last farthing. He knew the hatred the adorable Trinity have for sin and read its punishment in God. He knew the base ingratitude of sinners and the cowardice of His friends. He saw the whole of Hell let loose against Him: but what are all these? They are as nothing beside the suffering inflicted by the impress of the Finger of God's justice upon Him, for He writhed in agony of Soul beneath its touch. He was drawn into the divine Justice — all the weight of His wrath was upon Him. The floodgates of heaven were opened and the fountains of the great deep broken up and the torrent of God's vengeance rushed in upon Him, His thunderbolts were hurled against Him — Oh my God, Thy very words are works and what Thou dost is well done. When Hell was created to punish sin, how well qualified it was to do its work! But this is but a creature, but *here* God Himself touches the soul with the intent to cause it to suffer, how then can one be compared to the other, only so far as to say, as the Creator is above the creature, so is the suffering caused by one above the other, and beside this the flames of Hell grow cold. Oh, it really seems to me that these excesses are beyond the understanding of man, we have no words to speak, here the soul is launched out into the infinity of God and we know not really what we know, or as I said before we do not know anything.

"We may look at the external sufferings of our dear b. Lord during His awful bitter passion and see how each different agony is but a faint shadow of what is being effected in His holy Soul sorrowful unto death — see something of the dread — of His fear — something of His thirst for souls and the glory of His Father — something of the rending of His Heart and Soul — something of His love.

"Oh, the more God teaches us the less we can say, and that is why Mary was so silent. Her soul and heart were too full to speak, and I think she would not have lived if she had tried to speak.

"Oh my Father, you may think it very strange of me to write as I have, but you know my ignorance, you know my misery and I fear not to tell you, for I have asked Him who is the Wisdom of the Father to do that which I am unable to do and so He knows all. It seems strange that I should say God allowed me to partake more deeply in the agonies of His passion this year than ever, yet not be able to say even what I experienced, yet so it is. This year I had a terrible hard and dry passion, a passion of soul which none but He who graciously permitted it will ever realise. May His holy Name be blessed for ever. I do not think it is befitting that I should speak here about the temptations etc. which it pleased our dear Lord I should pass through, but I will finish about myself in the other letter and give it you in the morning or tonight.

"It seems as though the soul was rent asunder from the body and certainly I seemed to suffer more than the agonies of death. That was why I said to you about dying. Oh how terrible is God in His infinite justice and awful Purity.

"But on Holy Saturday the stone seemed rolled away from my poor soul and I began to feel the joys of the Resurrection, though not so fully as on Easter Sunday, but I will write all in detail.

"Begging your prayers and blessing

"I remain dear rev. Father

"Your obedient and devoted child in the s. Head and s. Heart

"TERESA HIGGINSON

"Enfant de Marie"[9]

"BOOTLE

"Ap. 20TH 1882

"In the holy Name of Jesus and in obedience I write of the light and joy which saturate my whole being through and through, for the Lord is truly risen. Alleluiah! Alleluiah! Alleluiah!

"Oh my Lord and Master, my Spouse and only Treasure, it seems that Thou art determined to make up to the soul that has suffered anything for Thee in a most extraordinary manner and

---

9   Letter 122.

APPENDIX A

Father Wilberforce's Memorandum

"HOLY CROSS, LEICESTER.
"NOV. 9 1882

"TO FATHER POWELL

"Opinion on the devotion to the Sacred Head of Jesus Christ."

"DEAR FR. POWELL,

"You ask me to express to you in writing my opinion regarding a volume of letters written by Miss T. H. containing among other matters an account of certain revelations which she considers to have been made to her by our Blessed Lord Himself, concerning devotion to the Sacred Head of Jesus as the Shrine of the Divine Wisdom. This would also include some opinion as to the spirit of the writer of these letters.

"I must first express the diffidence with which I give any opinion about matters so exalted in their nature and so widely removed from the beaten track of the spiritual life, especially as I have not any knowledge of the soul in question.

I. — As to the Devotion itself.

"The object of this, which in a certain sense may be called a *new* devotion, is the Sacred Head of the Divine Word Incarnate; but not simply that Sacred Head itself considered as the chief organic part of the material Body of Jesus Christ, but that Sacred Head considered as the Shrine or Tabernacle of the created Soul of the

God Man, united as that soul is, in one Person, with the uncreated and eternal Wisdom of God the Son. Thus the Devotion bears a striking analogy to the devotion in honour of the Sacred Heart which beat in the breast of our incarnate God, yet not simply as a material object of worship but as the Shrine and symbol of the Love of Jesus Christ, love residing in the Soul which was united in one Person with the Son of God.

"There would appear to be no theological objection to a devotion in honour of the Sacred Head as the Shrine of the intellectual faculties and powers of the Soul of our Lord Jesus Christ. For the soul is the Form of the whole body, and therefore of the head, the principal organ of the body; and as the Soul of our Blessed Lord is united in one Person with the Godhead, His Sacred Head is manifestly divine and worthy of the highest adoration or the worship of Latria.

"St. Thomas teaches that the Son of God assumed a created Soul and a created Intellect, and the holy Doctor quotes the words of St. Augustine who proves this truth from the teaching of Our Lord Himself: 'Firmly hold and nowise doubt that Christ the Son of God has true flesh and a rational soul of the same kind as ours, since of His flesh He says (Luke 24:39): 'Handle, and see; for a spirit hath not flesh and bones, as you see Me to have.' And He proves that He has a soul, saying (John 10:17): 'I lay down My soul [Douay: 'life'] that I may take it again.' And He proves that He has an intellect, saying (Matthew 11:29): 'Learn of Me, because I am meek and humble of heart.' And God says of Him by the prophet (Isaiah 52:13): 'Behold my servant shall understand.'"[1] St. Thomas then proceeds to prove this Catholic doctrine by three reasons against the Apollinarists and Arians.

"The same holy doctor (Sum. Pt. 3 Qu. 25. Art. 1) teaches that the Divinity of Christ and His Humanity are to be adored with one and the same worship. He quotes Canon 9 of the Council of Constantinople which defines the doctrine in these words: 'If

---

[1] See St. Thomas Aquinas, *Summa Theologiae* III, q.5, a.4. See also St. Augustine, *De Fide ad Petrum*, xiv.

anyone say that Christ is adored in two natures, so as to intro-
duce two distinct adorations, and does not adore God the Word
made flesh with the one and the same adoration as His flesh, as
the Church has handed down from the beginning; let such a one
be anathema.' Then the Angelic Doctor proceeds to show that, on
the part of the Person adored (*ex parte Ejus qui adoratur*), there is
only one and the same adoration of the two natures, because the
Person is One; but on the other hand, on the part of the cause for
which He is honored (*ex parte causae qua honoratur*), we can admit
that there is more than one adoration; for Christ is honoured by
one adoration on account of His uncreated Wisdom, but by
another on account of His created Wisdom.[2]

"In the Devotion now being considered, when the Sacred
Head is honoured, the Person is honoured, and as the Person is
divine, the honour due to the Sacred Head is divine.[3] This being
as above stated, in strict analogy to the worship of the Sacred
Heart, needs no further proof to show its perfect harmony with
the Catholic Faith.

"We may therefore conclude that the devotion to the Sacred
Head, as the Shrine of the divine Wisdom, can be defended
theologically and is in harmony with the teaching of the Catholic
Church.

II. — On the fitness of the Devotion.

"Having thus shown that the devotion to the Sacred Head is not
opposed to the teaching of Catholic Faith, the next question that

---

[2] See St. Thomas Aquinas, *Summa Theologiae* III, q.25, a.1. See also
Constantinople II, Anathema 9 against the 'Three Chapters': 'Si quis
in duabus naturis adorari dicit Christum, ex quo duae adorationes
introducuntur, sed non una adoratione Deum Verbum incarnatum
cum propria ipsius carne adorat, sicut ab initio Dei ecclesiae tradi-
tum est, talis anathema sit.'

[3] See St. Thomas Aquinas, *Summa Theologiae* III, q.25, a. 2.

arises may thus be put: 'Is the Devotion a congruous one? Is there any special fitness in it? 1. In itself. 2. At this particular time?'

"1. — If we consider the Devotion in itself, it will be acknowledged that there is a certain special fitness in it as a Devotion to the Eternal Wisdom. In support of this view the teaching of St. Thomas can again be adduced. The holy Doctor maintains that it was more fitting that the person of the Son of God should assume our nature than that either of the other Persons of the adorable Trinity should become Incarnate. One reason advanced by St. Thomas to prove this will throw considerable light on this devotion: 'Moreover, He has a particular agreement with human nature, since the Word is a concept of the eternal Wisdom, from Whom all man's wisdom is derived. And hence man is perfected in wisdom (which is his proper perfection, as he is rational) by participating the Word of God, as the disciple is instructed by receiving the word of his master. Hence it is said (Sirach 1:5): 'The Word of God on high is the fountain of wisdom.' And hence for the consummate perfection of man it was fitting that the very Word of God should be personally united to human nature.'[4] St. Thomas therefore considers that it was more fitting that the Son of God should become incarnate rather than the Father or the Holy Spirit because to the Eternal Son is attributed Wisdom (1 Co 1:24), Christ the Wisdom of God. For as man sinned and perished by an inordinate desire of wisdom and knowledge, so it is especially fitting that he should be restored by Him to whom Wisdom is especially attributed. From this we may rightly proceed to conclude that a most fitting object of special devotion for

---

4 St. Thomas Aquinas, *Summa Theologiae* III, q.3, a.8: 'Alio modo habet convenientiam specialiter cum humana natura ex eo, quod Verbum est conceptus Aeternae Sapientiae, a qua omnis sapientia hominum derivatur; et ideo per hoc homo in sapientia perficitur: quae est propria ejus perfectio prout est rationalis, quod participat Verbum Dei: sicut discipulus instruitur per hoc, quod recipit verbum magistri; unde Eccli. 1. dicitur: "Fons sapientiae verbum Dei in excelsis." Et ideo ad consummatam hominis perfectionem conveniens fuit, ut ipsum Verbum Dei humanae naturae personaliter uniretur.'

man after being redeemed is that very Wisdom by Whom the redemption has been accomplished. Now the Shrine of that Wisdom, its earthly tabernacle, is the Sacred Head of our Lord Jesus Christ. The devotion therefore in itself is most congruous and fitting.

"2. — It will not be difficult in the second place to show that there is a peculiar fitness in this devotion to the age in which we live. In order to suit a particular time, a devotion ought to meet the special dangers of the day, supplying an antidote to prevalent spiritual diseases. Now the spirit of this age is evidently one of spiritual rebellion. The human mind, intoxicated by modern scientific discoveries, is inclined to cast off all restraint and to refuse any longer to remain subject to the sweet yoke of Faith. Rationalism, pure and simple, is the prevailing spirit of the day. This spirit is at once most injurious to God and especially to the Wisdom of God on high, the Fountain of Wisdom, because it causes man to love and value the foolishness of human wisdom, despising what they consider to be the folly, but which truly is the eternal Wisdom of God. Moreover this spirit is most destructive to souls who are induced by it to love the darkness rather than the light.

"Against this pernicious spirit of evil and its consequences the devotion to the Sacred Head is especially directed. For as it consists in the adoration and praise of the Sacred Head as the Shrine of Divine Wisdom, it is particularly adapted to be used in reparation for all the insults offered to that Divine Wisdom by the sins of infidelity and intellectual pride. Just as the devotion to the Sacred Heart met the error of Jansenism so destructive of the spirit of Love, so the devotion to the Sacred Head will oppose the blighting errors of rationalism and infidelity, so insulting to the infinite Wisdom of God incarnate.

"Moreover a fervent devotion to the Divine Wisdom and its earthly shrine will bring down on the Faithful, we most confidently hope, a special grace to preserve their faith intact and to spread that 'precious gift' among many still out of the fold.

"We may then conclude that this devotion is thoroughly theological, in strict harmony with the devotion, already so solemnly and frequently approved, of the Sacred Heart, most congruous in itself, and lastly peculiarly suited to the special needs of the age in which we live.

"III. — What ought to be thought of the writer of these letters, her spirit and the truth of her visions?
"I feel that in attempting to answer this question I am treading on delicate grounds, and it would be presumptuous to assume too much certainty in a matter of such gravity, without personal knowledge of the writer.

"Still, however, this much I can assert with confidence, that everything that has come to my knowledge, through her letters and accounts given me by her confessor of her acts and dispositions, all lead me to conclude, not only that she is in a high degree of holiness, but also that her mind is wonderfully illuminated by the Light of God.

"I will give shortly the reasons that lead me to form this judgment, speaking first of her holiness, then of the reasons that appear to indicate that her visions are the work of the Holy Spirit.

"In order to judge of the holiness of a soul, in other words of the degree of divine Charity with which that soul is endowed, we should examine the four test virtues of humility, patience, obedience and mortification.

"A soul pretending to very exalted gifts of contemplation and yet failing to practise these virtues in corresponding perfection, would almost certainly be in a state of delusion.

"Of her *Humility*. To judge from her writings, taking for granted that they reflect the true dispositions of her soul, the person in question would appear to possess this fundamental virtue in high perfection. It would seem that she thoroughly despises herself, is truly anxious to be despised by others, is free from that self–will which would make her desirous to guide herself instead of submitting to others, has a fear of delusion, yet with confidence in God: is anxious that divine favours should remain hidden, yet mentions them with simplicity under obedience. Of course the grand point is to prove that these written sentiments are genuine by the test of practical trial. This, I am told, has already been done, and that her calmness under sudden and violent reproof and even abuse remain unruffled. Her confessor has been unable to detect any difficulty in bearing these things which to a soul gifted with extraordinary contemplation ought to occasion lively joy and satisfaction. Her conduct under the trial of desolation of spirit also proves her humility.

"Her *patience* under the pressure of extreme mental and bodily suffering, to judge from her writings corroborated by particulars I have heard, is shown to be heroic, because, not only does she endure these things without repining, but she displays an ardent thirst for more numerous and more painful afflictions, in order to unite her soul to Christ crucified.

"*Obedience* is proved by the promptitude and simplicity with which she lays bare her secret soul under authority in spite of all repugnance, and gives up at once any penance or exercise without agitation of mind when commanded. Moreover, her confessor after many trials is unable to detect any failing of obedience. The humble way in which she accuses herself of a very slight act of childish disobedience shows the light of the Holy Spirit and reminds us of St. Philip Neri.

"As to her spirit of *mortification* and *penance*, it would appear to be universal in extent and extraordinary in degree. Her penances from childhood have been extreme, and though undertaken without the sanction of obedience through simplicity of soul, she has never shown any disposition to persevere in them against the advice of her confessor, and since she understood that they ought not to be adopted without permission she never seems to have practised any exterior penance without leave. Her abstinence and fasting and the generosity with which she has mortified her sense of taste is, to judge from her letters, heroic, and by the testimony of her confessor, miraculous, but this she has ever striven to conceal.

"The Visions about the devotion to the Sacred Head.

"Is there solid reason to place confidence in those visions as described in the letters under consideration?

"Before applying the ordinary tests prescribed by spiritual writers, I will make three preliminary remarks, suggested by the case.

"1. — The person has read no books of mystical theology, even the ordinary spiritual books common among the faithful, yet she describes most accurately and in most striking terms how a vision which is neither imaginary nor even intellectual is infused by the action of the Holy Spirit in the centre of the soul itself (vid. letter 34).[5] It is impossible to avoid the impression that she is speaking from personal experience. 'Our Lord', she writes, 'when He wills to infuse the knowledge of anything into the soul, places it in the very centre of the soul without any words or any *image* being formed.' This description is decidedly in favour of the belief that the vision was from the Holy Spirit, whereas if she had described a vision seen by the bodily eyes or by mental images, the case would be more doubtful and she might mistake her own imagination for the working of God's grace.

"2. — The theological way in which this simple and unlearned person explains the doctrine of the Trinity and Incarnation and speaks of the devotion to the Sacred Head is a decided indication of superior illumination.

"3. — The fact that this person is unlearned, has read no books, and has ever lived secluded, makes it unlikely that she should have invented herself a devotion so admirably suited to the times in which we live.

"Lastly, to apply the rules laid down by theology for distinguishing between true and false visions.

"I. — As to the vision itself (the ones instructing her as to the Devotion):

---

5   See page 327.

1. — As above proved, the vision contains nothing contrary to faith, but is entirely conformable to the traditions of the Church.

2. — Nothing unbecoming, trivial or irreverent can be detected in it. We may therefore conclude that that there is nothing in the vision itself to prove that it could not be from God, but all the circumstances are such as are found in approved visions.

"II. — As to the person to whom the vision is made.

1. — She is an orthodox thoroughly obedient Catholic.

2. — She is fervent and holy in life.

3. — Her humility, obedience, patience and mortification are heroic.

4. — Does she desire visions and favours? 'Tale desiderium', says St. Vincent Ferrar, 'non potest reperiri absque radice et fundamento superbiae et presumptionis.'[6] I have seen no indication of this desire. On the contrary, she often humbly and lovingly expostulates with our Lord, reminding Him that by favouring so great a sinner in so extraordinary a way He may cause His gifts to be despised.

5. — She is no novice in spiritual life for she began very early to serve God and has persevered with the utmost fidelity in spite of all difficulties, desolation, etc. Moreover, a favourable sign is that in early life she was led to the solid virtues of penance, humility, obedience and hatred of sin and had no extraordinary favour till after these had become habitual in a high degree.

6. — Visions are certainly to be more cautiously received in the case of a woman, but manifestly, when other signs are satisfactory, the fact they have been vouchsafed to a woman is no sign of delusion. This soul has had diabolical visions and has detected them.

"III. — The effect of the vision.

1. — The visions seem to render the soul more humble by revealing to her the abyss of her own nothingness etc.

---

6 The Latin means: "Such a desire is rooted in pride and presumption."

2. — She has always been directed by the vision to reveal all to her spiritual guide and to follow exactly what obedience prescribes, even when contrary to the vision itself.

3. — In this message to the confessor, if terms too flattering to himself personally had been employed there might be grounds for suspicion, but in this case all that is said is simply 'tell my servant'. Now, as all priests are God's servants, there is here nothing excessive coming from the human spirit of a devout woman. Some soul is spoken of who is to help the devotion and in this case terms of the highest praise are employed, but the name is not given. We may think it most probable that the soul is T.H. herself though she does not seem to suspect it.

4. — Another favourable sign is that these visions seem to excite a genuine and fervent desire to suffer for and with Christ and thus nourish the spirit of mortification.

5. — As to whether they promote the peace of the soul at least substantially, I do not know, but if divine, this ought to be their effect.

Lastly I might mention that I was deeply impressed by the application of the texts of the Apocalypse to the devotion (vide letter 48). It struck me as extraordinary as coming from the mind of so simple a person.

"Two points in conclusion I would suggest.

1. — That the confessor would do well to try this soul by the test of mental obedience while she is in an ecstatic state.

2. — That the matter of the Communions received by her from our Lord Himself should be carefully examined. Were these sacramental or only spiritual? Once or often in the day?

"I humbly submit this opinion to the judgment of the wise and learned and to the authority of superiors.

"FR. BERTRAM WILBERFORCE, O.P.
"Holy Cross Priory, Leicester.
"Nov. 9 1882."

APPENDIX B

Bilocation

BILOCATION is a not infrequent phenomenon in the history of the saints. Several instances are recorded in the life of the Ven. Father Dominic, who so often carried Teresa in his arms as a little child, and her friends bear witness on more than one occasion to Teresa's own presence in two places at a given time. But besides these attested incidents Teresa had other experiences of a like nature, but so startling and remarkable that the letters relating them cannot be omitted. They record facts which are apparently unexampled in the lives of the saints — facts, moreover, for which no confirmatory evidence can be offered, for they rest on her own testimony alone. At the same time it may be noted that, even though they could be proved to be due to a mere hallucination, this need cast no shadow on the truth of her revelations. She herself bases no claim upon them and never brings them forward as proof of her veracity. Rather she owns to being completely mystified and attempts no explanation. At first she tried to persuade herself that she was being deluded and never spoke of her strange experiences, but at last their reality impressed itself so deeply on her mind that she felt bound by her obedience to relate them to her director.

The following are her letters to Father Powell:—

"Feast of the Circumcision 1882.

"DEAR REV. FATHER,

"In the Holy Name of Jesus and in obedience I will relate that which you desire me concerning Africa (at least so I suppose it to be, but I am not certain). Well, for some length of time I have from time to time found myself among the negroes, but how I am transported thither I really cannot say — I mean that I do not feel myself going (just as a person might close their eyes and when they opened them again they found themselves in a different place) not in spirit but personally present. I find myself with them whom it pleases our dear Divine Lord I shall assist, and yet I am able to continue where I was and go on with the duties I was performing here. I have all along tried to persuade myself that I was deceived and yet I feel so positive of what I did, for our Divine Lord would instruct me very clearly about all He wishes me to perform in each mission of this kind, and He impresses on me that I must not take of the productions of this soil nor of their industry. It is not always the same place that I visit nor the same people, though I have (been) most of all with a tribe whose chief is lately deceased, and whose name is Jaampooda. He and his people were savages and lived by hunting I should imagine, by the furs and ivory which they possessed in great abundance. It is now over four years since I first visited these people and they were stricken down by a sickness which turned their bodies purple and black and of which many of them died; then I did all I could to relieve their bodily suffering, and I was instructed to gather some bark off a tree which grew commonly there and make a beverage for them and which I understand they call bitter waters and waters of life.

"This has astonished me a little, that I perfectly understand all that they wish to communicate to me and they comprehend all that I say to them of the dear good God. I have told them all the necessary truths and they were very much moved at the history of the Incarnation and Death of our Divine Lord, and most of them I have baptised (though they were not in danger of death) they besought me so imploringly and they and their dear good angel guardians have raised hymns of praise, thanksgiving and admiration of that infinite wisdom, power and love which arranges and directs all things, to give glory to the adorable Three in One and the salvation of souls.

"At times when I know of scandals and slights and neglects shown to our dear divine Spouse Jesus, I conjure Him to allow me to do and suffer something in reparation and atonement. Then it seems to me that the holy angels (to whom I have a special devotion for I think God wishes the angels to be man's helpmates and man to help the angels in the care and salvation of souls) implore me to ask Him and Mary our dear Mother and their Queen that I may help *these* souls (of the negroes), redeemed by His most precious Blood and fashioned by the creative power of the most High. Then that burning flame of desire for souls seems to consume my whole being. I have learnt something of that ineffable beauty, that divine Image impressed on the soul of each child of Adam, and oh how I long to see the Sun of Justice, this Light of divine wisdom, faith, knowledge, and charity shine in upon these souls and expel the mist or cloud of sin which as a veil encompasses them, that so the Triune God may behold as in a mirror Their divine Image reflected therein, that so these people may know God; then they must of necessity love and serve Him, and when we consider the way in which they try to serve Him we may bow our heads in shame and confusion.

"It is about three weeks since the chief of whom I have before spoken, died, and I felt that he needed help and I asked my dear good angel to comfort him in my name, and on the Monday evening I said a special prayer for him, for I felt that he was dying or in great need, and I presently found myself by his side. I heard him distinctly call me and beg of God through that infinite Wisdom enshrined in His adorable Head to guide me to his side; and when I took out the Crucifix, he took hold of it and pressed it with reverential love to his heart and then with tears streaming down his cheeks he devoutly kissed the seven Wounds which caused Jesus such agonising torture, and I begged of God to forgive him all his sins he had committed by the different senses of his body, and I tried to comfort his people and console him and he asked me to leave him the sign for man's redemption till he should stand before that Jesus whom it represents dying in ignominy and shame. And then I hardly knew what to do, I mean I did not like to refuse him and still I felt that I had only the use of it and I should ask of you before I did so.[1] Then the thought came that this would be some sort of a proof to me whether it was a reality or if I was being deceived, for although things that happened seemed to me to be so strange yet I could not but believe them to be realities. So I left him the crucifix and on Wednesday I again found myself with Jaampooda and I stayed with him till he died.

"I found too that nearly all the holy water was used out of the bottle I had and I had to refill it. These people burn the bodies of their dead, and after the Wednesday I had the crucifix the same as usual, but from Monday night till Wednesday I was without. Then I thought I should ask about whether persons could be in two or more places at the same time or not. Blessed be His Name who is all wise and powerful yet chooses the weakest and the most wretched worms to do His Holy Will. I will write or tell you about the other places I have found myself in, and what God has done for these various people. Have I done wrong in not telling you of this sooner? I really don't know why I have never mentioned it. I know I have been determined to tell you several times and when I would have told you it was taken completely out of my mind. I mean I have forgotten it. I know two or three times I have said to you in the confessional that I wanted to ask you

---

[1] This crucifix belonged to Father Wells who wished to make a gift of it to her, but she would only borrow it. She always wore it in her belt and would often cure the children's little ailments by applying it to them. Miss Catterall recalls how one Wednesday, at the dinner hour, Teresa came to her with a radiant expression and whispered, "I have got back my crucifix." Miss Catterall was completely mystified as to her meaning at the time and only learnt later on what she meant.

about something very particular, but I could not think of it then, and yet I never troubled myself in any way about it. I have often told our dear Lord about these things over and over again, and I always felt that He ruled all things and that I was but as a little feather or even less in a great wind, I mean that I am as power-less and wish to be as willing to be governed by Him as the feather is blown hither and thither according to the direction of the wind.

"Begging your prayers and blessing.

"I remain dear Rev. Father

"Your obedient and devoted child

"in the S. Head and S. Heart.

"TERESA HIGGINSON, Enfant de Marie."[2]

AMDG et in hon BVM et ST. J.

"Jan. 2nd 1882.

"DEAR REV. FATHER,

"In the holy Name of Jesus and in obedience I will continue about the little missions on which it has pleased our dear good God to send me.

"The people of whom I have already written are certainly the darkest in complexion but by no means the lowest in intelli-gence. I have been five or six times among a people who make beds for themselves in the low brushwood (almost like birds' nests) and they climb up the rocky crags and leap from one projection to another like animals. These are certainly the most degraded people I have ever been among and could never imag-ine human nature to be able to sink so low, for they live upon insects and crawling reptiles, and in form they are very diminu-tive and in features the least beautiful (I should imagine) of any of the nations of the earth. These people have not that brave and noble spirit of self–sacrifice which struck me very much in the

---

2   Letter 115.

people of whom I have written. These appear indolent and self–indulgent, though confiding and friendly, and they lay much store upon bright and shining and useless baubles which they will fasten in the hair, ears, and around their necks and arms, and they paint themselves with different coloured dyes on different occasions. They are not black like negroes; I hardly know what colour they are and rather fancy that they do not wear any clothing; at least if they do I have not noticed it. They also dig up a kind of earth nut of which they are very fond with their long claw–like fingers. They are timid and very slave–like in their service of anyone in power. I have noticed when I have spoken to them they have crawled towards me, many times rolling their heads in the dust so as to prove to me that they were as slaves waiting to do whatever I should wish them. And I have baptised many young children here, and have tried to instruct the older ones, but I do not think as yet they have at all a proper idea of God though they are anxious to learn, yet they are not naturally bright and intellectual and everything I have to explain by comparisons; they have no idea of anything spiritual, though they have an idol to which they offer human sacrifice and in whom they place all their hope and trust. I really believe that at first they would almost have worshipped me though through a sense of fear. They fancied I had some magic power over them for they brought a number of children whom they had decorated beautifully with flowers (different kinds of cactus and primulas) and holding in their hands some of the earthnuts I have before mentioned, and I saw them wind round these children a garland of flowers and this bound them very closely together, and I saw them place a quantity of beautiful blossoming bushes and ar-ranged the children upon it. Three or four young girls followed and I noticed in the hand of one a small cross made of twisted twigs and I noticed she held it up in her hand — I hoped for an instant that she knew something of the love and wisdom of our dear Blessed Lord, but I was mistaken. Taking out the crucifix to my use I held it up and said three times, 'In the name of the

Father etc.' and all the people again rolled their heads in the dust and I hardly understood what to do. Then I heard a most unearthly noise which they made with their voices, and I saw them carrying an old man whom it turned out was their chief and he was covered all over with fearful holes and ulcers, poor thing. He tried too to crawl upon the ground but he was not strong enough to do as he would wish and his brother crawled behind him. The old chief too was to be sacrificed, at least as soon as this brushwood was burning. Amid the cries of the dying children and clapping and singing and shouting of the whole tribe he was to throw himself upon his own funeral pile, and his brother would succeed him as chief. It pleased our dear divine Lord that I should see these things that so I might understand in what way to deal with them, and so as to make these people see and know that I was their friend, God allowed the cure of the chief, as soon as the shadow of the crucifix fell upon him, making the sign of the cross over him. And then I asked him in the name of the most Holy Trinity what all these things meant, and I told him also to rise and be healed, and he was cured at once and rose and explained all to me. Then I told him I was one of the least of the servants of that great Almighty God who gave life, maintained life in the body, and when this poor body died He took us to live with Him forever in His Kingdom. Then I told them of that One True and living God in Three, of all His love, mercy, and goodness to us and of that unspeakable wisdom which directs all things, and Who had said, 'Thou shalt not kill', and 'I am the Lord thy God', etc. This they seemed to understand for they asked me to take them to this great King, and I told them as yet they could not come, they must do many things and leave off many practices which they then followed, before they could come to Him. The sun at the time shone out with more magnificent splendour than I have ever before or since observed, and pointing to it I told them how the soul of man was created far brighter and more beautiful than that radiant sun, for it had impressed upon it the image of the eternal Three in One. It had a knowledge too within it to which the light of the sun was a darkness, for it knew that God whose holy image was sealed therein. Then as a fearfully dark cloud passed over the sun, I told them, so sin hid the glorious light of that Image — man did not see or know God because he could not remove the great cloud or stain of sin from off his soul, and when God looked down into the souls of men He saw that beautiful image covered all over with this dark, ugly cloud (sin). I instructed them in all that is really necessary. I baptised a number of children and a few very aged. I taught them to make the holy sign of the Cross (the next time I saw them I found that they mixed up a great many pagan practices with the truth, and I visited them four times closely after each other), the mysteries of religion and short prayers. I have taught them to sing for I find all these heathen people learn much better and remember them longer when they are sung, they are attracted by music. The last time I was with them, which was about four months since, during September, I found a number whom I had baptised were gone. I showed them how to baptise and tried to make them see the necessity of baptism so I trust that all may now be baptised before they die.

"Another people I have been among are copper–coloured, they are quick and intelligent, brave and noble–spirited, and I found that two of the very oldest could make the sign of the Cross and I knew at once they had been baptised and by the hands of a priest. They knew many truths and had partly instructed their people. These too had prayed and asked God to send someone to instruct and baptise their people, and they seemed to expect my arrival. I raised the crucifix and told them in short the great mysteries of our holy religion. I taught them the short acts of Faith, Hope, Charity and Contrition, the Our Father, Hail Mary, Creed, etc. and little prayers to S. Head and S. Heart. The elders of the tribe brought me water from a neighbouring stream and I baptised nearly all, for they seemed to have a wonderful faith. These people paint their bodies and wear clothing of skins and wear long feathers in their hair standing straight up, and I think they live by hunting principally. I have many times been with them and they can sing many hymns and prayers and they unite in spirit at holy Mass, and some of these men promise to go out in the name of God and under the protection of our Blessed Lady and St. Joseph, and in honour of the S. Head and love of the S. Heart, to find a priest of whom the two old men have told them. And the last time I was with them, they asked me and I blessed them in their undertaking in the name of the most holy Trinity, for they have a great and longing desire to receive Him into their hearts and souls in the holy Communion and they long also to be really present at the holy Sacrifice of the Mass.

"I have on several occasions taken the most holy Sacrament to the dying, twice to nuns and once to a poor priest who communicated himself, and twice to young people. I have taken the ciborium from churches where the sacred particles were consecrated by sacrilegious hands (I think in Germany) and taken it where I have been instructed. I don't know how the others received, I mean by whose hands, but in each case I stayed with them till they died, and I have always been careful about replacing the sacred vessel. I have been often at death–beds and joined with the good angel in helping the struggling soul to defeat its arch–enemy. And God sent me once by night into a prison to a young man who was praying that his innocence might be proved and that he might be restored to his friends, and God told me to tell him that He had heard his prayer, and would graciously grant his petition.

"I think now I have told you about the different missions on which the all–powerful God has sent me, and I know you will return thanks with me for the souls whom He has chosen for His service, and who before were adoring idols, but now praising, believing in and blessing that all wise Creator who spared not His own most beloved Son to redeem them and us, and gave us His Holy Spirit to make us holy.

"Begging your prayers and blessings,

"I remain, dear Father,

"Your obedient and devoted child

"In the S. Head and S. Heart

"T. HIGGINSON

"E de M."[3]

Father Powell evidently asked for further particulars about the tribe whom Teresa thus visited, for at the end of her next letter she says:

"I asked our dear Lord after Holy Communion about the people you told me. I don't know where you said, but I thought you said Polynesia, but I understand that they are Africans of that race which we call Hottentots, and I feel that those others are North American Indians as you say, but I am by no means certain."[4]

---

[3] Letter 116.

[4] Letter 116.

APPENDIX C

Prayers and Devotions

LITANY TO THE SACRED HEAD OF JESUS

Lord have mercy on us	Lord have mercy on us
Christ have mercy on us	Christ have mercy on us
Lord have mercy on us	Lord have mercy on us
Christ hear us	Christ graciously hear us
God the Father of heaven	have mercy on us
God the Son, Redeemer of the world	have mercy on us
God the Holy Spirit	have mercy on us
Holy Trinity, One God	have mercy on us

Sacred Head of Jesus, Formed by the Holy Spirit in the womb of the Blessed Virgin Mary: Guide us in all our ways

Sacred Head of Jesus, Substantially united to the Word of God:
                    Guide us in all our ways

Sacred Head of Jesus, Temple of Divine Wisdom:
                    Guide us in all our ways

Sacred Head of Jesus, Hearth of eternal clarities:
                    Guide us in all our ways

Sacred Head of Jesus, Sanctuary of infinite intelligence:
                    Guide us in all our ways

Sacred Head of Jesus, Providence against error:
                    Guide us in all our ways

Sacred Head of Jesus, Sun of heaven and earth:
>Guide us in all our ways

Sacred Head of Jesus, Treasure of science and pledge of faith:
>Guide us in all our ways

Sacred Head of Jesus, Beaming with beauty, justice and love:
>Guide us in all our ways

Sacred Head of Jesus, Full of grace and truth:
>Guide us in all our ways

Sacred Head of Jesus, Living lesson of humility:
>Guide us in all our ways

Sacred Head of Jesus, Reflection of God's infinite majesty:
>Guide us in all our ways

Sacred Head of Jesus, Object of the delights of the heavenly Father:
>Guide us in all our ways

Sacred Head of Jesus, Who received the caresses of the Blessed Virgin Mary:
>Guide us in all our ways

Sacred Head of Jesus, On whom the Holy Spirit reposed:
>Guide us in all our ways

Sacred Head of Jesus, Who allowed a reflection of Thy Glory to shine on Tabor:
>Guide us in all our ways

Sacred Head of Jesus, Who had no place on earth to lay:
>Guide us in all our ways

Sacred Head of Jesus, To whom the perfumed ointment of Magdalen was pleasing:
>Guide us in all our ways

Sacred Head of Jesus, Who deigned to tell Simon that he did not anoint Thy Head when Thou entered his house:
>Guide us in all our ways

Sacred Head of Jesus, Bathed in a sweat of blood in Gethsemane:
>Guide us in all our ways

Sacred Head of Jesus, Who wept over our sins:
>Guide us in all our ways

Sacred Head of Jesus, Crowned with thorns:
>Guide us in all our ways

Sacred Head of Jesus, Disgracefully outraged during the passion:
Guide us in all our ways

Sacred Head of Jesus, Consoled by the loving gesture of Veronica:
Guide us in all our ways

Sacred Head of Jesus, Which Thou inclined towards the earth at the moment Thou saved us by the separation of Thy Soul from Thy Body on the cross: Guide us in all our ways

Sacred Head of Jesus, Light of every man coming into this world:
Guide us in all our ways

Sacred Head of Jesus, Our Guide and our Hope:
Guide us in all our ways

Sacred Head of Jesus, Who knows all our needs:
Guide us in all our ways

Sacred Head of Jesus, Who dispenses all graces:
Guide us in all our ways

Sacred Head of Jesus, Who directs the movements of the Divine Heart: Guide us in all our ways

Sacred Head of Jesus, Who governs the world:
Guide us in all our ways

Sacred Head of Jesus, Who will judge all our actions:
Guide us in all our ways

Sacred Head of Jesus, Who knows the secrets of our hearts:
Guide us in all our ways

Sacred Head of Jesus, That we want to make known and adored by the whole world: Guide us in all our ways

Sacred Head of Jesus, Who ravishes the angels and the saints:
Guide us in all our ways

Sacred Head of Jesus, That we hope to contemplate one day, unveiled: Guide us in all our ways

V. We adore Thy Sacred Head , O Jesus,
R. And we submit ourselves to all the decrees of Thy infinite Wisdom.

Let us pray:
O God who sent Thy only begotten Son into the world in human nature, grant that by adoring His Sacred Head, we may be filled with holy wisdom and come one day to contemplate Thy glory. Through Christ Our Lord. Amen.

A PRAYER

O WISDOM of the Sacred Head, guide me in all my ways.

O LOVE of the Sacred Heart, consume me with Thy fire.
Three Glory be's, in honour of the Divine Will, Memory and Understanding.

O SEAT OF DIVINE WISDOM, and guiding Power, which governs all the motions and love of the Sacred Heart, may all minds know Thee, all hearts love Thee, and all tongues praise Thee, now and for evermore. Amen.

O WILL, which was always in meek subjection to Thy Heavenly Father's, control me in all things, as Thou didst govern all the affections and motions of the Sacred Heart of the God made man.

O UNDERSTANDING, which knows all things, ever guide me with Thy light.

O MEMORY, in which past, present and future are at once reflected, which is ever mindful of me, and always seems studying some new means of giving fresh favours, force me to love Thee more and more.

TERESA HIGGINSON'S MEDITATIONS
ON THE
FIVE SORROWFUL MYSTERIES

First Sorrowful Mystery

Soul of a sinner–turn aside with me,
To walk awhile in sad Gethsemane!
Shut out the world–let every care depart!
Bring nothing with thee, but a humble heart!
Wash in the wave of Cedron–as it flows:
Just cross'd by Him– who has endur'd thy woes:
For see yon garden with the dew–drops wet
That Paradise of pain–Mount Olivet!
There hath the "Man of Sorrows" entered now
With the calm victim's sign upon His brow.
That hour is come which none but He could bear,
Wrapt in His crimson agony of prayer:
Nature nay sink through sadness unto sleep,
But love at least shall watch, and wail and weep.

Second Sorrowful Mystery

Soul of a sinner–child of guilt and shame,
Now let another sight thy heart inflame!
With arms uplifted–merciless and bare.
See the sweet Victim in His love reveal'd,
By whose rich stripes alone our souls are Heal'd:
Wrapt in His purple of descending gore,
He yields Him to the smiters more and more!
Dread Flagellation! shall its tortures tell
In vain– how we should have the doom of hell,
Had not for us the Word Incarnate trod

The doleful winepress of the Wrath of God!
Hail, Thou Rejected Lamb! in all Thy woe;
Let the hot tears of deep contrition flow:
Till sin, and self, and sense, be all abhorr'd,
Lost in the wounds of our once suffering Lord!

Third Sorrowful Mystery

Soul of a sinner–subject to a Lord
For thee once mock'd and crown'd and yet abhorr'd;
Come to this coronation; lo': the scorn
With which they weave His diadem of thorn!
Eye the vile splendour of that scarlet robe
Vesting the veil'd Creator of the globe!
Hear the rude jest–behold the bonded knee,
The mirth infernal–and the homage see:
That Hand–once reach'd to each one in his need,
Now spurn'd by all–and sceptr'd with a reed;
That Brow of majesty and might divine,
A throne of woe–with love in every line!
Here let me linger through life's pensive day,
Till this poor heart in tears shall melt away:
And death approach with liberation sweet
To let me fall–and worship at His feet!

Fourth Sorrowful Mystery

Soul of a sinner–here without a home,
Art thou a pilgrim for the world to come?
See, then, thy Great Exemplar on His way
A path of colours–cloth'd in red array!
The sight of Calvary His heart inspires
And lights eternal love with ardent fires.
Lo! where His Holy Mother stands opprest,
The sword of sorrow piercing through her breast!

See where the Cross–that purchase of the Crown
Weighs on His wounded frame, and sinks it down!
See where yon woman wipes His sacred face,
And wins a likeness of the King of Grace!
Hear where the daughters of sad Salem wail,
While Siloa's brook sighs softly through the vale;
These with sweet sympathy dissolv'd in fears,
That to be shortly swollen with their tears!
Lord! let each eye o'erflow with contrite grief,
And in the road to Calvary, seek relief!

Fifth Sorrowful Mystery

Soul of a sinner–turn with me once more
Upon a scene excelling all before!
And as the mighty Moses, when he saw
The Burning Bush with overwhelming awe,
Put off his shoes, before the fire of God,
That he might worship on the sacred sod;
So thou from sin, and self, and sense set free,
Ascend the Holy Hill of Calvary!
Behold the Cross, in wreaths of sable furl'd,
The atoning Altar of a guilty world!
Look on thy Jesus in His final hour,
Till the look thrills thee with transforming power:
Hear His last, words–the prayer–the bitter cry
That rends the Veil–and rocks the earth and sky:
Lo! how He bows–when He resigns His breath,
That Head–which holds the crown of life and death.
And now the spear hath pierc'd His rifted side,
Whence flows for sinful man a double tide:
Oh! Glorious Cross! the "Tree of Love" art Thou!
To Thee I kneel–beneath Thy shade I bow:
To Him–whom thou didst lift from earth to heaven,
Be my whole heart in sweet affection given!

TERESA'S PRAYER TO OUR LADY

O Mary, I implore Thee by all the love and homage Thou hast bestowed on this Seat of Divine Wisdom before which the Cherubim and Seraphim lie prostrate in awe and trembling, fear and love, by this Sacred Head which Thou hast so often pressed on Thy Immaculate Heart and pillowed on Thy bosom. Oh Mary and Joseph, oh ye Choirs of Angels and glorious Assembly of Saints, raise now your minds, your hearts, and your hands to the adorable Trinity and beg the Holy of Holies to look upon these warm vermilion drops of priceless worth, the Precious Blood of Jesus that have obeyed to the orders of His Divine Wisdom; ask Him through His obedience unto death, through the Wisdom and Love He has displayed towards His creatures, to arise and spread this light over the whole face of the earth. Where should we all be if it were not for His Infinite Wisdom and Love? In the Nothingness out of which He called all things. Then let all creatures acknowledge, praise, bless and love this Wisdom, let them adore the Sacred Head of Jesus as its Seat. Not my will but Thine be done. I mean that I am ready to await Thy good pleasure, but Oh Lord. Thou knowest how this fire burns within me, Thou knowest all things. My love and my desires are not hidden from Thee

TERESA'S LAST WORDS

Do not fear, dear child,
but put your hand with loving confidence into your Father's hand
and He will guide you safely through every path.
Where the road is rough and stony
He will carry you in His arms.
We worship Jesus, The seat of divine wisdom

and we submit our souls and bodies to all her decrees.
Jesus my true, my only Good
I wish for naught but Thee
Behold me all Thine own, my God,
Do what thou wilt with me
Holy Mary, Our Lady of Wisdom,
Saint Joseph, Foster father of Jesus
and patron of the Universal Church,
Pray for us.

After Teresa's death,

the following lines were found in her writing book

Father of all, we fain would say, as did Thy only Son,
In every hour of every day, Oh let Thy Will be done.
In thought, in word, in deed, in death, things finished or begun,
Let every transitory breath whisper, Thy Will be done.
In daily cares to thousands known, or known perchance to none,
Let this request be beard above, Oh! Lord, Thy Will be done.
In sickness though some stroke unseen may oft the senses stun,
Let grace suggestive intervene to feel Thy Will be done.
In health, when in its full career the race of man is run,
Let joy be taught by holy fear to pray, Thy Will be done.
Amid the rocks and shoals of life which few can ever shun,
Let peace compose each spark of strife and cry, Thy Will be done.
And when the bow of hope shall blend all colours into one,
Time with eternity shall end with LORD, THY WILL BE DONE.

Lightning Source UK Ltd.
Milton Keynes UK
14 January 2011

165730UK00002B/1/P